# NIXON AND THE ENVIRONMENT
## THE POLITICS OF DEVASTATION

# NIXON AND THE ENVIRONMENT
## THE POLITICS OF DEVASTATION

INTRODUCTION BY THEODORE ROOSEVELT

THIRTEEN ESSAYS
EDITED BY JAMES RATHLESBERGER

A VILLAGE VOICE BOOK
PUBLISHED BY TAURUS COMMUNICATIONS, INC., NEW YORK, NEW YORK

Copyright © 1972 by The Village Voice

All rights reserved under International and Pan-American Copyright Conventions. No part of this book may be reproduced or transmitted in any form or by any means, electronic or mechanical, including photocopying, recording or by an information storage and retrieval system, without permission in writing from the publisher.

Cover photograph by Arthur Tress
Cover design by Eugene Beck

Published in the United States by The Village Voice/Taurus Communications, Inc., New York, New York, and simultaneously in Canada. Distributed by Random House, Inc., and in Canada by Random House of Canada, Ltd.

Library of Congress Catalog Card Number: 72-83641. ISBN: 0-394-70790

Printed in the United States of America

THIS BOOK IS PRINTED ON RECYCLED PAPER
Second Printing

# CONTENTS

| | |
|---|---|
| INTRODUCTION<br>Theodore Roosevelt | 5 |
| AIR POLLUTION<br>James Miller | 9 |
| WATER POLLUTION<br>David Zwick | 30 |
| WATER RESOURCES DEVELOPMENT<br>Brent Blackwelder | 59 |
| ENERGY<br>Wilson Clark | 80 |
| THE PUBLIC LANDS<br>George Alderson | 110 |
| WILDLIFE<br>Tom Garrett | 129 |
| PESTICIDES<br>Harrison Wellford | 146 |
| POPULATION<br>Carl Pope | 163 |
| TRANSPORTATION<br>Bob Waldrop | 180 |
| THE INNER-CITY ENVIRONMENT<br>James Rathlesberger | 200 |
| THE WORKPLACE ENVIRONMENT<br>Franklin Wallick | 222 |
| SOLID WASTES<br>Janet Schaeffer | 239 |
| DECISION-MAKING IN THE WHITE HOUSE<br>Joe Browder | 257 |
| INDEX | 271 |

# PREFACE

"The 1970's absolutely must be the years when America pays its debt to the past by reclaiming the purity of its air, its waters, and our living environment. It is literally now or never," said President Richard M. Nixon on signing the National Environmental Policy Act (NEPA) on January 1, 1970. It was his first official act of the new decade. Later that year, he warned that "we face the prospect of ecological disaster," and he called for "a total mobilization by all of us." In his State of the Union Address on January 22, 1971, President Nixon pledged that environmental quality would be the "third great goal" of the "New American Revolution."

But the militancy of the rhetoric was short-lived. Just seven months after the State of the Union Address, the President attached a message to the Council on Environmental Quality's (CEQ) 1971 annual report warning the country "not to expect environmental miracles." And one month later, on September 23, 1971, before the Detroit Economic Club, the President spoke in words indicating that his caution had led him to a complete reappraisal of his environmental policies. Reassuring the auto executives that he would not permit environmental concern "to be used sometimes falsely and sometimes in a demagogic way basically to destroy the system," President Nixon made it clear that the Administration would be looking for approaches less revolutionary than he had earlier led the nation to expect.

Actively involved in the shaping of Nixon's environmental programs have been several agencies established during his Administration, most notably the Council on Environmental Quality, the Environmental Protection Agency (EPA) and the Office of Management and Budget (OMB). The activities and interactions of these three agencies provide a key to the President's personal commitment.

The Council on Environmental Quality was established by the National Environmental Policy Act of 1969 despite objections from the White House. The Council has the job of advising the President and coordinating environmental policy. Nixon previously had established a cabinet level committee called the "Environmental Quality Council," but Senator Henry Jackson (D-Wash.), who authored NEPA, expressed the feelings of both Congress and environmentalists when he said that the President's committee "promises more rhetoric than action."

Proposals for an Environmental Protection Agency, which now has authority over air and water pollution, solid waste, noise, and limited jurisdiction over pesticides and radiation, also met initial opposition from President Nixon. The President wanted instead to reorganize the government's executive branch into four super-departments, one of which would have jurisdiction over all natural resources and environmental programs. But increasing pressure from Congress, especially from Senator Edmund Muskie (D-Me.), led Nixon to propose the EPA on July 9, 1970.

Part of the President's motivation for establishing EPA may have been an attempt to isolate Walter Hickel, then Secretary of the Interior and increasingly a thorn in the side of the White House. The Interior Department lost to EPA, upon its creation, its largest agency, the Federal Water Pollution Control Administration; and the National Oceanic and Atmospheric Administration (NOAA), established by the President at the same time as EPA, absorbed the Interior Department's Bureau of Commercial Fisheries. Interior officials complained openly, and Hickel's dream of a new department of natural resources and environment was destroyed. Hickel was subsequently dismissed, and the President's reorganization plans now call only for a Department of Natural Resources, leaving EPA intact.

The White House Office of Management and Budget, in contrast to the CEQ and EPA, is President Nixon's own invention. A Bureau of the Budget previously existed in the Executive Office of the President, but the Office of Management and Budget, established by the President on May 16, 1970, created a much broader executive capacity for coordinating, and controlling, governmental policy. OMB oversees the daily activities of each federal agency and makes certain they are in strict accordance with the policies of the President.

The writers of this book believe a comprehensive review of these policies is essential in this election year, and hope this book will contribute to enlightened debate on national environmental goals.

JAMES RATHLESBERGER
*Research Director*
League of Conservation Voters
Washington, D.C.

# NIXON AND THE ENVIRONMENT
## THE POLITICS OF DEVASTATION

# INTRODUCTION

## THEODORE ROOSEVELT

The natural resources of our country are in danger of exhaustion if we permit the old wasteful methods of exploiting them longer to continue.

With the rise of peoples from savagery to civilization, and with the consequent growth in the extent and variety of the needs of the average man, there comes a steadily increasing growth of the amount demanded by this average man from the actual resources of the country. Yet, rather curiously, at the same time the average man is apt to lose his realization of this dependence upon nature.

Neither the primitive man nor the pioneer was aware of any duty to posterity in dealing with the renewable resources. When the American settler felled the forests, he felt that there was plenty of forest left for the sons who came after him. When he exhausted the soil of his farm he felt that his son could go West and take up another. So it was with his immediate successors. When the soil-wash from the farmer's fields choked the neighboring river he thought only of using the railway rather than boats for moving his produce and supplies.

In Washington's time anthracite coal was known only as a useless black stone; and the great fields of bituminous coal were undiscovered. As steam was unknown, the use of coal for power production was undreamed of. Water was practically the only source of power, save the labor of men and animals; and this power was used only in the most primitive fashion. But a few small iron deposits had been found in this country, and the use of iron by our countrymen was very small. Wood was practically the only fuel, and what lumber was sawed was consumed locally, while the forests were regarded chiefly as obstructions to settlement and cultivation.

Since then our knowledge and use of the resources of the present territory of the United States have increased a hundredfold. Indeed, the growth of this nation by leaps and bounds makes one of the most striking and important chapters in the history of the world. Its growth has been due to the rapid development, and alas! that it should be said, to the rapid destruction, of our natural resources.

Since the days when the Constitution was adopted, steam and electricity have revolutionized the industrial world. Nowhere has the revolution been so great as in our country. The discovery and utilization of mineral fuels and alloys have given us the lead over all other nations in the production of steel. The discovery and utilization of coal and iron have given us our railways, and have led to such industrial development as has never before been seen. The vast wealth of lumber in our forests, the riches of our soils and mines, the discovery of gold and mineral oils, combined with the efficiency of our transportation, have made the conditions of our life unparalleled in comfort and convenience.

The steadily increasing drain on these natural resources has promoted to an extraordinary degree the complexity of our industrial and social life. Moreover, this unexampled development has had a determining effect upon the character and opinions of our people. The demand for efficiency in the great task has given us vigor, effectiveness, decision and power, and a capacity for achievement which in its own lines has never yet been matched. So great and so rapid has been our material growth that there has been a tendency to lag behind in spiritual and moral growth.

Disregarding for the moment the question of moral purpose, it is safe to say that the prosperity of our people depends directly on the energy and intelligence with which our natural resources are used. It is equally clear that these resources are the final basis of national power and perpetuity. Finally, it is ominously evident that these resources are in the course of rapid exhaustion.

This nation began with the belief that its landed possessions were illimitable and capable of supporting all the people who might care to make our country their home. We began with an unapproached heritage of forests; more than half of the timber is gone. We began with coal fields more extensive than those of any other nation and with iron ores regarded as inexhaustible, and many experts now declare that the end of both iron and coal is in sight.

The mere increase in our consumption of coal during 1907 over 1906 exceeded the total consumption in 1876, the Centennial year. The enormous stores of mineral oil and gas are largely gone. Our natural waterways are not gone, but they have been injured by neglect, and by the division of responsibility and utter lack of system in dealing with them. We are over the verge of a timber famine in this country, and it is unpardonable for the nation or the states to permit any further cutting of our timber save in accordance with a system which will provide that the next generation shall see the timber increased instead of diminished. Finally, we began with soils of unexampled fertility and we have so impoverished them by injudicious use and by failing to check erosion that their crop producing power is diminishing instead of increasing. In a word, we have thoughtlessly, and to a large degree unnecessarily, diminished the resources upon which not only our prosperity but the prosperity of our children must always depend.

We have become great because of the lavish use of our resources and we have just reason to be proud of our growth. But the time has come to inquire seriously what will happen when our forests are gone, when the coal, the iron, the oil, and the gas are exhausted, when the soils shall have been still further impoverished and washed into the streams, polluting the rivers, denuding the fields, and obstructing navigation. The questions do not relate only to the next century or to the next generation. It is time for us now as a nation to exercise the same reasonable foresight in dealing with our great natural resources that would be shown by any prudent man in conserving and wisely using the property which contains the assurance of well-being for himself and his children.

We are coming to recognize as never before the right of the nation to guard its own future in the essential matter of natural resources. In the past we have admitted the right of the individual to injure the future of the Republic for his own present profit. The time has come for a change. As a people we have the right and the duty, second to none other but the right and duty of obeying the moral law, of requiring and doing justice, to protect ourselves and our children against the wasteful development of our natural resources, whether that waste is caused by the actual destruction of such resources or by making them impossible of development hereafter.

*The White House, 1908.*

# AIR POLLUTION

## JAMES MILLER

By the late 1960's, air pollution had ceased being an aesthetic hazard. It had become an outright danger. In the fall of 1969, Dr. Leonard Greenberg (Albert Einstein Medical College) and Dr. Martin Glasser (New York Medical College) released a study finding that when the daily levels of sulfur dioxide were between 0.2 and 0.4 parts per million, the number of "excess deaths" in New York City ranged between ten and twenty persons. These levels of sulfur dioxide were reached on about 30 percent of the days included in the study, which spanned a five-year period from 1960 through 1964. The Council on Environmental Quality noted in its 1970 report that "it is well established that air pollution contributes to the incidence of such chronic diseases as emphysema, bronchitis, and other respiratory ailments. Polluted air is also linked to higher mortality rates from other causes, including cancer and arteriosclerotic heart disease." Despite clean air legislation in 1963, 1965, and 1967, nationwide emissions of carbon monoxide (CO), particulate matter, sulfur oxide ($SO_x$), hydrocarbons (HC), and nitrogen oxides ($NO_x$), five major pollutants, actually increased from 272.5 million tons in 1968 to 281.2 million tons in 1969.

Air pollution, by 1970, had become a significant po-

---

*James Miller, who graduated from Princeton University in 1970, has been a co-director of the Natural Resources Defense Council's Project on Clean Air.*

### Estimated Emissions of Air Pollutants by Weight, Nationwide, 1969*

(in millions of tons per year)

| Source | CO | Particulates | $SO_x$ | HC | $NO_x$ | Total |
|---|---|---|---|---|---|---|
| Transportation | 111.5 | 0.8 | 1.1 | 19.8 | 11.2 | 144.4 |
| Fuel combustion in stationary sources | 1.8 | 7.2 | 24.4 | .9 | 10.0 | 44.3 |
| Industrial processes | 12.0 | 14.4 | 7.5 | 5.5 | .2 | 39.6 |
| Solid waste disposal | 7.9 | 1.4 | .2 | 2.0 | .4 | 11.9 |
| Miscellaneous | 18.2 | 11.4 | .2 | 9.2 | 2.0 | 41.0 |
| Total | 151.4 | 35.2 | 33.4 | 37.4 | 23.8 | 281.2 |

* Most recent information available.
SOURCE: The Mitre Corp. MTR-6013. Based on Environmental Protection Agency data.

litical issue, so it was no surprise when President Nixon's first environmental message, sent to Congress on February 10, 1970, strongly emphasized proposals for national air quality standards, under which each state would have to prepare pollution abatement plans within one year. Federal authority to seek court action would be extended to include intrastate pollution, whereas before it had been limited to interstate problems. Nixon also proposed that failure to meet the standards or implementation plans be made subject to court-imposed fines of up to $10,000 per day.

Bold as these proposals sounded, they were filled with restrictive and weakening loopholes. "One is hard put to imagine," said the Ralph Nader task force report, *Vanishing Air*, "a more ineffective measure [than President Nixon's]. But the Nixon Administration has managed to draft one. . . . Suffice it to say that the proposal incorporates all the weaknesses and most of the delays that have hamstrung enforcement of the present law. . . . In the journey up the echelons [of the Administration], every meaningful provision of the earlier drafts was systematically pruned. Private rights of action to enforce violations of standards, power to subpoena information, and expedited enforcement provisions were only a few of the Nixon proposals that fell unceremoniously to the cutting room floor at the White House."

The President's proposal was, in part, an attempt to wrest the initiative and therefore the credit for air pollution legislation from Senator Edmund Muskie (D-Me.), Chairman of the Subcommittee on Air and Water Pollution and in 1970 the major Democratic contender for the Presidency. "At that time," the *National Journal* later recalled, "it appeared that the President had effectively challenged Muskie's political preeminence in environmental matters and was well on the way toward claiming the environmental protection cause as his own." But Nixon's proposal awakened the political and competitive instincts of Senator Muskie.

## The Clean Air Act of 1970

Many new air pollution proposals were offered in both the House and Senate in early 1970, and during March and April hearings were held before Muskie's Subcommittee on Air and Water Pollution, and its counterpart in the House. On June 10, the House, after defeating a series of toughening amendments, passed its version of the bill, a thirty-page piece of legislation incorporating President Nixon's proposals. Muskie's original bill, while somewhat stronger, still was not remarkably fierce. But in August, during executive sessions with his subcommittee, and shortly after a serious smog had hit the East Coast, Muskie inserted definite cleanup deadlines into the bill: automobile emissions, for example, would have to be reduced 90 percent by 1975.

## Highlights of the 1970 Clean Air Act Amendments

### Automobiles

- Emissions of carbon monoxide and hydrocarbons must be reduced by at least 90 percent of 1970 levels for 1975 models. Emissions of nitrogen oxides must be reduced at least 90 percent for 1976 models.
- The Administrator of the Environmental Protection Agency (EPA) is authorized to grant a one-year extension to each of these deadlines.
- Manufacturers or sellers who violate these standards are subject to $10,000-per-vehicle fines.
- The manufacturers must warranty the effectiveness of pollution control devices for five years or 50,000 miles.

### Stationary Sources

- The establishment of national air quality standards of two kinds (regulating the general purity of the air): primary standards, those judged necessary to protect public health, and secondary standards, to protect public welfare. Primary standards must be achieved within three years after federal approval of state implementation plans. There is no specific deadline for meeting the tougher secondary standards.
- Standards for sulfur oxides, particulates, carbon monoxide, hydrocarbons, and oxidants must be issued by EPA one month after enactment of Amendments.
- After holding public hearings, states must submit implementation plans for those five standards within nine months after standards are issued.
- EPA then must approve the state's plans within four months or substitute its own plan within six months if the state plan is not satisfactory.
- EPA may grant a state no more than two years of extensions for meeting primary standards.

- Criteria (compilations of scientific data on which standards are based) for other major pollutants are to be issued within thirteen months of enactment. Issuance of standards will follow, and the same deadline mechanism will take effect.

## Emission Standards for Stationary Sources

- State implementation plans must include emission standards regulating amounts of pollution various sources may emit.
- The Environmental Protection Agency is authorized to issue special emission standards for hazardous substances, such as mercury, asbestos, and beryllium. These may be set at zero-emission level.
- Major *new* sources of pollution, such as power plants and industrial plants, are required to meet new national performance standards which set emission ceilings.

## Enforcement

- To enforce compliance with national air quality and emission standards, EPA is given concurrent jurisdiction with states.
- EPA may issue an abatement order against a polluter and refer the matter to the Justice Department for prosecution if the pollution does not stop. If the Justice Department does not act, the EPA may do so itself.
- EPA may issue orders for immediate abatement where pollution poses an imminent and substantial danger to health.
- Violations of standards are punishable by $25,000-a-day fines and one-year jail sentences. Second offenders are subject to $50,000-a-day fines and two-year sentences.
- Citizen suits are authorized against polluters and government agencies for violations of standards. The Administrator of EPA is also subject to suit for failure to carry out certain mandatory functions.

Industrial polluters, wary of the Nixon bill, were amazed by Muskie's, and tried to mount a campaign to weaken it. But Muskie had skillfully won bipartisan support from the other subcommittee members, and the complex 100-page bill moved through the Senate before industrial lobbyists had much time to react. As Joseph Mullen of the National Coal Association later said, "The bill that came out of the Senate was not the bill that anybody had testified to." On September 22, 1970, the "Muskie bill" passed the Senate by a vote of 73-0.

The Administration was faced with a dilemma. To oppose the Senate bill would obviously be seen as favoring polluters, and ruin the President's newspaper image as a fighter of air pollution, but on the other hand the bill went further than the White House wanted to go. While the President proposed national air quality standards, for example, the Administration's bill dropped all of the 1967 law's essential procedural safeguards for standard setting. No longer would the law require that air quality standards be set on the basis of a comprehensive body of scientific evidence, nor would the law specifically require that standards be set at levels protecting the public health and welfare. No longer would public hearings even be required on proposed standards. The Secretary of HEW would be given virtually unlimited discretion to set these critical standards at whatever levels he chose.

During October and November a series of meetings was held at the White House Office of Management and Budget and at the office of John C. Whitaker, the President's deputy assistant for natural resources. Among the agencies represented were the Department of Health, Education and Welfare, the Department of Commerce, the Department of Justice and the White House Council on Environmental Quality. Elliot Richardson, Secretary of HEW, argued against opposing Muskie's deadlines, but the Commerce Department felt that they had to be weakened one way or another.

Two weeks after the 1970 congressional elections the

Administration sent a letter, under the signature of Elliot Richardson, to the members of the House and Senate conference committee which was negotiating the differences between the House and Senate bills. The letter asked that almost all the tough provisions in the Senate bill be deleted from the final legislation:

• The Administration endorsed the "target date" of 1975 for automobile emission controls, but asked for permission to continue indefinitely giving auto-makers one-year extensions, instead of the single one-year extension Muskie had allowed.

• The Senate bill required that auto-makers warrant the performance of their anti-pollution devices for 50,000 miles. Richardson said the Administration supported the principle, but asked that this requirement be dropped in favor of a provision allowing the Secretary (later the Administrator of the Environmental Protection Agency) to set his own warranty requirements "as he determines that such requirements can be justified."

• Realizing that some urban states have more severe air pollution problems than the nation as a whole, the Senate had written its bill to allow the states to set their own stricter auto pollution standards where necessary. Richardson asked that the provision allowing them to do this be deleted.

• The Senate bill authorized citizen suits against both polluters and federal enforcement authorities not in compliance with the law. Richardson accepted suits against polluters, but asked that citizen suits against the Secretary of HEW be prohibited.

• The Senate bill allowed states three years to meet new national air quality standards, and, to separate politics from pollution control, stated that only a court could grant a one-year extension. Richardson asked that the Secretary of HEW be given discretion to extend this key deadline.

Richardson's recommendations would have reduced the Clean Air Act Amendments of 1970 to the same flabby level of previous air pollution laws. The Senate bill was an attempt to eliminate the loopholes, delays, and ineffectual enforcement occurring under existing law by assigning direct responsibility for specific tasks to be accomplished by specific deadlines. The Administration's recommendations ran consistantly counter to this purpose by releasing the Secretary from specific duties, by increasing his discretion to release others from their duties, and by shielding him from direct accountability for his actions.

The House and Senate conferees reported on December 17, and Congress cleared the following day a bill with the Senate provisions prevailing on nearly all important points. Concessions had been made: states, with the exception of California, are not allowed, for example, to set auto emission standards tougher than the Federal government's. But the Clean Air Act Amendments of 1970 are an enormous improvement over previous law, tougher even than many environmentalists would have thought politically possible just a few months before.

## The Nixon Administration's Performance

President Nixon decided to take credit for the amendments even though he had fought them throughout their passage. The President signed the law on December 31, 1970, in a ceremony before newsmen and expressed pleasure that the bill incorporated all his recommendations (which, to say the least, it did). He also said the bill was a "cooperattive effort" of both political parties. Conspicuously absent from the Congressmen and Senators invited to witness the event, however, was the bill's chief architect, Senator Muskie. A Nixon aide explained that the ceremonial room was too small to accommodate all forty sponsors of the bill. One persistent reporter argued that the bill was so much Muskie's that it was even known as the "Muskie bill," but the aide said, "I don't believe it's been called that . . . in this room."

If nothing else, this effort to claim credit for the law gave increased hope that the Nixon Administration would implement it vigorously. The appointment of William Ruckelshaus as the Administrator of the new Environmental Protection Agency (EPA), which would be responsible for the clean air program, was also encouraging.

Up to this time, the Administration's record had not been impressive. Appropriations for the National Air Pollution Control Administration for fiscal 1970 totaled only $108.9 million, while $179.3 million had been authorized. At the time the new law was passed, NAPCA's personnel total was only 971, against a previous projected requirement of 1,900. The Clean Air Act Amendments of 1970

## Budget for EPA's Clean Air Programs
(in thousands of dollars)

|  | Fiscal 1972 | 1973 |
|---|---|---|
| Research and Development |  |  |
| Pollution Process and Effects | $ 23,416 | $ 31,065 |
| Pollution Control Technology | 34,715 | 39,647 |
| Abatement and Control |  |  |
| Standards, Guidelines and Regulations | 9,691 | 9,708 |
| Monitoring and Surveillance | 8,759 | 11,756 |
| Planning | — | — |
| Control Agency Support | 42,930 | 51,548 |
| Technical Information and Assistance | 6,807 | 7,278 |
| Federal Activities | 902 | 847 |
| Manpower Planning and Training | 5,632 | 4,575 |
| Enforcement | 1,353 | 2,320 |
| TOTAL | $134,205 | $158,744 |

SOURCE: *The Economics of Clean Air*, Environmental Protection Agency, February, 1972.

substantially increased existing authorizations. At Ruckelshaus' confirmation hearings, Muskie stressed the need for more staff and money, and Ruckelshaus agreed that more had to be done.

Officials in the Environmental Protection Agency frequently complain of insufficient resources for the air pollution program. But the President has been requesting, and the Office of Management and Budget budgeting, only half the amounts authorized by the Clean Air Act (See table on page 17). For fiscal 1972, the Amendments authorized $225 million; for fiscal 1973, $300 million. When the Amendments were being debated in Congress in 1970, the Administration claimed the measure would require $320 million in fiscal 1973.

## State Implementation Plans

> "OMB will simply have nothing to do with the final approval of these individual state plans."
> William Ruckelshaus, February 17, 1972.

The Environmental Protection Agency (EPA) issued on April 7, 1971, proposed regulations under which states are to prepare their plans for meeting national air quality standards. The standards themselves spell out what amounts of the various pollutants may be emitted into the air without damaging human health; the state plans are to spell out the specific measures states will use to reduce pollution to meet the standards. EPA's proposed regulations were guidelines as to what it would consider an appropriate plan.

The regulations were submitted to the public for comment and then revised, with marked attention to the suggestions of environmentalists. Administrator Ruckelshaus received the revised guidelines on June 28, 1971, along with a memo from Dr. John T. Middleton, head of the EPA air pollution program, describing the major revisions and recommending speedy promulgation. Shortly after, the White House asked that the guidelines be sent to its Office of Management and Budget (OMB) for review, a review that was closed to the public. A month and a half later, on August 17, Ruckelshaus promulgated the regulations as revised by the White House. He had accepted drastically weakened guidelines.

Peter Bernstein, of the Newhouse News Service, was one of the few reporters who covered the White House revisions. By his account, OMB officials "intervened at the request of Commerce Secretary Maurice Stans, Federal Power Commissioner John Nassikas, and several other federal officials who share big industry's viewpoint. Government sources say Ruckelshaus defended the original draft at subsequent meetings, but finally lost out when two key White House aides intervened on the side of big industry. They were presidential assistants John D. Ehrlichman and Peter M. Flanigan."

The changes made by OMB made it clear that Nixon's promises to fight pollution were little more than rhetoric. A key appendix to the guidelines was badly mauled. Nearly all of Appendix B's original sample regulations dealing with permit systems, emissions monitoring, air pollution emergencies, and compliance schedules vanished. The remaining six sections, each suggesting feasible emission limitations for a major pollutant, no longer appear as sample regulations but merely as a listing of possible control levels. With all regulatory language removed, the suggestive power of the Appendix was substantially reduced.

The proposed guidelines would have required states to obtain authorization from their legislatures to inspect motor vehicles and to enforce land use and transportation control measures before they submit their implementation plans. Now states only have to demonstrate that, if such measures are necessary, they will get that authorization from their legislatures at a later date, often a difficult task.

The Clean Air Act was intended "to protect and enhance the quality of the Nation's air resources." But OMB deleted from the guidelines a regulation which would

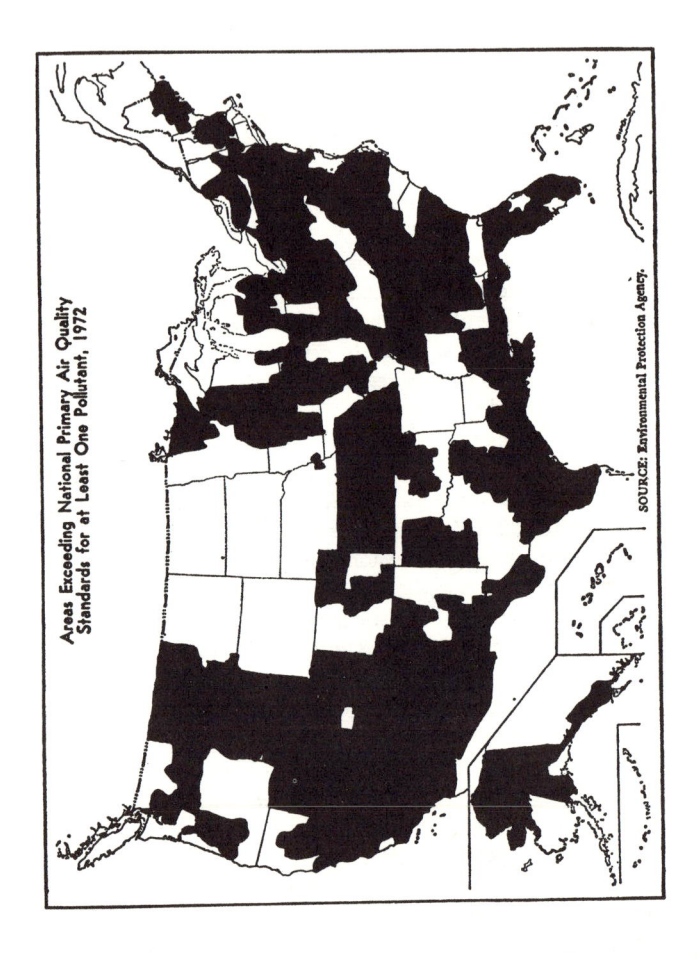

Areas Exceeding National Primary Air Quality Standards for at Least One Pollutant, 1972

SOURCE: Environmental Protection Agency.

have required states to prevent degradation of air already cleaner than the national standards.

The final guidelines also reduced by a considerable number those heavily polluted regions classified as "Priority I." Since the guidelines' requirements are strictest for these regions, OMB's changes released whole areas of the country from the obligation to pursue vigorous clean-up programs.

OMB's worst offense, however (and the best evidence of how effective the Commerce Department was in weakening the guidelines), was to encourage states to take costs into account when choosing control strategies to meet national air quality standards. States are now to consider the "cost-effectiveness," the "costs and benefits" and the "social and economic impact" of any control measure before using it. In 1970 Senate and House conference members had, in fact, struck all mention of such cost factors from those sections in the final law dealing with state plans. In March, 1972, EPA had issued a document calling such language "inappropriate" and "an unaccountable digression from the proper emphasis of the law." The thrust of the law "should be protection of public health and welfare, first and foremost." Now OMB had put the loopholes back and opened the way for more delay.

The impact of the interference from the White House Office of Management and Budget is already being felt. Only a handful of the state plans submitted to EPA have included non-degradation clauses, and only a handful of states have made any serious attempt to incorporate comprehensive land use or transportation controls in their plans, though many have asked for extensions of deadlines they could well have met with such measures.

Polluters have also used OMB's changes to try to evade tough standards and deadlines. In Montana, for example, Anaconda Copper Company and American Smelting and Refining Company pressed the State Board of Health to back down from a strong 90 percent limitation

## Projected National Annual Damage Costs[1]
## by Pollutant in 1977
(1970 dollars in millions)

| Damage Class | Pollutant | | | | | Total |
|---|---|---|---|---|---|---|
| | Part. | SO$_x$ | O$_x$[2] | NO$_x$ | CO | |
| Health | $3,880 | $ 5,440 | $—[3] | $—[3] | $—[3] | $ 9,320 |
| Residential Property | 3,330 | 4,660 | —[3] | —[3] | —[3] | 7,990 |
| Materials and Vegetation | 970 | 3,680 | 1,700 | 1,250 | 0[4] | 7,600 |
| TOTAL | $8,180 | $13,780 | $1,700 | $1,250 | $—[3] | $24,910 |

[1] Based on "The Cost of Air Pollution Damages: A Status Report" by Larry B. Barrett and Thomas E. Waddell, Public Health Service, Department of Health, Education and Welfare, July 1970.

[2] Assumed proportional to HC emissions.

[3] Not available due to lack of data.

[4] Assumed to be negligible.

SOURCE: *The Economics of Clean Air*, Environmental Protection Agency, February, 1972.

on sulfur emissions from copper smelters. The copper company arguments relied heavily on the cost-benefit language. When the Board resisted their pressure, the copper companies went to White House aide Peter Flanigan, and EPA was eventually forced to retreat from its support of the 90 percent standard. The Board has courageously refused to reverse its position, but Montana's governor, claiming the cost of meeting the standard is too high, has refused to submit the implementation plan to EPA.

The final blow came in early 1972, in hearings before Senator Muskie's Senate Subcommittee on Air and Water Pollution, when an EPA document revealed that all state plans are required to be sent to OMB for twenty-two days for final approval. Having worked its will on state plans by rewriting EPA's guidelines, the White House apparently intends to make sure the job is done right by rewriting the plans themselves.

## Automobile Pollution

The major source of air pollution is the automobile. Contributing well over 50 percent of the air pollution in many urban areas, the nationwide emission of the five major pollutants from automobiles alone amounted to 97,500,000 tons in 1969.

The 1970 Clean Air Act Amendments called for at least a 90 percent reduction in the emissions of three major auto pollutants: carbon monoxide (CO) and hydrocarbons (HC) were required to be reduced at least 90 percent from 1970 levels by 1975, and nitrogen oxides (NOx) to be at least 90 percent reduced by 1976. The Administrator of EPA is authorized to grant extensions of only one year. Sooner or later, the Amendments require Detroit to clean their engines up, if the Administration enforces the law. (For the control of lead content in gasolines, see page 207.)

The 1970 Amendments, for example, clearly direct EPA to set the hydrocarbon standard for 1975 cars so as to reduce the emissions "at least" 90 percent from the emissions allowed by standards already set for 1970 cars. As the 1970 Amendments were being drafted, the old National Air Pollution Control Administration assured Congress that 90 percent reductions, measured by the 1970 Federal Test Procedure, would be adequate to protect public health and welfare. But when EPA actually set the 1975 standard, it adopted a new test procedure. The 1970 cars, meeting the 1970 hydrocarbon standard of 2.2 grams per mile under the old test, showed up emitting 4.1 grams per mile under the new test. EPA took its 90 percent reduction from the 4.1 instead of the 2.2 figure, and ended up with a 1975 standard two-and-one-half times as lenient as the one Congress intended.

Ruckelshaus and other Administration spokesmen usually talk tough in public, but what's said behind closed doors is anyone's guess. A two-day meeting at the Western White House in San Clemente, California in January,

1972, gives some indication. Representatives from the Environmental Protection Agency, the General Services Administration, the National Science Foundation, the Justice Department, Ford, General Motors, Chrysler, American Motors, and Union Oil Company—altogether fifty-five industry, government, and "scientific" representatives—"reportedly concluded," said the *Washington Post,* "that amendments should be sought to the Clean Air Act." The meeting, reputedly organized by Rep. Victor V. Veysey (R-Cal.), was strictly a closed-door affair. But obviously, regardless of whatever good intentions Ruckelshaus and the Environmental Protection Agency might have, pressure is mounting for a change in the 1970 Clean Air Act itself.

In an interview in July, 1971, Ruckelshaus was asked what the Nixon Administration would do if Ford, General Motors, or Chrysler failed to meet the 1975 emissions standards and "haven't even made a decent try. Could you imagine the government really closing one of them down?" "No," replied Ruckelshaus. Asked what would happen, he explained that "Congress might come along and amend the law. We would bring the situation to Congress."

On January 1, 1972, the National Academy of Sciences (NAS) submitted to Congress and the Environmental Protection Agency the first in a series of reports on the technological feasibility of meeting the 1975 auto emission standards. Unfortunately, the Academy's study placed primary reliance on data supplied by the auto industry and its conclusions were immediately called to question. Senator Thomas Eagleton (D-Mo.), who chaired hearings before the Senate Subcommittee on Air and Water Pollution during Muskie's presidential campaign, charged that "a nice mutual admiration society" existed between NAS and Detroit.

NAS reported that, under certain conditions, most manufacturers possibly could comply with the standards, but warned that the cost would be high and suggested that an extension would allow the manufacturers necessary time to improve their cars' performance. NAS also suggested averaging the results of emission tests on production-line automobiles and using only the average to compare to the standard. The inevitable result would be the approval of some cars not up to the standards. The second condition urged by NAS is that car owners be compelled to replace emission controls before their automobile has been driven for five years or 50,000 miles. This condition could circumvent the Clean Air Act requirement that the auto makers warranty the effectiveness of their air pollution controls for the useful life of the automobile (defined by the law to be five years or 50,000 miles).

Shortly before EPA began holding the first hearings on auto-makers' requests for a one-year extension of the 1975 standards, the White House Office of Science and Technology released on February 28, 1972, its own "scientific" study which concluded that the standards were too stringent. This report proposed even more loopholes than the NAS study. Ralph Nader attacked it as "a mockery of scientific integrity . . . and another effort to intimidate the federal regulatory agencies responsible for motor vehicle air pollution." Senator Muskie charged, "Once again, the Nixon Administration is putting special interests ahead of public interest. It puts the interests of the boardrooms ahead of those of Main Street." Lee A. Iacocca, president of Ford Motor Company, praised it as the "best news the public has had in many years."

Despite this pressure on EPA for a relaxation of the standards, it came as no surprise to clean air advocates when Ruckelshaus announced on May 12, 1972, that "presently available technology is adequate" for the manufacturers to meet the 1975 standards and that he had therefore decided against a one-year extension. His decision was admirable, and, although it technically only applies to Ford, Chrysler, General Motors, International Harvester and Volvo, Ruckelshaus made it clear that he would make the same decision on requests from other companies. In addition, Ruckelshaus has apparently rejected the averaging of the emissions loophole urged by NAS, and has indicated that EPA's maintenance requirements will be of a sort acceptable to environmentalists.

But even these EPA decisions may not stop Detroit's attack on the Clean Air Act. The auto companies have two remaining recourses: they can, and probably will, seek a reversal of Ruckelshaus' decision in the courts, in which a victory for them is unlikely; or they could go to Congress after the 1972 election for changes in the law. To keep the law from being further weakened, a commitment to clean air must therefore come from the White House. An Administration which fought the law before it passed, and which admitted it would ask Congress to weaken the law even if the auto makers don't make a decent try to comply, can not yet be counted on to see that the 1975-1976 requirements are really achieved.

## The Sulfur Tax

President Nixon proposed in his second Environmental Message, February, 1971, that a tax be put on sulfur emissions. "Sulfur oxides," he said, "are the most damaging air pollutants. High levels of sulfur oxides have been linked to increased incidence of diseases such as bronchitis and lung cancer. In terms of damage to human health, vegetation, and property, sulfur oxide emissions cost society billions of dollars annually."

The Environmental Protection Agency estimates that in 1969, the last year for which figures are available, a total of 33.4 million tons of sulfur oxides were emitted into the nation's air. By far the largest sulfur polluter is the electric power industry, which contributes about 55 percent of total sulfur emissions.

The following table from the National Academy of Engineering and the National Research Council shows an alarming projected increase in sulfur emissions if they remain unabated. Note the increase from 1967 to 1970, a period of only three years:

## Estimated Potential Sulfur Pollution

| Source | \multicolumn{5}{c}{Annual Emission of Sulfur Dioxide (millions of tons)} |
|---|---|---|---|---|---|
| | 1967 | 1970 | 1980 | 1990 | 2000 |
| Power Plant Operation (Coal and Oil) | 15.0 | 20.0 | 41.1 | 62.0 | 94.5 |
| Other Combustion of Coal | 5.1 | 4.8 | 4.0 | 3.1 | 1.6 |
| Combustion of Petroleum Products (Excluding Power Plant Oil) | 2.8 | 3.4 | 3.9 | 4.3 | 5.1 |
| Smelting of Metallic Ores | 3.8 | 4.0 | 5.3 | 7.1 | 9.6 |
| Petroleum Refinery Operation | 2.1 | 2.4 | 4.0 | 6.5 | 10.5 |
| Miscellaneous Sources | 2.0 | 2.0 | 2.6 | 3.4 | 4.5 |
| TOTAL | 30.8 | 36.6 | 60.9 | 86.4 | 125.8 |

The EPA estimated that in 1968, sulfur pollution caused damages worth a total of $8.3 billion, and further estimates that these damages may climb to $13.8 billion by 1977. Significantly, sulfur causes more than half of the total damages from pollution, even though it contributes a fairly small proportion of total pollutants by weight.

One year after its proposal, the President's sulfur tax finally emerged. But like many of his proposed "reforms," the sulfur tax recommendations have the look of a strong new law but little of the substance.

A sulfur tax could make it more expensive to pollute than to clean up. Even if a company chose to litigate rather than comply with emission standards, the tax, unlike regulatory standards, is still imposed while litigation proceeds, and polluters are forced to weigh the cost of the tax plus legal fees against the cost of cleaning up.

If the tax is not high enough, however, this mechanism breaks down, and the tax only encourages polluters to pay up and continue polluting. It seems likely that the President's tax proposal will have this effect. It would assess 10 or 15 cents per pound of sulfur, depending on how dirty the surrounding air already was. The Coalition to Tax Pollution, which speaks for a group of major environmental organizations, maintains that at least a uniform 20-cent charge is necessary, since cleanup costs are often more than 10 or 15 cents per pound, and since EPA estimates that society pays at least 25 cents per pound for damage caused by sulfur dioxide pollution.

As it became clear that the Administration would not allow EPA to use the 1970 Amendments to prevent degradation of existing clean air, it was hoped that the new sulfur tax would help serve that purpose. Without a specific directive to the contrary, ambient air quality standards can also become a kind of license to pollute, since a mass of clean air can legally be filled with pollutants up to the level of the standards. A uniform sulfur tax, on the other hand, applies to every pound of pollutant emitted by every polluter, and therefore provides a continuing incentive to foul a given air mass as little as possible and to reduce the total load of pollutants being dumped into the atmosphere.

The President's proposed legislation neatly subverts this purpose by failing to make its tax uniform. Polluters would pay 15 cents in regions with air already worse than the national primary air quality standards, and 10 cents where air pollution exceeds the tougher secondary but not primary standards. No tax at all would be imposed where the air is still cleaner than the secondary standards. The practical effect of this scheme would be to provide a strong incentive for polluters to move to areas where the air is now clean in order to pollute tax-free. The total pollution load would not be reduced; it would simply be spread out.

Another major defect of the President's proposal is its timing. Though the measure's professed purpose is to stimulate compliance with the 1970 Clean Air Act Amendments, the tax would not go into effect until after 1976—well after the law requires the primary air quality standards to be met.

In the midst of rising public concern over environmental deterioration, President Nixon proclaimed in his January, 1970, State of the Union Message that clean air, clean water, and open spaces ought once again to be the birthright of every American. "If we act now," said the President, "they can be." The Environmental Protection Agency, under Administrator Ruckelshaus, has done at least a creditable job of trying to implement the Clean Air Act. But after two years, it has become clear that, at least with regard to clean air, the President has no intention of responding to his own call for quick action. Instead, his Administration has consistently sought to delay the fight against air pollution by urging weak legislation and by undermining enforcement of the existing law.

# WATER POLLUTION

DAVID ZWICK

Faced with the need to control a rampant water pollution problem, the Nixon Administration started out, like much of the American public, almost sound asleep. The President climbed aboard the environmental bandwagon in 1970 when the fare was cheap, but quickly jumped off again as soon as the stakes began to rise. By the end of 1971, Administration forces were working actively with representatives of big business to block stronger water pollution control policies.

To put the Nixon response to water pollution in perspective, it is important to appreciate the extent to which our water is threatened. First of all, we don't have much of this precious resource available to waste. National water-use projections show that if current growth rates continue, the demand for water by industry, agriculture, and our domestic population will outrun useable supplies by 1980 or shortly thereafter.

What little we do have of this indispensable, life-giv-

---

*David Zwick directed the Nader Task Force on Water Pollution and co-authored* Water Wasteland *(Grossman, 1971), the report based on the two-year pollution study. A 1963 graduate of the U.S. Coast Guard Academy, he is currently on leave from graduate studies in law and public policy at Harvard. He serves as a consultant to several consumer/environmental groups on water pollution matters and is director of the Nader-sponsored Fishermen's Clean Water Action Project.*

ing commodity is being destroyed by pollution. According to the 1971 report of the President's Council on Environmental Quality (CEQ), over ninety percent of our watersheds are more than "moderately" polluted. Many of our major urban waterways have become so overburdened with municipal and industrial excretions that they are fit for little else besides navigation and continued dumping. A number of rivers, heavily laden with oil and industrial chemicals, are fire hazards. Cleveland's Cuyahoga River, for example, burst into flame in the summer of 1969, causing extensive damage.

Our nation's waters, overall, continue to grow more polluted every day. On the bright side, the 1971 CEQ report pointed out that the implementation of waste treatment controls over the past decade had almost kept pace with increases in organic wasteloads, which consume the oxygen in waterbodies. Thus the organic pollution of our lakes and streams was only slightly worse in 1968 than it was in 1957. But, the Council lamented, we have not yet come close to holding the line against many other forms of pollution: nutrients (such as the phosphates in detergents), which stimulate the growth of algae and promote accelerated oxygen deficiencies of waterbodies; sediment runoff, much of it from irresponsible construction practices; and the rapidly-increasing assortment of new and dangerous industrial contaminants (toxic synthetic chemicals, heavy metals, and many others).

Water pollution has long been associated in the American public's mind with aesthetic deprivation—ugly sights and nauseous smells—and with loss of recreational opportunities. Many people are also vaguely aware that the same waterbodies that our polluters use as their private sewers often do double duty as the source of many food items, including our most important foodstuff—drinking water. (An estimated one half the U.S. population drinks water discharged "only hours before . . . from some industrial or municipal sewer," in the words of Dr. Daniel Okun, chief of environmental sciences at the University of North

Carolina.) Still, until very recently it has been widely assumed that serious health hazards posed by water pollution were a relic of past centuries, before the widespread use of chlorination and the technology of drinking-water purification. Such comforting notions are mistaken. Available evidence points increasingly to water pollution as a possible contributor to many human ailments, including heart disease, cancer, birth deformation, and genetic damage.

The drinking-water treatment technology now being used across the country is typically not capable of screening out many of industry's exotic new pollutants. A nationwide drinking-water survey released in July, 1970, by the Department of Health, Education, and Welfare's Bureau of Water Hygiene revealed that 30 percent of the samples taken at consumers' taps contained quantities of chemicals exceeding limits recommended by the U.S. Public Health Service (PHS). Little is known about most of the 12,000 toxic or potentially toxic chemicals now being used by industry. An estimated 500 new chemicals are produced each year, with little or no information provided to an unsuspecting public about the extent or the dangers of their dispersal into the environment.

What we do know is not encouraging. Poisons like arsenic, lead, or methyl mercury, for example, can produce damage to the brain and central nervous system which may not show up for several years and is easily misdiagnosed when it does appear. All have been found in water in amounts exceeding PHS limits. Cadmium, another toxic metal found in municipal water supplies, has been linked to high blood pressure and arteriosclerotic heart disease. Nitrates, a component of farm runoff from artificial fertilizers and animal wastes, as well as of domestic and industrial effluents, can cause acute methemeglobinemia ("blue babies"). Excessive nitrate levels have been found in drinking water in several states, and the average nitrate concentrations in California's San Joaquin Valley are almost as high as the PHS limit. PHS nitrate limits themselves are inadequate, as evidenced by findings of behavioral disturbances and mental deficiencies associated with levels of nitrate only slightly above or even below the "safe" limit. The hormone diethylstilbestrol (DES), a known dangerous carcinogen used in cattle feed to produce rapid weight gains, may be excreted in animal wastes and carried by runoff into streams, which supply the drinking water of millions of Americans.

The viruses in domestic sewage and other wastes are another of the contaminants that can evade modern drinking-water purification systems and infiltrate their way through to the consumer's tap. In April, 1972, EPA scientists revealed the development of new techniques for isolating viruses, which led to the discovery of viruses in "properly treated" drinking water. Viruses capable of causing respiratory and heart diseases, nonbacterial meningitis, muscular paralysis, hepatitis, diarrhea, vomiting, and flu were found in the tap water of Bellerica and Lawrence, Massachusetts. The water purification systems in both these cities are superior to those used throughout most of the United States.

Beyond damage to human health are the more measurable indices of increasing water pollution. Six million fish were recorded killed by pollution in 1960; the number had soared to 23 million in 1970. Mercury pollution has led to warnings and restrictions on sport and commercial fishing in twenty-one states and Canada, as well as to the virtual demise of the swordfish industry in this country. Health authorities have closed more than 400 different shellfishing areas in the United States. Countless waters are off limits for swimming. (The lower Hudson River, for example, with bacteria counts of 170 times the safe limit, is so laden with pathogenic organisms and other filth that merely touching it is considered dangerous from a health standpoint.) Annual economic losses from water pollution in the United States were placed at nearly $13 billion in 1968.

## Municipal Sewage Treatment

The amount of federal money spent to help municipalities construct sewage treatment plants is a measure of the lower limit of any administration's environmental concern. Giving out federal sewage treatment subsidies steps on nobody's toes and politically is relatively easy to do. That the Nixon Administration has so frequently balked at committing the funds needed to curtail our burgeoning municipal wasteload does not inspire confidence that the Administration might also commit itself to the politically more difficult task of cracking down on industrial polluters.

Little more than half of the U.S. population is served by any form of municipal sewage treatment. Nearly 30 percent of the "treated" waste receives only primary treatment, which consists of screening and settling out the largest solid chunks before it is dumped into the nearest waterbody. Most of the rest receives no more than secondary treatment: a biological process that removes from 50 to 85 percent of the oxygen-demanding organic waste in sewage. Secondary treatment is not sufficient in many places to keep municipal pollution from increasing. And most sewage plants are too small to handle the wastes of the population they serve.

While many cities are ill-equipped to handle the heavy capital costs of municipal sewage treatment entirely on their own, President Nixon asked Congress for only $214 million of the $1 billion authorized for fiscal 1970. The Administration then fought a concerted but losing battle against Congress and the Citizens' Crusade for Clean Water (a coalition of conservation and citizen groups and municipal and county government associations, formed to press for the full authorization) to keep the appropriations low. Over White House objections, Congress upped the appropriation to $800 million. The following fiscal year, President Nixon again requested less than the authorized sum, this time successfully ($1 billion out of an authorized $1.25 billion).

The feuding over municipal construction grant appropriations between congressional clean water advocates and the Nixon Administration has led to a debate over how much money is actually needed to do the job. Congress' cost estimates have always been much higher than the Administration's. In July, 1970, for example, a survey taken by the National League of Cities–U.S. Conference of Mayors, at Senator Muskie's request, projected public expenditure requirements of $33 to $37 billion between 1970 and 1976 in order to meet the pollution control needs already identified by local authorities. An Administration survey came up with a $12 billion requirement for the fiscal 1972–1974 period ($6 billion of which the Administration proposed to finance out of Federal funds). Apart from the difference in the time spans for the two surveys, the difference in the cost estimates is accounted for primarily by the fact that the Mayors' figures include money for items not included by the Administration: more advanced treatment, for example, and the separation of combined storm and sanitary sewers to prevent raw sewage from running off into the rivers when it rains.

The funding debate has, naturally, become part of the controversy between the White House and Congress over

## Federal Grant Funds for Municipal Waste Water Treatment Construction
(in millions of dollars)

| Fiscal Year | 1970 | 1971 | 1972 | 1973 |
|---|---|---|---|---|
| Authorized by Congress | 1,000 | 1,250 | * | * |
| Requested by Administration | 214 | 1,000 | 2,000 | 2,000 |
| Appropriated by Congress | 800 | 1,000 | * | * |
| Obligated by Administration | 425 | 1,228 | 2,081 (e) | 2,000 (e) |
| Spent by Administration | 262 | 478 | 908 (e) | 1,100 (e) |

(e) Budget estimate
* Authorizations and appropriations for fiscal years 1972 and 1973 will be established by pending legislation.

SOURCES: Office of Management and Budget, and Environmental Protection Agency.

the new water pollution control bill. The Senate version (the "Muskie bill"), passed in November, 1971, allocates $14 billion in Federal funds over four years. The House raised the Federal four-year contribution to $20 billion, in response to pleas from the states and cities that the Senate bill was too stingy. The Administration still clings to the $6 billion grant proposal, spread over a three-year period, that accompanied its $12 billion estimate of total costs.

Regardless of how the bill comes out, the Administration is in a position to have the last laugh on sewage treatment funding. It can simply refuse to spend the money. Judging from President Nixon's past performance, cities and states would be well advised not to begin counting their municipal grant dollars until they have them firmly in hand.

## Refuse Act of 1899

American industry was credited by the Federal government with responsibility in 1968 for more than four times the water pollution (measured by "biochemical oxygen-demand," or BOD, the standard unit for measuring how much oxygen is consumed by the decomposition of organic wastes) caused by our domestic population. Industry expands that commanding lead with every jump in the GNP. Though industrial wastes account for more than half the waste load in our overburdened municipal treatment plants, less than one quarter of industry's total waste output goes into municipal sewer systems. The rest of the factory filth in industry's wastewater gets poured directly into our lakes, streams, and bays. An estimated 40,000 industrial establishments discharge their wastes into the nation's navigable waterways. Whatever the exact number, virtually all of them are breaking the law.

The law they are breaking is the now-famous Refuse Act of 1899. This archaic statute makes it a Federal crime to put "any refuse matter of any kind whatsoever" (a phrase that has been construed by the courts as including all "foreign substances and pollutants" except municipal sewage, which the 1899 law specifically exempts) into the navigable waters of the United States without a permit from the U.S. Army Corps of Engineers. Prior to 1969, less than one percent of U.S. industries had ever bothered to apply for a Corps permit and only a handful have been granted since then. Violators of the Refuse Act are subject to criminal sanctions of up to $2,500 per violation in fines and up to one year in jail. The Supreme Court has ruled that the government may also seek an injunction against a violator, to require him to stop polluting and clean up the mess he has already made.

Until it reached the venerable age of 70, when it was "rediscovered" by environmentalists, the 1899 Refuse Act lay almost completely dormant. To appreciate the significance of the law's 1969 reawakening, it is important to understand how great the contrast is between its simple and speedy enforcement procedures and the cumbersome abatement mechanisms of the "modern" pollution control laws.

Under the feeble Federal Water Pollution Control Act, which dates from 1948, the prescribed remedy for pollution is the so-called "enforcement conference," an elaborate bull session between state and Federal authorities, the polluters, and interested members of the public, which results in "recommendations" that the states are asked to carry out. To shield polluters from anything stiffer than recommendations, the designers of the Pollution Control Act threw up a series of statutory obstacles. Federal inspectors have no right, but must seek permission, to enter the polluter's property. In practice, polluters keep the inspectors out until incriminating evidence is cleaned up or swept under the table. Then there's a series of two six-months waiting periods before the polluter can be taken to court, and the government has the almost impossible burden of proving that the polluter's effluents are causing damage outside of the state from which they come (federal authority is limited to interstate pollution). Should the government ever overcome all the obstacles and arrive at a court showdown with a polluter (which has happened only once since the law's inception), the Pollution Control Act permits no penalties to be assessed. The court can issue an order to abate the pollution, but only if the order is "economically feasible." The intended net result of this complex charade is that pollution regulation is left to the states, which typically are firmly under the thumb of their large local polluters. Under this scheme, industries have been able to play one state off against another, "bargain hunting" for the weakest control standards.

Amendments to the Federal Water Pollution Control Act in 1965 added another layer to the Act's labyrinthine structure: water quality standards. The standards, to be set by the states and approved by the Federal government, were to specify permitted levels of pollution on all interstate waters. Enforcement of the standards was tied to most of the same delays and difficulties in the original Pollution Control Act. The process of merely setting the standards, let alone enforcing them, has been so complicated that as of April, 1972, almost five years after the June, 1967, final deadline for their submission, eight states still did not have a complete set of approved standards.

The Nixon Administration, during its first two years in office, slightly stepped up the use of these flimsy abatement tools in the Pollution Control Act from the state of near-paralysis which prevailed during the final LBJ years. But despite this gradually increasing pace of activity, environmentalists despaired of seeing any pollution cleaned up until the long-forgotten Refuse Act was resurrected late in 1969. Apart from its flat prohibition on dumping and its promises of rapid relief (criminal penalties and immediate injunction), this exciting "new" law offered an attractive fringe benefit. The Refuse Act encourages citizen involvement by awarding half the fines assessed to persons who furnished information leading to convictions. And existing legal precedent strongly suggests that the law could be extended to cover municipal pollution as well as industrial, notwithstanding the statutory exception for domestic sewage, where industries dump their wastes into municipal systems.

To environmentalists, the 1899 law was a godsend. To the Nixon Administration, it was an embarrassment. No longer could it hide behind the weaknesses in modern-day statutes as its excuse for not achieving visible cleanup results. In its simplicity, the Refuse Act points up the hypocrisy of the government's entire approach to controlling water pollution. Despite public praise by Administration officials for the 1899 law's virtues, behind-the-scenes efforts by the Nixon Administration have been aimed at narrowing the law's scope or quietly killing it off altogether.

The first Administration effort to restrict the scope of the Refuse Act came in the form of Justice Department guidelines issued to all U.S. Attorneys in the field on July 10, 1970. The directive instructed U.S. Attorneys that only in the case of "accidental or infrequent" violations of the 1899 law could they initiate a prosecution without seeking permission from higher up. Where violations were of a "continuing nature resulting from the ordinary operations of a manufacturing plant" (or, in other words, as the guidelines conceded, the kinds of cases that constitute "the greatest threat to the environment"), no one was to prosecute without clearance from Washington. In this way, Nixon Administration officials could keep tight control over use of the law. The basic Administration policy was to defer to the states—and to the polluters that so heavily influence state control programs—by deliberately withholding use of the Refuse Act where polluters were in compliance with state standards (no matter how weak or incomplete those standards might be) or where the state claimed it was (however feebly) conducting enforcement. Thus the Administration was able to saddle the Refuse Act with all the disadvantages of the "modern" pollution control laws. From the beginning of 1970 through June, 1971, U.S. Attorneys could only get Justice Department clearance for injunctive actions against a grand total of thirty-seven of the estimated 40,000 corporate law-breakers who violate the law on a continuing basis.

Public criticism, and hounding by Congressional clean water proponents like Rep. Henry Reuss (D-Wis.), prompted the Administration to come up with a new scheme, announced with great fanfare by President Nixon in December, 1970, for administering the Refuse Act: the "national permit program," scheduled to begin in July, 1971. Under the new Administration plan, industrial polluters would be required to apply for Federal permits from the Army Corps of Engineers. Before a polluter could receive a permit, EPA would have to certify that the permitted discharge would be acceptable from a water quality standpoint. What the ultimate outcome of the Nixon permit program will be is unclear. But so far it has had the same net effect as the restrictive Justice Department guidelines it replaced: to shield industrial polluters from Federal action under the Refuse Act.

It should be noted that the permit program has been accompanied by two positive benefits so far. It has enabled the government to collect, for the first time, accurate information on industrial discharges. (Federal law provides criminal penalties for false statements on permit applications.) And the Administration has, at the commencement of the permit program, increased the number of Federal personnel working in enforcement, a trend that, if continued, could produce significant dividends in tougher Federal enforcement in the future. But environmentalists were suspicious of other aspects of the permit program from the beginning.

It is important to understand that granting industries permits to dump is hardly an environmental improvement in itself. It simply gives official blessing to polluting activities that were previously illegal. The potential of a permit program rested in the possibility that its commencement would signal an end to the Nixon Administration's deliberate underenforcement of the Refuse Act. Administration spokesmen assured environmentalists this would be the case, and changed the restrictive Justice Department prosecutorial guidelines to require only that U.S. Attorneys in the field clear their actions with EPA regional offices. But since the possession of a permit insulates its holder from prosecution under the 1899 law as long as he complies with its terms, the permits themselves can be no better than the conditions that accompany their issuance. The Refuse Act gives the Federal government sweeping authority to attach stringent conditions, up to and including the elimination of discharges altogether. Early indications, however, were that the Administration's intentions were to grant permits with such weak conditions that most of them would simply be "licenses to pollute."

At February, 1971, joint House-Senate hearings on the Refuse Act permit program, EPA General Counsel John Quarles confirmed environmentalists' fears when he explained that the Administration planned to treat polluters on interstate waters differently from polluters on *intra*state (i.e., within a single state) waters, even though the Refuse Act makes no such distinction. The 1899 law gives the government authority to set tough Federal standards on all navigable waters. But as Quarles explained it, since Federal water quality standards under the "modern" Federal Water Pollution Control Act applied only to interstate waters (only 14 percent of the nation's stream mileage), EPA's procedure would be, with only minor exceptions, to rubber-stamp whatever requirements the states had imposed on industries on intrastate waters. This was a back-door way of continuing to defer to moribund state regulation under the modern pollution control laws. It would mean that Federal permits would be little more than licenses to pollute on as much as 86 percent of the nation's rivers and streams.

As public criticism of the Administration's stance again began to mount, the Administration issued several "clarifications" of its position. EPA Administrator William Ruckelshaus' response to the Nader report, *Water Wasteland*, contained the first public pledge that where

"State Water Quality Standards are inadequate or so weak as to be inconsistent with the purposes of the Federal Water Pollution Control Act, EPA will override State recommendations and apply appropriate water quality standards." The policy that ultimately emerged after several clarifications was to apply tough Federal review to the 10 percent of polluters that, according to EPA estimates, cause 90 percent of the problem, be they on interstate or intrastate waters. The only condition that would be applied to the remaining 90 percent of the permits, however, is that the polluter comply with applicable water quality standards, which are often so meaningless as to make such a condition virtually worthless from an enforcement standpoint.

At least the Administration was intending to focus its very limited resources on the most serious problems. But Administration officials have not been able to explain satisfactorily their plan to hand out the vast bulk of the pollution tickets with only the most cursory review and the vaguest definition of conditions. Perhaps the most honest explanation was given by one EPA official, who said, "They paid their $100 filing fee, and we have to give them something for their money." In any event, the Administration has not even gone so far as to promise to limit the duration (to one year, for example) of permits which do not contain strict discharge limitations, so that, as soon as the government's limited manpower allows, tough cleanup requirements can be imposed. The permit program still looks like a device to grant immunity from Federal control to the vast majority of polluters.

The permit program's most significant success to date has been in diverting public attention away from the continued non-enforcement of the Refuse Act. All the while the Administration and environmentalists have been trading shots over the plans for granting the permits, the polluters have had less to worry about than before. The Corps of Engineers' regulations for administering the permit program say that the fact that a polluter has applied for a permit will not be a bar to prosecution for failure to obey the law. Corps regulations notwithstanding, EPA's working policy has been not to trouble polluters who have applied for permits. From July, 1971, when the permit program officially started, until the middle of January, 1972, injunctive actions against the approximately 20,000 polluters with pending permit applications totaled only twenty-seven. During the same period the Justice Department also filed cases against forty-one polluters who did not even bother to apply for a discharge permit. The rest of the 40,000 industrial lawbreakers remain at large, free to dump to their hearts' content.

Other developments may make the whole debate over weak permit conditions academic. In the fall of 1971, Jerome Kalur, a Cleveland attorney and Sierra Club member who likes to canoe on Ohio's Grand River, sued the Secretary of the Army. Kalur argued that the National Environmental Policy Act (NEPA) requires that an environmental impact statement be filed by the Corps on each permit application, before the permit can be granted. In a December, 1971, decision, Judge Robinson of the District of Columbia U.S. District Court agreed. Up to that time, permit-granting had been a complex, agonizingly slow process. A total of only twenty-one permits had been granted nationwide in the first six months of the program. Rather than issue the impact statements required by law on each permit, the Administration responded by shutting down its permit granting operation entirely. While permit applications are still being internally processed, the entire program is now in a state of limbo. The tough Federal permits that were promised are nowhere to be seen, enforcement is negligible, and water pollution cleanup minimal.

In the meantime the Administration has persistently declined to attempt to expand the Refuse Act to cover municipal pollution. The last thing the Administration apparently wants is more enforcement authority to go unused, which would only be an additional source of embarrassment.

Beginning in late 1971, the Nixon Administration's efforts against the Refuse Act escalated from the level of ignoring it to the point of active assault. The Administration has favored a House of Representatatives version of the new water pollution bill which surrenders the permit granting authority back to the states, with no workable Federal check, over a Senate version that preserves the Federal government's power to deny the granting of state-approved discharge permits. Passage of the House version would reverse the progress of the past twenty years toward more uniform national control and leave the Refuse Act, and the entire water pollution control program, only half alive.

And (perhaps inevitably) on February 1, 1972, Nixon forces made an abortive attempt to deliver the *coup de grace* to the aged statute. Timothy Atkeson, general counsel for CEQ, carried up to Capitol Hill a draft letter, the original of which had been signed by CEQ Chairman Russell Train, urging that after July 1, 1973, (when the state-run permit program under the House version of the pending new water pollution legislation would be in effect) the Refuse Act be made applicable only to anchorage or navigation matters, thus effectively repealing it as an antipollution tool. The execution was supposed to have been performed neatly and quietly. In what was supposed to be a confidential session with staffers of the House Public Works Committee, Atkeson asked them to insert the Administration's draft language repealing the Refuse Act in the new water pollution bill. But the House staffers were not sympathetic, and the entire effort backfired when the confidential letter leaked out, setting off outraged denunciations from clean water advocates.

The ostensible Administration rationale for killing off the Refuse Act is that the new law will render it redundant if not obsolete, an explanation that has a hollow ring to citizens who are familiar with the workings of the 1899 statute. Under the Refuse Act, U.S. Attorneys can initiate actions on their own upon receiving a citizen complaint, a feature not provided in the pending new legislation, which forces citizens to rely exclusively on the good graces of EPA or the states. The designers of the pending House and Senate bills were also loathe to give citizens a percentage of fines assessed, as the Refuse Act does. And finally, the Refuse Act has been tried and tested, and it works. The same cannot be said of any new law, much less of the convoluted draftsmanship contained in the new water pollution proposals pending before Congress.

It would be folly to assume that the Refuse Act of 1899 is safe, as long as it remains in the custody of the Nixon Administration. The Administration never really wanted the law in the first place. Citizens who care about clean water would be well advised to watch over this elderly statute with great care, lest we wake up some morning to learn it has passed away mysteriously in the night.

## Phosphate Detergents

In lakes and slow-moving streams throughout the United States, fish and other marine life are being killed in vast numbers by reductions in the oxygen supply in the water. The loss of oxygen is caused by the artificially-induced overgrowth of algae in the water, and the water process involved is known as cultural eutrophication.

Phosphate detergents have been identified as a major contributor to cultural eutrophication, an acceleration of the normal aging process in slow moving bodies of water, such as lakes and meandering streams. Algal growth chokes oxygen out of the water and suffocates many types of marine life. The algal growth is caused by a number of nutrients, but the elimination of just one would be enough to stop what has now become widespread deterioration of the nation's water.

Phosphorus is the nutrient most capable of being eliminated, because it is the only one being added largely by man. Phosphate detergents, which the soap and detergent industry substitued for soap during the 1950's, contribute about 2,000,000,000 pounds, or about 50 percent of the total phosphate load, to our waters each year.

The problem would not seem that difficult to solve, were the government of a mind to solve it. Phosphates could be phased out of detergents coupled with a requirement that any new ingredient introduced into detergents in large quantities be pre-tested and pre-cleared. At the same time, the Federal government could require localities with known eutrophication problems to take necessary steps to solve them, including immediate bans on phosphate detergents. Where necessary, detergents could be replaced altogether by going back to soap. There are nonphosphate detergents now being marketed that have been judged effective, safe, and nonpolluting. And EPA has known for some time, based on laboratory studies that are being performed, that even more promising substitutes for phosphates are just around the corner. Yet the Nixon Administration has advocated none of these forward steps. The Administration has instead not only cut back on earlier government commitments to get the phosphates out of detergents, but upon occasion even seems to promote them.

Meanwhile, eutrophication is growing more serious. Lake Erie, for example, has seen at least 5,000 years of its natural life span disappear in the last twenty-five years. One recent study by the Environmental Protection Agency found that a "mat of algae two feet thick and a few hundred square miles in extent floats in the middle of the lake in mid-summer. . . . The zone of zero oxygen is spreading, bringing the threat that eutrophication will soon become self-sustaining." EPA estimates there are additional eutrophication problems in at least thirty-two states and 1,000 bodies of water.

The Administration has never denied that eutrophication and prosphate detergents are a problem. In fact, the White House Council on Environmental Quality said in its 1970 Annual Report that "eutrophication is emerging as perhaps the single most difficult water pollution control problem," and that "phosphates are still the most important nutrient to control if eutrophication is to be successfully attacked."

But, incredibly, just one year later, on September 15, 1971, the United States Surgeon General Jesse Steinfeld, held a press conference at which he announced, "My advice to the housewife would be to use the phosphate detergent." Lever Brothers, one of the big three detergent makers, ran this statement in full-page newspaper ads around the country, and joined Procter & Gamble, and Colgate-Palmolive to fight local ordinances passed to restrict phosphate detergents. Officials from the EPA and the Department of Health, Education and Welfare (HEW) also testified at local hearings in Miami and in other parts of the country suggesting that restrictions on phosphates may be unwise. Even the international agreement between the United States and Canada on the protection of the Great Lakes was delayed, endangered and weakened before it was finally signed by President Nixon and Prime Minister Trudeau on April 15, 1972.

Behind this pattern of events was the careful lobbying of the detergent industry, coordinated by Bryce Harlow. Harlow had worked in the White House during President Nixon's first two years of office as the President's chief lobbyist on Capitol Hill. Having agreed to replace Rogers Morton as the chairman of the Republican National Committee, Harlow left the White House in December, 1970, to return instead to his old job with Procter & Gamble. As columnist Jack Anderson reported on April 5, 1972, "Procter & Gamble . . . officials thought he would be more valuable working for them full time."

The detergent companies had known for several years that public pressure to eliminate phosphates might eventually force the government to take restrictive action. By early 1970, they were beginning to experiment with a phosphate substitute called sodium nitrilotriacetate, an organic compound commonly known as NTA. But on December 18, 1970, Surgeon General Steinfeld and EPA Administrator Ruckelshaus requested the companies not to market NTA until further tests could determine whether or not it caused cancer and birth defects. The manufacturers agreed, but at a substantial financial loss. In fiscal 1971, for example, Procter & Gamble wrote off $7,100,000 of binding contracts to purchase NTA. The detergent industry's full NTA investment is well over several hundred million dollars.

Thus, as government studies of NTA went on and on, Harlow held a strategy session on April 22, 1971, with the other partisans of the detergent industry. According to Jack Anderson, who obtained a transcript of the secret meeting, Harlow "told the group that he was working inside the White House with presidential aides Peter Flanigan, John Whitaker and Charles Colson. Harlow had also consulted, he said, with Tim Atkeson, general counsel for the President's Council on Environmental Quality, and Jim Lynn, then general counsel for the Commerce Department." The soapmakers are anxious for obvious reasons to see NTA get the green light. They also wanted a guarantee that phosphates would not be banned and assurances that they would not have to put up with the nuisance of varied local phosphate ordinances.

The Administration's September 15, 1971, news conference was just what the detergent industry needed. It was now doubtful whether NTA would be cleared as a phosphate substitute for some time to come. Surgeon General Steinfeld wanted additional studies on NTA which could take up to two years for completion. Having geared up production and marketing machinery for detergents, the industry cannot conceive of a return to soap. Thus, from the viewpoint of men like Harlow and Flanigan, a whitewash of phosphates must have seemed like an ideal solution.

To justify the position of September 15th, Steinfeld and Ruckelshaus argued that the nonphosphate detergents were unsafe for human health. "Certain of the nonphosphate detergents now on the market," read their press release, "contain ingredients that, if accidentally ingested, aspirated, or introduced into the eyes, may be extremely injurious to humans, particularly to children. These particular products utilize materials as a substitute for phosphates that are highly caustic and that clearly constitute a health hazard, which phosphates do not." This argument ran directly counter to the results of tests done by HEW's Food and Drug Administration. The FDA found that the safety ranges of phosphate and nonphosphate detergents completely overlapped. There are, in fact, phosphate detergents that are highly toxic and there are nonphosphate detergents that FDA considers safe. Malcolm Jensen, the FDA's Director of Product Safety, answered Jesse Steinfeld's assertion that phosphates "are safe for human health" by stating, "I would not have given the same advice."

If the government refused to force an elimination of phosphates from detergents, it did promise to take phosphates out of municipal sewage by improving waste water treatment. But as a recent report from Rep. Henry Reuss' (D-Wis.) House Subcommittee on Conservation and Natural Resources points out, control of eutrophication will require *both* improved waste water treatment and elimination of phosphates from detergents. Half of the country's treatment plants are already overloaded, and each year an additional thousand communities outgrow their systems. Fully 34 percent of our domestic sewage load now receives no treatment whatsoever. The construction of all the needed facilities will take billions of dollars and many years. In the meantime, many bodies of water will be further degraded.

The Great Lakes are in the greatest danger of all, and, according to one official close to the negotiations, Jesse Steinfeld's "advice" became "a major stumbling block" in the pending agreement between the United States and Canada. The Canadians had already taken steps to reduce their detergents to a phosphorus content of only

2.2 percent by the end of 1972, and were understandably wary of the new position taken by the White House. Phosphate detergents from Lever Brothers and Colgate-Palmolive have a phosphorus content of 8.7 percent and those from Procter & Gamble range from 9.7 percent to 14.8 percent.

The agreement, signed April 15, 1972, came under immediate fire. Back in June, 1971, the Canadian-United States Joint Working Group had called for an agreement to "essentially eliminate phosphates in detergents" in order to achieve an 80 percent reduction in the total phosphorus loadings of the Lakes by 1975. As it happened, the agreement signed by President Nixon and Prime Minister Trudeau, however, did not call for the U.S. to take phosphates out of detergents; and, as a result, only aimed for a 60 percent reduction of the phosphorus load. This reduction will allow 16,000 tons of phosphorus to be dumped into Lake Erie each year. Senator Muskie charged that the omission of curbs against detergents "will make the agreement a retreat instead of an advance." Rep. Henry Reuss called the agreement "a victory for Procter & Gamble, but a potential disaster for Lake Erie."

Why did Canada sign such a weak agreement? As Rep. Reuss explains, Trudeau was simply put in the position of signing what Nixon wanted "or having no agreement at all."

## Water Pollution Legislation

The Nixon record on new water pollution legislation has been distinguished by its solicitude toward polluters, particularly industrial polluters. It is a record that displays a reluctance to extend the basic principles of law and order to outlaws of the big business variety.

Under the 1970 Nixon water pollution proposal, for example, a polluter caught red-handed dumping in willful violation of the law could not be penalized, nor could he even be given an administrative order to stop. Before any government fines could be assessed, the Nixon bill required control officials first to give the lawbreaker a notice to stop and then wait six months, during which time the violator would be free to pollute with impunity.

The 1971 Nixon bill was improved, but it still suffered from severe structural defects. For example, pollution controls could not be imposed by the government without "taking into account the practicability of compliance," a phrase that could be used by business firms to argue for exceptions from control requirements on the ground that they might cut unduly into the company's profits. This phrase was inserted during interagency meetings before the proposed legislation was made public, reportedly at the insistence of the Commerce Department's National Industrial Pollution Control Council (NIPCC), the government-funded lobby for weaker pollution controls made up of the representatives from the nation's biggest industrial polluters. The day the Administration's water bill was sent off to Congress, on February 10, 1971, the President was entertaining the Council's industrialists and their business colleagues at a special White House reception. He pledged to his guests that they would not be allowed to become the "scapegoats" of his Administration's environmental effort: "The Government—this Administration, I can assure you—is not here to beat industry over the head." It was widely suspected that the "practicability" phrase was intended to insure that the Administration would make good on this pledge.

Additionally, the 1971 Nixon proposal set no final deadline for polluters to be in compliance with water quality standards. Nor would the Nixon bill oblige the Administrator of EPA to prosecute even the most flagrant violators of the law. Enforcement was left an optional matter for the Administrator to conduct, or fail to conduct, as he chooses. The Administration bill would perpetuate the discredited policy of deference to state regulation by actually forbidding penalties against a polluter if the states are taking the "appropriate and sufficient action" to secure eventual compliance. The one redeeming factor of the

Nixon bill was its requirement that industries discharging wastes into municipal systems pay back a fair share of the construction costs of municipal sewage treatment plants, thus ending a longstanding loophole in the Federal Water Pollution Control Act that permitted the giveaway of billions of dollars in Federal funds as a hidden subsidy to private industries.

Fortunately, Senator Muskie's Subcommittee on Air and Water Pollution did not consider itself bound by the Administration's limited aspirations. The Subcommittee got down to the business of drafting a new water pollution law in June, 1971. The "Muskie bill" passed the Senate by an 86-0 vote in November, 1971, and was unlike anything President Nixon had proposed.

Its objective is the attainment of truly clean water (restoration of the "natural chemical, physical, and biological integrity of the Nation's waters"). To get there, the Senate bill sets forth a national policy calling for the elimination of discharges of pollutants from their source into the navigable waterways by 1985 (the "zero discharge" standard). The bill would give polluters until 1976 to comply with national minimum effluent limitations, to be developed under guidelines promulgated by EPA, and to meet existing water quality standards. By 1981, industries would have to stop their dumping altogether, unless they could show that they could not make the shift to zero discharge at a "reasonable cost." In that case their 1981 control requirements would be based on the "best available" technology.

The no-discharge concept of the Senate bill is aimed at stimulating the recycling and reclamation of wastes and wastewater, to turn what would otherwise be harmful pollutants into valuable resources whenever possible. The Senate committee had been impressed in its deliberations by the degree to which existing methodology for waste recycling is being ignored by state and Federal control officials, typically sanitary engineers bent on running sewage treatment pipes straight to the nearest river.

Available evidence on more than twenty-five land disposal systems in this country, for example, indicates that using the earth as a filter for sewage can produce clean water (i.e., water which typically meets Public Health Service drinking water standards) for less money than it costs to meet existing low water quality standards by conventional technological treatment. Muskegon County, Michigan, actually anticipates making a net profit from its spray-irrigation style pollution control system, when it totals up revenues from crops grown on the newly fertilized land and from "cooling fees" to be charged to an electric utility which wants to dump its heated effluent into the system's wastewater treatment lagoon (where, incidentally, it aids the treatment process). Similar results have been reported by industries (Dow Chemical, for instance) which have been compelled to install closed-loop recycling systems and found, to everyone's amazement, that they have begun to realize money savings by reclaiming valuable products from the waste streams.

The Senate committee had also become convinced that the old water quality standards approach of existing law (i.e., the notion that different levels of dirtiness should be permitted on different bodies of water) not only was causing serious harm to our waters but also was so complicated to administer that it would continue to frustrate clean water results and keep the public thoroughly confused.

The Nixon Administration had been hoping for a business-as-usual water quality standards bill, so Administration officials were appalled when they saw what the Senate was doing. At the same time, they sensed a potentially powerful backlash against the Senate-passed legislation in the business community and several states. The Administration capitalized on the opportunity by stepping in and assuming leadership of the environmental backlash, mobilizing the various forces for an all out attack in the House of Representatives on the Senate bill.

Here's how the *National Journal* described the Administration effort:

> Spokesmen for industrial interests . . . credited the Administration with galvanizing opinion and action against the Senate bill in the business community.
>
> "The notion that somehow industry 'got to' the Administration and pushed them into this campaign is really the reverse of what happened so far as I can tell," said Douglas Trussell, vice president of government relations for the National Association of Manufacturers.
>
> "The Administration took the initiative." he said, "and many executives were ignorant of what was in the Senate bill when this all started."
>
> John J. Coffey, Jr., senior associate for natural resources and environmental quality for the Chamber of Commerce of the U.S., said: "Actually, the Administration's effort bucked up some industries who had thought the situation hopeless after the bill passed the Senate."
>
> Several industry spokesmen said that the Commerce Department and its National Industrial Pollution Control Council were highly influential in moving the Administration's counterattack into high gear.
>
> Said David R. Toll, general counsel for the National Association of Electric Companies: "My impression is that [Secretary of Commerce] Stans and [Executive Director of NIPCC] Walter Hamilton over at Commerce put the fire under the Administration."

The Administration began orchestrating the industrial attack on the Senate bill at a strategy session on November 4, 1971, just two days after its passage, when the White House called together representatives of seven trade associations. Presidential aide John Whitaker and his assistant Richard Fairbanks were in charge of the meeting, along with Commerce's Walter Hamilton, and Howard Cohen, director of EPA's legislative office. The *National Journal* describes what happened this way:

> "Fairbanks made an incredible speech," said one association representative. "His pitch was: 'We fought a lonely battle over here on this bill. Where the hell were you guys when we needed you? We could have gotten some of the worst provisions changed if you had gotten into this in a big way.'
>
> "Cohen also got up and talked about how we'd blown it, and both clearly felt that industry had let them down."

That meeting was followed up by one the next day between Commerce Secretary Stans and some thirty executives who belong to the Commerce Department's NIPCC. P. Nick Gammelgard of the American Petroleum Institute recalls that the Administration wired four of the largest oil companies asking them to take action in the House against the Senate bill.

The Nixon Administration's principal weapon, apart from the army of industrialists it set into motion, was misleading and distorted information. The main Administration argument, echoed faithfully by its industrial allies, was that the legislation would cripple industry and wreck the economy. To frighten the House Public Works Committee into backing down from the Senate's strong controls, the Council on Environmental Quality cooked up a phony price tag of $316 billion for attainment of the bill's objectives.

The CEQ cost estimate was particularly deceptive, since the Senate bill contained explicit economic loopholes to guarantee against the astronomical costs the Administration projected. Industries were not to be required to eliminate their discharges unless they could do it at a "reasonable cost." The 1981 "best available technology" requirements were carefully hedged with the qualification that the Administrator of EPA must take into account "the cost of such controls."

A main thrust of the Administration's effort to sow confusion was painting the 1985 no-discharge target as though it were a legislatively enforceable mandate, when in fact both the language of the bill and Senator Muskie's comments on the Senate floor left no doubt that it was not a binding requirement but rather a policy goal, to stimulate research and planning. Furthermore, the CEQ had arrived at its incredible $316 billion estimate of national costs for no-discharge by calculating the cost of *distillation* of our nation's entire wastewater volume, thus disregarding completely both the intent of the Senate bill and the availability of low-cost recycling methodology like land disposal/spray irrigation and closed-loop systems for industry. A special study conducted for Friends of the Earth concluded that the Administration may have overstated the cost of cleanup by as much as six times, and possibly more.

At the same time the Administration was conjuring up its bogus cost figure, in late October, 1971, EPA Administrator Ruckleshaus was writing a letter to the Secretary of the Army demanding that the Army Corps of Engineers immediately discontinue studies into the cost of curtailing pollutant discharges into the waterways by shifting to land disposal/spray irrigation schemes in several major metropolitan areas. Ruckleshaus later retracted the demand, but no one could figure out exactly why it had come in the first place. One possibility is that the Administration wanted to squelch any chance that the Corps might come up with cost estimates that would have exposed the Administration's scare campaign as a fraud.

The possibility that it was fraudulent did not prevent the campaign against the Senate bill from being successful. Under the massive pressure being brought by industry and the Administration, the House Public Works Committee inserted a proviso in its version of the bill that not only rendered the Senate's 1985 goal null and void but also scrapped the 1981 requirement that industries use the best available technology. That having been done, the House Committee then proceeded to dismantle the Senate bill section by section, inserting loopholes for industry and other polluting special interests in strategic spots throughout. By the time the House Committee bill came up for a floor vote in March, 1972, its key provisions had been rendered so impotent that corporate lobbyists and the Administration were working hard together for the bill's passage, insisting that not a single comma be changed on the House floor. An effort by environmental, labor, and citizen groups to get the emasculated bill strengthened on the floor with a "Clean Water Package" of amendments, sponsored by Reps. Dingell (D-Mich.), Reuss (D-Wis.), and Saylor (R-Pa.), ran into an onslaught of industrial opposition that Dingell later described as "the best financed and most energetic lobbying effort I've ever seen." The key amendments in the Clean Water Package were defeated, and the bill passed with loopholes intact.

Contributing to the defeat of the Clean Water Package amendments on the floor was more self-serving manipulation of information by the Administration. In the middle of March, 1972, the Army Corps of Engineers had finished a study (one of the studies EPA Administrator Ruckleshaus had tried to get halted the preceding fall) comparing the cost of recycling the entire domestic and industrial wasteload of metropolitan Chicago, by using spray irrigation on land, to the cost of conventional technology sewage treatment. To apologists for the old waste-dumping ways of handling the sewage problem, the results of this study could not help but be mind-boggling: the cost of irrigation/recycling Chicago's domestic and industrial wastes is approximately one-half the cost of the cheapest conventional sewage treatment alternative. For approximately $1.80 per month per person, the citizens of Chicago could eliminate the water pollution they have become accustomed to tolerating and could have clean water instead. By comparison, the per capita cost of going to advanced biological treatment—the most comonly recommended advanced treatment scheme—was figured at over $4 per month.

If the Chicago cost figures can be projected nationwide, national cleanup costs come out to $59.88 billion over the next twenty years, compared to the Administration's inflated $316 estimate.

When White House assistant John Whitaker saw the Corps study's explosive results, about ten days before the House vote on the water pollution bill, he immediately placed it under wraps. Officials of the Corps who were familiar with the report were muzzled on White House instructions. Upon learning of the suppressed report, Ralph Nader sent a letter to OMB head George Schultz asking for its immediate release, noting the report's "critical significance to the debate now going on in the House of Representatives." The report, said Nader, "could give a major boost to House proponents of tougher controls on industrial pollution. By withholding this information from the public at the very time the Congress and the American people most need it to make rational legislative decisions for the future, the Administration demonstrates again its willingness to place the interests of corporate polluters ahead of the public's interest in a clean and healthy environment."

The Nader charges succeeded in shaking the study loose on March 27, but too late to make most Congressmen aware of its findings. The day after the report's release, the Clean Water Package was defeated on the House floor.

It remains to be seen whether the Administration's campaign for dirty water has delivered the clean water cause a permanent setback, for representatives of the House and Senate have yet to attempt to settle their differences in conference committee. Some observers think the differences between the House and Senate versions of the new bill may be so great as to prevent agreement being reached at all. Others are concerned that the water pollution bill that emerges may be so weak that cleanup will continue to be frustrated. If tough water pollution control legislation is not passed in the 1972 session of Congress, the failure, as in the case of the 1899 Refuse Act, phosphate control, and the Canadian Great Lakes Agreement, must be attributed directly to the Nixon Administration.

# WATER RESOURCES DEVELOPMENT

BRENT BLACKWELDER

On January 19, 1971, President Nixon announced that he was ordering a halt to further construction of the Cross-Florida Barge Canal, "to prevent potentially serious environmental damages." Designed during the Second World War, the barge canal was to provide a short route from the Gulf of Mexico to the Atlantic Ocean. It also would have destroyed the unique Oklawaha River, a beautiful semi-tropical stream, and quite possibly would have polluted the region's aquifer and water supply. The Florida Defenders of the Environment had released a study condemning the project as a disaster, and a group of 150 scientists had written the President asking that the construction be stopped. Four days before the President's decision, conservationists had even obtained a temporary court injunction against the project. In announcing his action, the President said that the "Council on Environmental Quality has recommended to me that the project be halted, and I have accepted its advice. The Council pointed out to me that the project could endanger the unique wildlife

---

*Brent Blackwelder is a Washington, D.C. representative of the Environmental Policy Center and co-chairman of the Citizen's Committee Against Channelization. He previously worked with Friends of the Earth. He earned his Bachelor's degree from Duke University in 1964, his Master's degree in mathematics from Yale in 1966, and is presently working on a Doctorate in Philosophy at the University of Maryland.*

of the area and destroy this region of unusual and unique natural beauty."

The President's action was especially commendable and bold in light of the fact that the canal was already one-third complete, with $50 million of the project's total cost of $180 million already spent. "The step I have taken today will prevent a past mistake from causing permanent damage," the President said. "But more important, we must assure that in the future we take not only full but also timely account of the environmental impact of such projects—so that instead of merely halting the damage, we prevent it."

Unfortunately, great damage has already occurred because of water resources "development." Each year, more than $2 billion of taxpayers' money is spent making harmful alterations of rivers and streams. Historically known as "pork barrel projects," the projects involve dam building, canal digging, and channelization of streams. Each year, more and more free-flowing scenic rivers and streams succumb to the bulldozer and dredging bucket. All the major river basins from the Columbia to the Potomac have been damaged or compromised by dams, pollution, dredging, or channelization.

Channelization turns streams into unsightly ditches. Fish and wildlife habitat is destroyed, stream productivity is lowered, species diversity is reduced, and many food chains are wiped out entirely. Channelization also aggravates downstream flooding, erosion and siltation, lowers the water table, and spreads pollution such as pesticide contamination.

Large dams flood out scenic valleys and canyons, and the trapping of nutrients behind a dam often causes accelerated eutrophication (excessive growth of weeds and algae). Damming large rivers also eliminates wildlife habitat. The passage of spawning fish is often blocked, and the dams can increase the water's nitrogen content to the point where fish get the bends.

Canals often cause a harmful mixing of ecosystems.

The Welland and Erie Canals, for example, can be blamed for the presence of the sea lamprey and the alewife, which have seriously damaged the lake trout population, in the Great Lakes. The industry which follows the canal route almost inevitably increases the pollution.

## Army Corps of Engineers

The Army Corps of Engineers is by far the largest of the four water development agencies. Now working on projects having a total cost of well over $17 billion, the Corps' activities include harbor dredging, canal digging, channelization, dam building, levee construction, and control of beach erosion. Corps programs for harbors and navigation date back to the 1880's, but it was not until the 1936 Flood Control Act that the Corps began its accelerated program of dam building and channelization. In that act Congress declared that flood control was a proper federal activity and gave the Corps the green light. Since 1936, the Corps has completed 250 flood control dams at a cost of more than $5 billion.

## Soil Conservation Service (SCS)

The Soil Conservation Service (SCS) was established in 1935 as part of the Department of Agriculture and was given the assignment of preventing erosion, preserving soil fertility, and promoting land conservation. The SCS did good work at first, and brought about much needed reform in the disastrous farming practices that led to the dust bowl era. But in 1954, the SCS was given the job of flood prevention in small watershed areas, and it began to adopt more of the destructive techniques used by the Corps of Engineers. With its motto of "holding the raindrop where it falls" lost to the past, the SCS began channelizing streams into straight ditches, rushing water off as fast as possible. Already having channelized over 4,000 miles of streams, the SCS has plans approved for 12,000 additional miles. With the Corps projects on bigger rivers and streams, and the SCS activity with the smaller streams, the two agencies combined can accomplish great destruction.

## Bureau of Reclamation

The Bureau of Reclamation was created within the Department of Interior by the Reclamation Act of 1902, which Congress passed in order to promote development of the arid West. The Bureau's work is confined to the seventeen westernmost states, and consists primarily of irrigation, development of hydroelectric power and flood control, and the provision of water for municipalities and industry. Some irrigation and development in the West was surely desirable, but the Bureau has gone overboard and spent $1 billion building dams and altering rivers and streams. There is now a $5.5 billion backlog of projects awaiting funding for construction. A recent Nader task force report, *Damming the West,* has pointed out the serious ecological impact of the Bureau's work, the hidden subsidies it has provided to big landowners and speculators, and the unrealistic economics used to justify the Bureau's projects.

## Tennessee Valley Authority (TVA)

The Tennessee Valley Authority (TVA) was created in 1933 as a public corporate entity and was given the responsibility for development in the Tennessee River Basin. TVA activities include navigation improvement and flood control, provision of electric power, and promotion of agriculture and industrial development. It spends about $28 million each year for development of water resources. Since 1933, TVA has been damming up Tennessee's rivers and streams and flooding out one valley after another. It boasts that it has created over 11,000 miles of shoreline, more than surrounds the Great Lakes. But there are not many free-flowing rivers left in Tennessee. Undaunted, the TVA is planning dams for those that remain, such as the Duck River and Little Tennessee. TVA is also venturing into North Carolina, with a proposed Upper French Broad project involving fourteen dams.

Plugging up the pork barrel is no easy task. These projects find favor with many Congressmen and Senators anxious to bring jobs and money into their districts and states. Happy construction contractors obligingly reciprocate with campaign contributions of a not altogether ungenerous nature. The need for reform is long overdue.

Despite more than $7 billion spent for flood control since 1936, flood damages continue to exceed $1 billion each year. The water development agencies look for big structural solutions, such as dams and channelization, while less costly and ecologically sound alternatives are rarely considered. Floodplains should be zoned to prevent development, while the pork barrel projects are justified as making such development possible. Floodproofing of those buildings and structures which do exist is rarely adequate, and the Federal Flood Control Insurance Act of 1968 has been poorly implemented.

The public works projects also spend millions of taxpayer dollars destroying streams for the purpose of putting more land into agriculture despite the fact that one third of the nation's cropland is now idle. The result is the growth of big farms, while the small family farmer is squeezed out of business. Figures from the U.S. Department of Agriculture show a steady and continuing decline in the number of American farms: 5.6 million in 1950, 4.0 million in 1960, and only 2.9 million in 1970.

Thus President Nixon's stopping of the Cross-Florida Barge Canal promised a much needed honest reappraisal of water development projects. It was not an easy decision for him to make, and he received blistering criticism from those who had their hands in the pork barrel. Rep. Joe Evins, (D-Tenn.), chairman of the House Appropriations Subcommittee on Public Works, for example, asked: "What is coming to this country if the people's elected representatives in the House and Senate are ignored, and some one individual can stop things like this?" Conservationists were jubilant. After all, the President said that vigorous action had to be taken in the future to prevent damage from occurring, rather than simply halting it after it already had begun. But environmentalists sadly discovered in May of 1971 that the promise was empty. On May 25, four months after he halted the Cross-Florida Barge Canal, the President arrived in Mobile, Alabama, to join Gov. Wallace in the ground-breaking ceremonies for the Tennessee-Tombigbee Waterway—a project twice as expensive and probably more damaging to the environment.

The Tennessee-Tombigbee is designed to link the Tombigbee River in Alabama with the Tennessee River by means of a canal. At an estimated total cost of $365 million, the project will mean dredging hundreds of miles of rivers and streams and the movement of 258 million cubic yards of earth (100 million more than were moved in building the Panama Canal). The project would require digging a 186-mile-long channel in the Tombigbee River, a 45-mile-long lateral canal, and a 39-mile-long deep canal piercing the high ridge which separates the basins of the Tennessee and Tombigbee. The project not only would have a severe impact on rivers and streams, but would lead to the devastation of northern Alabama by strip mining. One major goal of the project is to provide a direct route for export to Japan of this large reserve of strip minable coal.

President Nixon's personal endorsement of the Tennessee-Tombigbee is especially regrettable since completion of the waterway would increase the pressure to reopen the construction of the Cross-Florida Barge Canal and to build a canal known as the "missing link" across the Gulf Coast along the Florida panhandle to connect the Tenn-Tom with the barge canal. Tenn-Tom completion would also add pressures to construct other canals linking into what would become a vast network.

The President's endorsement was made in spite of a report from the southeastern regional office of the Environmental Protection Agency (EPA) which said the Tennessee-Tombigbee would "irreversibly" damage the scenic and natural area. Relatively pure streams would be polluted with such contaminants as mercury and DDT from the heavily industrialized Tennessee River. EPA's report concluded that "a reevaluation of the project should be made." But throughout the decision-making period, the White House Council on Environmental Quality was strangely silent. In the Cross-Florida Barge Canal decision, President Nixon said he took CEQ's advice. Now when confronted with a project twice as big and possibly more destructive, the Council argued against it in private but had nothing to say in public.

Shortly after the President's trip to Mobile, conservationists filed suit to halt the Tenn-Tom construction on the basis of the glaring inadequacies in the Corps' environmental impact statement, required under the National Environmental Policy Act of 1969 (NEPA). U.S. District Court Judge John Lewis Smith granted a preliminary injunction, agreeing with the conservationists that the Corps had not fully met the requirements of NEPA. Nevertheless, the President's budget for Fiscal 1973 includes a $12 million request for funding construction.

## Budget Increases

The President's new budget for fiscal year 1973 dispels any belief that the President is de-emphasizing pork barrel projects. With $2.4 billion spent on water resources development in fiscal 1971, the budget estimates increases of $596 million in fiscal 1972 and $190 million in fiscal 1973. These sharp increases in funding can hardly be described as an effort to curtail destructive manipulation of rivers and streams.

The White House Office of Management and Budget (OMB) claims that the Administration is simply trying to get rid of the enormous backlog of projects which are lingering on but not yet completed, but this argument has economic merit only if we assume that a project will eventually be constructed. Many projects have already been delayed, and their costs have skyrocketed in the meantime. In addition, many projects which have not yet reached the construction stage were authorized back in the 1950's and 1960's, some even date back to the 1930's and 1940's. All of these should be thoroughly reevaluated to make certain they still have the required favorable cost-benefit ratios.

### Outlays for Water Resources and Power
(in millions)

| Fiscal Year | 1971 | 1972 | 1973 |
|---|---|---|---|
| Soil Conservation Service | $118 | $136 | $148 |
| Corps of Engineers | 1,365 | 1,631 | 1,810 |
| Bureau of Reclamation | 501 | 598 | 672 |
| Tennessee Valley Authority | 367 | 582 | 507 |
| TOTAL | $2,351 | $2,947 | $3,137 |

SOURCE: *U.S. Budget, Fiscal 1973*

Some credit must be given the Administration for limiting the number of new starts in Fiscal 1973 on Corps and Bureau of Reclamation projects, and for not including such potentially destructive projects as the Big Darby Dam in Ohio and the Cascadia Dam on the South Santiam River in Oregon. The Administration is also not asking for funding of the TVA's Upper French Broad project in western North Carolina. But all in all, the 1973 budget reflects a failure to come to grips with the pork-barrel issue. Far too many projects funded in the budgets for 1973 and the previous two years represent environmental and economic boondoggles. Here are just a few of the projects being funded for the Corps of Engineers which should be considered prime targets for budget cutting:

• Sprewell Bluff Dam on the Flint River in Georgia. The Flint River has been called the most scenic river in the Georgia piedmont by the Georgia Natural Areas Council, and it's been recommended for status as a state scenic river. Building the Sprewell Bluff Dam, at a total cost of $121 million, is the height of insensitivity to the river's many natural values. The Georgia Recreation Commission is opposed to the dam because of the growing demand for recreation on natural streams.

• Cache River project in Arkansas and the West Tennessee Tributaries project in Tennessee. These channelization projects, with a total cost of over $80 million, would destroy very significant fish and wildlife habitats in order to put more land into agriculture. To justify the Cache project, the Corps has counted the destruction of more than 250,000 acres of bottomland hardwoods as a benefit. This would destroy more than 12 per cent of the remaining forest cover in the Mississippi delta section of Arkansas. Of the original 10 million acres of delta forest in eastern Arkansas, only two million remain.

• Trotters Shoals Dam on the Savannah River in Georgia. This project, with a total cost of $148 million, would create a lake between two already existing lakes on the Savannah. The Corps counts an increase in recreation benefits as a plus for the project, even though the state has no need for more flat water recreation. No account is given to the eutrophication which will occur in the lower lake once the oxygen producing section on the Savannah now connecting the two lakes is inundated.

• Tocks Island Dam on the Delaware River. Here again the $295 million project can only be justified as producing enormous recreation benefits, yet the project would flood out a beautiful valley which has tremendous recreational potential just as it is.

• Oakley Dam on the Sangamon River in Illinois. This $76.3 million project has been shown by the local Committee on Allerton Park to be "ecologically and economically unsound, and will not provide the benefits claimed for it." A non-structural project could be developed at less than half the cost, and would not harm Allerton Park, farmers, or the Sangamon River.

New Hope Dam in North Carolina, Salt Creek Dam in Ohio, Trinity River Canal in Texas—the projects, spread from coast to coast, could go on and on.

## Bureau of Reclamation

Second only to the Corps in its "development" and destruction of our country's water resources is the Bureau of Reclamation. The Bureau has already spent $1 billion for its projects, and has a backlog of proposed construction which will cost the taxpayers over $5.5 billion. Much of this money goes for putting more land into farm production, despite the fact that one-third of the nation's cropland is now idle. The Bureau's irrigation projects provide huge subsidies to big farming and irrigation interests, and further encourage the replacement of the small farmer by the big corporate farm. In the Bonneville Unit of the Central Utah project, for example, irrigators would be getting an annual subsidy of $23 million. Hearings before the Senate Appropriations Committee in the spring of 1971 revealed that ten other ongoing Bureau irrigation projects will cost from $1,045 to $2,803 per acre, while the land-owners will be repaying $637 at most, and in some cases as little as $77, per acre. The Bureau's dams have had serious environmental consequences, causing deterioration of water quality, blocking the passage of spawning fish, and aggravating downstream flooding. Between 1960 and 1968, for example, over 1.4 million fish died in massive fish kills because the Bureau failed to maintain adequate water quality in its reservoirs in the Snake River Basin. The Bureau's construction of Hoover Dam caused serious flooding in Needles, California.

Clearly, some sort of action is necessary, but the Administration has initiated no reform. The new budget for fiscal 1973 funds only two new construction starts, but it continues 57 ongoing projects. The Bureau's Teton Dam on the lower Teton River in Idaho is one of the projects included in the budget. Costing a total of $71 million, the dam will destroy a uniquely beautiful canyon, inundate

17 miles of free-flowing river having a high-quality trout fishery, and eliminate wildlife habitat especially important for big game animals. The economics used to justify the project reveal the typical unrealistic assumptions and exaggerations of anticipated benefits used by most water resources development agencies. Of the $2,975,000 in projected annual benefits, more than $2,142,000 is attributed to irrigation. Inclusion of irrigation benefits is totally unjustifiable considering that the Federal government doles out more than $4.5 billion each year for price support and soil bank payments. That the government pays this much each year to keep the prices on farm goods up, and to keep farmland unplanted, makes the expenditure of millions of dollars for increased irrigation an unwise use of funds. It can only contribute to the displacement of small farmers in other parts of the country. The inclusion of recreation benefits for the artificial lake created by the dam is hardly legitimate since the project will destroy a unique and valuable recreational resource which now exists. To justify flood control benefits of $238,000 annually, a major flood equaling the magnitude of the area's most serious flood in history would have to occur once every three years.

The Administration is also funding the massive Central Arizona Project (CAP), despite the fact that an adequate environmental impact statement has not yet been completed. CAP would involve the construction of a series of pumping stations, dams, and aqueducts to take water from the Colorado River and deliver it to the Tucson and Phoenix areas. At a total cost of perhaps more than $2.5 billion, CAP will result in Federal expenditures of as much as $1,250 per acre to irrigate land worth $700 an acre. By any analysis, further irrigation is unwise and unnecessary. While crops and livestock account for only 12 percent of the state's total personal income, these industries account for 90 percent of the water used in Arizona. The water supply from the Colorado River already has been seriously overdrawn, to the extent that water flowing into Mexico often is not fit for use due to the high salt content.

There will not even be enough water in the Colorado River to make CAP operable in the long run, so project sponsors are looking into the possibility of diverting some of the water flowing into the northwest's Columbia River down into the Colorado.

Perhaps the most serious of all threats to the rivers of the West will come from development of oil shale, a sedimentary rock which yields oil when heated to 900 degrees Fahrenheit. President Nixon proposed in his 1971 Energy Message that these deposits be developed beginning in early 1973. Fifty-two and one-half percent of the Federal revenues from oil shale development will go into the Bureau of Reclamation's general fund, and this money could then be used for Bureau projects damming most of the West's still free-flowing rivers. Oil shale development itself, considering that a full scale industry would require about 450,000 acre-feet of water each year, will add to the pressure to start these additional projects. Oil shale development would also be an environmental disaster for Colorado, Utah and Wyoming, which together have about 2 trillion barrels worth of oil shale worth about $300 billion. For a full scale industry, 4.5 million tons of oil shale would have to be mined each day, mostly by strip mining. At this rate, disposal of spent shale would require 4,640 surface-acres each year. Oil shale would nourish the Bureau of Reclamation, and the Bureau of Reclamation would nourish oil shale. Together, they spell additional big trouble for the West.

## SCS, CEQ & Stream Channelization

Growing controversy is surrounding stream channelization, which turns meandering tree-lined streams into straight sterile ditches. Trees along the stream banks are bulldozed and the streams dredged wider and deeper. The habitats of fish and wildlife are destroyed, to say nothing of scenic beauty. Done in the name of flood control by the Soil Conservation Service (SCS), the Tennessee Valley Authority (TVA), and the Corps of Engi-

## WATER RESOURCES DEVELOPMENT 71

*The Corps' Cross-Florida Barge Canal on the Oklawaha River. An unharmed portion of the Oklawaha is shown below.*

neers, channelization drains swamps and wetlands to put more land into agriculture.

Hearings in both the House and Senate in 1971 documented the wide range of environmental degradation caused by channelization. Representatives from eleven state game and fish agencies came to Washington to tell how the SCS and the Corps consistently ignored fish and wildlife considerations. Nathaniel Reed, the assistant secretary of Interior for fish, wildlife, and parks, testified at the House hearings in June of 1971, saying: "A large part of the morale problem within my Department is the result of rarely being listened to when we offer relevant recommendations to other agencies on this problem. It is discouraging for our biologists and field personnel to stand by helplessly and watch the wetlands resource succumb to the dredge bit or dragline bucket with little or no regard for the natural system." Reed further stated that "it has been the observation of the majority of our personnel that those agencies engaged in stream channelization activities are still largely paying nothing more than lip service to earnest environmental protection."

These charges are backed up by reports made by the Agriculture Department's own Inspector General (the SCS is part of the Department of Agriculture) and by the Interior Department's Bureau of Sport Fisheries and Wildlife. Neither have been released officially as of this writing, but copies have been obtained and reported by such Washington-based columnists as Jack Anderson.

The report from Agriculture's Inspector General Nathaniel Kossack charged that "there were no organized procedures at the department level to assure that environmental statements," required by the National Environmental Policy Act (NEPA), were prepared for the SCS projects. Indeed, as of January 31, 1972, the SCS was preparing environmental impact statements on only 20 out of 273 authorized projects in 19 key states. The Kossack report says that even those impact statements which have been written were "made to justify proposed actions" rather than to describe them objectively for the public. On December 9, 1971, this report was delivered to Agriculture's assistant director for science and education, Dr. Theodore C. Byerly, who quickly exempted it from public disclosure under the Freedom of Information Act.

The report from Interior's Bureau of Sport Fisheries and Wildlife was written because of continued frustration with the SCS, which under existing law is supposed to heed the Bureau's advice on matters affecting fish and wildlife. The Bureau's advice has most often been ignored.

In February, 1971, in a document known as Watershed Memorandum 108, SCS chief Kenneth Grant promised to reform his agency. The memo ordered his staff to review every pending channelization scheme and to place it in one of three categories—Group 1 for "minor" environmental impact, Group 2 for "adverse" impacts, and Group 3 for "seriously adverse" impacts. But very few of the projects were put into Group 3, and it became obvious that the Memorandum 108 study was not an honest evaluation. After lambasting the SCS during the congressional hearings, Assistant Secretary of Interior Reed ordered his department to launch a case-by-case survey of all 440 channelization projects reported in the Memorandum 108 review.

Still unreleased to the public, this study has been reported in a *Los Angeles Times Syndicate* column by Stewart Udall and Jeff Stansbury. The Reed report, according to Udall and Stansbury, says that SCS has issued no environmental impact statements for the vast majority of its proposed channelization projects, and, in violation of NEPA once again, it did not consult with the Bureau of Sport Fisheries and Wildlife on half of the 83 statements it did file with the White House Council on Environmental Quality. This fact led Reed to offer an implicit criticism of the White House agency. "The bureau believes," he wrote, "that 45 of the environmental statements filed should have been rejected by CEQ as not being in compliance with the law or with the CEQ guidelines."

To stop the controversy of both the Kossack and Reed reports, the White House and the Council on Environmental Quality held a meeting with Interior and Agriculture officials on March 27, 1972. CEQ, SCS, and White House officials ordered the Interior Department to tone down its criticism of the channelization program. The Interior representatives, already resigned to the views of SCS officials, were shocked when CEQ's Stephen Sloan backed up the demands from the SCS.

Furthermore, Sloan recently wrote to Richard Bryan Jr. of the Louisiana Wildlife Federation asserting that the SCS Memorandum 108 review can be substituted for environmental impact statements in assessing the environmental impact of any channelization project. This runs directly counter to the letter and spirit of NEPA, and Bryan responded that Memorandum 108 was "an intra-agency cop-out, subject to no public participation and no authority other than that of the agency which has devised the project being reviewed."

Udall and Stansbury report that this action by CEQ has convinced environmentalists that "the White House does not wish to offend either the Southern congressmen who control the funds for the CEQ and the SCS or the wealthy farmers who get big hidden subsidies from U.S. taxpayers whenever the SCS drains their marshlands." Gus Speth, of the Natural Resources Defense Council, said "the CEQ appears to be dominated by political considerations emanating from the White House."

In the midst of this battle, during the spring of 1971, CEQ organized its own study of channelization. Selecting 36 projects, it contracted with A. D. Little, Inc. to prepare a study. Conservationists became alarmed when it was learned that CEQ was only planning to study non-controversial projects. Of the 36 selected projects, 33 had been selected by the water resources development agencies themselves. The very agencies accused of wrongdoing were asked to choose the projects to be studied. Conservationists were also angered to learn that the A. D. Little study team was being given guided tours of the projects by the Corps and SCS without adequate representatives from the state fish and wildlife agencies which have considerable knowledge of the adverse impacts of channelization.

After protesting to the CEQ, environmentalists succeeded in getting six controversial projects into the study; but when A. D. Little's report was released on April 1, 1972, it was obvious that it was designed to whitewash channelization and divert attention from the types of projects which had been under fire. Still, the section of the report on biological effects done under subcontract by the Philadelphia Academy of Natural Sciences has real merit. It found that even the noncontroversial projects sometimes have devastating effects on wildlife and stream organisms. Some of the comments from the Philadelphia Academy:

"Our conclusion with regard to channelization of Crow Creek is that a highly productive, unique stream has been destroyed."

"In summary, the hydrological regime of Caw Caw Swamp has been completely altered by channelization."

"Channelization of the middle Rio Grande Valley has had profound effects upon the wildlife resources.... Rare or unusual species such as river otter, Brewster and American egrets, and the Mexican duck, constituting in some cases the only representatives in the Southwest, have been almost if not completely eliminated."

## A Role for the EPA

In contrast to the White House Council on Environmental Quality, the Environmental Protection Agency (EPA) has been quite helpful to conservationists and other citizens attempting to reform traditional pork barrel practices. The National Environmental Policy Act of 1969 (NEPA) requires EPA to comment on the effects which the Corps, Bureau of Reclamation, SCS, and TVA projects might have on such things as water quality, recreational sanitation, and solid waste management. Many of the comments made by EPA's regional offices have provided citizens with valuable information, and some have even raised questions as to the advisability of the projects. The EPA report mentioned earlier on the Tennessee-Tombigbee, for example, is representative of the good job the agency has done on commenting on a number of Corps and TVA proposals.

Concerning the Corps' draft environmental impact statement on the Lincoln Dam on the Embarras River in Illinois, EPA pointed out that "failure to control adequately the pollution sources will subject the reservoir to rapid siltation and nitrification, degrading the water quality so as to make it unusable for municipal supplies or recreation." EPA warned that unless nutrient and waste discharges upstream from the proposed dam are controlled, "the project will cause a significant adverse environmental impact." EPA thus argued that "the cost of treatment should be considered a cost of the project."

EPA's comments on the New Hope Dam in North Carolina pointed to the facts "that overall stream temperatures will be elevated; that the overall assimilative capacity of the stream will be lessened; and that the overall water quality in the stream will be lowered." EPA also estimated that the cost of controlling algal blooms expected to occur behind the dam would likely range from $2.3 million to $5.8 million each year.

In commenting on TVA's draft environmental impact statement for the Duck River project, EPA said, "This statement is lacking in sufficient information to enable an accurate environmental appraisal of the total project. In general, proper consideration has not been given to problems of water quality, project alternatives, secondary environmental effects, environmental degradation during construction, or operational procedures."

Comments like these have forced agencies like the TVA and Corps of Engineers to rethink and reevaluate some of their projects. EPA's remarks have also served to alert the public to the undesirable effects of certain projects.

The EPA contracted in 1970 the Institute for the Study of Health and Society to do a study of the Corps of Engineers as part of an advanced studies program in environmental education. Under project director Charles Clusen, authors Thomas Clement, Glenn Lopez, and Pamela Mountain completed a hard-hitting report entitled "Engineering a Victory for our Environment: A Citizen's Guide to the U.S. Army Corps of Engineers." Unfortunately, the report was not released until March, 1972, even though it was ready in July, 1971. Because of pressures from the Corps, it might not have been released at all had it not been for counter pressures exerted by conservationists and columnist Jack Anderson. Now published, the report is just the sort of information needed by citizens concerned about the destruction caused by the Corps. One chapter explains all eighteen steps through which the projects must pass before being authorized, and tells how citizens can have an impact in each stage. Other chapters are devoted to the adverse effects of Corps projects, an analysis of pork barrel economics used for justification of the destruction, and case studies of how citizens have been effective in struggles with the Corps.

## New Standards for Water Projects

During the 1969-1972 period the Water Resources Council (WRC) has been working on new standards for planning water resources projects. The proposed new standards would affect all projects of the Corps, Bureau of Reclamation, TVA, and SCS. Developers and conservationists have closely followed the WRC's proceedings since the direction of the multi-billion dollar dam and canal building enterprise depends upon the form the final standards take. Construction interests, developers, and dam building agencies want broader standards which would allow more projects to be justified. Conservationists want restrictive standards to curtail the number of destructive projects which can be built. The proposed standards were finally published on December 21, 1971, and climaxed a long dispute between the White House Office of Management and Budget (OMB) and the WRC.

The Water Resources Council was established in 1965 by the Water Resources Planning Act and was assigned the task of coordinating water development projects, recommending water policy, and formulating standards for planning water projects. Members of the WRC include the chairman of the Federal Power Commission and the Secretaries of Agriculture, HEW, Interior, Transportation, and the Secretary of the Army. On August 12, 1970, a WRC task force gave the council its recommendations in the form of four volumes know as the *Salmon Books*. The *Salmon Books* recommended a discount rate of 5½ percent, and this proposal proved the basic bone of contention between OMB and the WRC in the dispute which delayed publication of the proposed standards for a year and a half.

The discount rate plays a prominent role in the computation of the cost-benefit ratio of a project, and without a favorable cost-benefit ratio a project stands little chance of receiving Administration approval. The benefits which a project brings in ten or twenty years from now, however, are discounted, on the theory that because of the interest which money can earn, future benefits are worth less than real money now.

Many projects were authorized many years ago under discount rates as low as 2⅝ percent. During the 1960's, the rate was gradually increased, and it now stands at 5⅜ percent. Developers and agencies like the Corps have become alarmed at the upward swing because it makes it harder to justify projects. The Corps recently reviewed 578 projects in various stages of planning and reported that 440 would be justified at a rate of 5⅜ percent, 295 at 7 percent, and only 143 at 10 percent.

Being well aware of the specious economics used to justify pork-barrel projects, and under pressure to trim the budget, OMB argued that the discount rate should be set at 10 percent, roughly the rate of return on investments in the private sector. Conservationists supported the 10 percent rate too, and applauded OMB's efforts to prevent unsound economics from being inserted into the project planning standards. Powerful members of Congress also got into the dispute. Senator Ellender (D-La.), chairman of the Senate Appropriations Committee, warned solemnly that, "If the OMB view is allowed to prevail, it will effectively sound the death knell of water and land resource projects." Rep. Bob Jones (D-Ala.), an important backer of the Tennessee-Tombigbee Waterway, asserted that, "In the event the Water Resources Council is prevented from carrying out the responsibility granted to it by the Congress, the Congress may find it necessary to reassert its authority in this field."

When the standards were finally published in proposed form in December, 1971, OMB's views had been partially adopted. The discount rate was set at 7 percent, a compromise between the 10 percent OMB wanted and the 5½ percent proposed in the WRC's *Salmon Books*. The hearing record is closed and it is unclear what changes, if any, the WRC will make in response to the criticisms presented in the comment period. The most important test of the President's commitment to environmentally sound water resources development will come when he receives the standards from WRC for official signature. Through OMB, the President will be able to make last minute alterations if he doesn't like what he is given. If he signs ecologically enlightened and sound economic standards, this would indicate a real commitment to protecting and preserving the environment. If he signs poor standards designed to allow continued wasteful and destructive alterations of rivers and streams, this will show that his commitment lies only in rhetoric. Tough standards are essential to halt the damage caused by Nixon's emphasis on pork-barrel politics over environmental advocacy. But with all the controversy which has surrounded the issue, the President will likely view the standards as too hot to handle until after the election.

# ENERGY

## WILSON CLARK

Although persistent efforts have been made by government officials, citizens, and industries, the United States has no national energy policy. Energy policy under President Nixon's Administration is largely the creation of the industrial interests involved. In effect, the various federal regulatory and administrative agencies rubber-stamp the growth plans of energy industries. Control over energy utilization and extraction is held largely by massive oil and gas companies, coal companies, and to a lesser extent, electric utilities, manufacturers of equipment, and the like, who present to the country a picture of increasing national need for energy in all its forms. Americans already use more than six times as much per capita energy as the world average. The entire nation of 200 million people burns more energy than the 500 million of Japan, Great Britain, Germany, and the Soviet Union combined.

Agencies such as the Federal Power Commission, the

---

*Wilson Clark is an energy consultant to several environmental organizations, including the John Muir Institute for Environmental Studies and the Environmental Policy Center. He has written extensively on social and technological solutions to the energy crisis, including articles in* Not Man Apart, Environmental Action, *and* Smithsonian *magazines. He was a contributing author to* Earth Tool Kit *(Pocket Books, 1971) and is currently completing a book on new sources of energy to be published by Doubleday & Co.*

## Sources of Energy

|  | 1970 (actual) | 2000 (projected) |
|---|---|---|
| Oil | 43.0% | 34.6% |
| Natural Gas | 32.8% | 26.4% |
| Coal | 20.1% | 13.7% |
| Waterpower | 3.8% | 2.6% |
| Nuclear | .3% | 22.7% |

## U.S. Consumption of All Energy by Consumer, 1970
(in trillion B.T.U.'s)

| | |
|---|---|
| Industrial | 21,192 |
| Electrical Generation, Utilities | 16,967 |
| Transportation | 16,436 |
| Residential and Commercial | 14,098 |
| Miscellaneous | 180 |
| TOTAL | 68,810 |

SOURCE: U.S. Department of Interior

## U.S. Consumption of Electricity by Consumer, 1970
(in million kilowatt-hours)

| | |
|---|---|
| Industrial | 571,271 |
| Residential | 468,514 |
| Commercial | 308,296 |
| Miscellaneous | 48,424 |
| TOTAL | 1,396,505 |

SOURCE: U.S. Federal Power Commission

Atomic Energy Commission, the Department of the Interior, and the Environmental Protection Agency have little power to regulate the energy industries, much less know the intricacies of their operations. President Nixon has proposed the consolidation of energy management and regulation under his plan for a Department of Natural Resources. According to the President's Energy Message to Congress of June 4, 1971, this plan would "provide a focal point where energy policy in the executive branch could be harmonized and rationalized."

The following analysis of the President's existing "energy policies" should provide some idea of what this rationalization means.

## Petroleum Policies

President Nixon's policies toward oil and gas are focused on four primary goals:

1) Maintaining high oil prices by keeping oil import quotas.
2) Expanding domestic petroleum resources through increased federal land- and offshore-leasing.
3) Building the Trans-Alaskan Pipeline to Prudhoe Bay.
4) Increasing gas prices and deregulating gas to the extent the public will permit.

The path to the White House has been greased with oil for at least the last half-century. An industry with billions of dollars each year in tax preferences would certainly be expected to spend money to assure the continuation of the policies which protected them, and the oil industry does exactly that. No less than sixty-one Washington offices are now being staffed by petroleum lobbyists to be sure that legislation affecting them gets favorable treatment in Congress. This doesn't include the vast array of attorneys hired by the oil companies to represent their interests before the Federal Power Commission, the Federal

## U.S. Energy Consumption

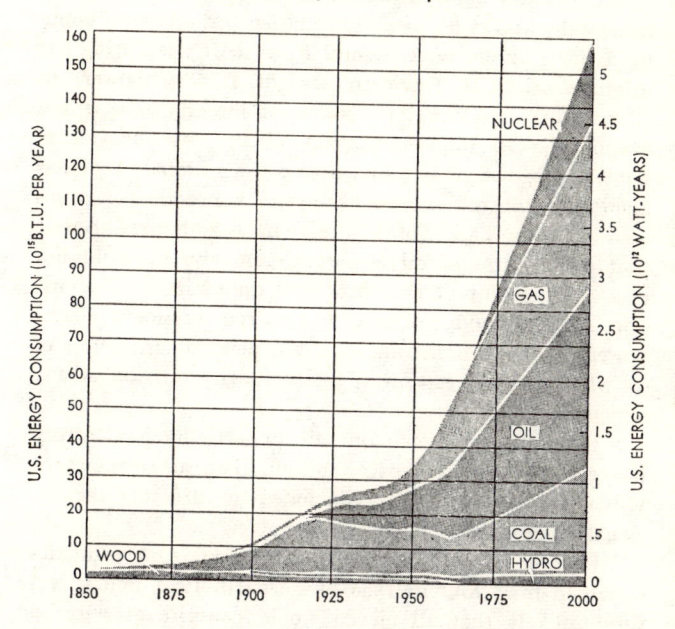

From "Energy and Power" by Chauncey Starr. Copyright ©, September 1971, by Scientific American, Inc. All rights reserved.

During the last 40 years, the American population has grown 70 percent but our energy consumption has grown 310 percent. In just the next thirty years, between now and the year 2000, the United States will consume more energy than it has in its entire history. If fossil fuels are consumed at present rates, the U.S. could be left only with coal by the year 2000. The nation already has passed its peak oil production, and is on the verge of reaching its peak gas production. Huge increases in nuclear energy, and in fossil fuel imports, are thus projected.

Trade Commission, the Supreme Court, and other Washington forums.

The warm ooze of petroleum campaign contributions historically knows no party boundaries, but oil and Republicans have always mixed especially well. It was during the Administration of President Dwight D. Eisenhower, in 1959, with Vice President Nixon at his elbow, that the Mandatory Oil Import Program (OIP) was undertaken. Under the guise of national defense—a rationale that has been dismembered thoroughly even by President Nixon's own Cabinet Task Force—President Eisenhower decreed that the amount of oil imported from abroad could not exceed 9 percent of that produced domestically. The nation simply could not afford, declared President Eisenhower, to let itself become overly dependent on a flow of oil which another nation might arbitrarily turn off at any moment.

Nixon's Task Force on Oil Import Quota Controls, headed by conservative Republican, then as Secretary of Labor, George P. Schultz, concluded in 1970 that the national defense argument was untenable.

First, it noted, the number of oil exporting countries increased from four in 1956 to eleven in 1970, and it was very unlikely that all eleven would conspire at once to deny oil to the U.S. Secondly, the Middle Eastern countries were in special need of hard currency from the U.S. Third, controlling imports from Canada did not make sense because the U.S.-Canadian economic ties were sufficiently close that oil exports were not likely to be jeopardized. Fourth, in a nuclear attack, oil supplies would not be crucial anyway. Fifth, risks of submarine attack would be no greater for ships sailing from Venezuela than for those bringing oil from Louisiana and Texas to the East Coast. And finally, synthetic fuel development, increased storage capabilities, and government exploration and production from its own sources could adequately fulfill the nation's petroleum needs in the event of an extended war.

John O'Leary, deputy assistant Secretary of Interior

in 1962, recently recalled at a meeting of the American Association for the Advancement of Science that the OIP had never been set up primarily for national security purposes, but had been designed chiefly "to protect surpluses" and keep oil prices up. This was further substantiated by Eisenhower's own "deputy president," Sherman Adams, who acknowledged in his memoirs that "the imposing of import quotas on oil was primarily an economic decision brought about by an economic emergency," i.e., the influx of foreign oil "at such a rate that the American oil-producing centers were being forced into desperate straits."

By blindly following the oil industry's prodding, the Nixon Administration has embarked on what its own former energy specialist, Dr. S. David Freeman, calls a "drain America first" policy. In continuing to drain America's own petroleum resources, while barring most imports, President Nixon is not only jeopardizing fuel resources in the future, but is costing every family in America an extra $100 per year in the process. That's what experts in the field are saying Americans would save if the oil import quotas were removed and oil actually had to compete in a free market.

## Oil Leasing

The only remaining oil booms in the U.S. are probably Alaska and the outercontintental shelf (OCS). Whereas 90 percent of the potential land regions has been explored, only 10 percent of the potential outer continental shelf sources has been. That 10 percent has turned up proved reserves of some 4.3 billion barrels of oil and 34.2 trillion cubic feet of gas on the U.S. outer continental shelf, according to recent estimates.

There is little or no agreement about the amount of oil and gas that might ultimately be produced in the U.S. and the OCS. M. King Hubbert of the U.S. Geological Survey has conservatively estimated that about 190 billion barrels of crude oil remain available both in the U.S. and offshore. The Potential Gas Committee of the oil and gas industry has estimated that the U.S. has an ultimate supply of 1,290 trillion cubic feet of natural gas. But in 1971, the U.S. consumed 5.6 billion barrels of oil and 22.1 trillion cubic feet of natural gas, and the consumption rates are increasing.

The Nixon Administration's oil policy advocates rapid acceleration of OCS leasing. In earlier administrations, oil lease sales were spasmodic and appeared to be primarily geared toward raising revenue. While the Nixon Administration also has counted on income from oil lease sales to help reduce its budget deficits, its major purpose is to increase oil and gas production.

In 1971 the Interior Department anounced its intentions to reopen OCS leasing with a lease sale of 366,000 acres off eastern Louisiana in the Gulf of Mexico. However, it made only a superficial effort to comply with the requirements of the National Environmental Policy Act (NEPA), which calls for filing an environmental impact statement examining potential environmental effects as well as the alternatives available and the benefits compared to risks.

The Natural Resources Defense Council, Inc., filed suit to halt the sale until the Interior Department assessed alternative forms of meeting the needs that would have been served by the OCS drilling, a step required by NEPA. In January, 1972, the U.S. Court of Appeals for the District of Columbia ruled in favor of the environmentalists, and the Interior Department was forced to reschedule the sale for 1972.

The Administration, particularly through the public remonstrances of Interior Secretary Rogers Morton, has denounced environmentalists for slowing down the flow of oil in the face of shortage, and continues to push for two major off-shore lease sales each year.

A major decision now facing the Nixon Administration in the realm of offshore leasing involves tapping the apparently extensive oil and gas reserves that lie off the Atlantic Coast. But it has become apparent that the

Nixon Administration is going to dodge the issue of OCS leasing off the East Coast until the Presidential campaign is over. Whether Nixon wins or loses the election, it is probable that once it's over, the Administration will give offshore leasing the go-ahead along the Eastern seaboard.

In terms of national oil policy and environment, Malcolm Baldwin of the Conservation Foundation, recently noted in the *Ecology Law Quarterly* (Vol. 1, No. 2) that "if our ability to rely on oil is limited by time, and if the need to develop other sources of energy is pressing, our public policy ought to avoid irrevocable environmental commitments in the interim to insure that there are in fact 'no insuperable physical or biological difficulties' during this period of transition.

"Continuation of present oil policies," Baldwin maintained, "will result in increasing oil trade and production, and it is unclear whether the rapid consumption of petroleum will cause widespread ecological dislocation." This suggests, he added, that "the appropriate environmental policy is one of buying time to assess the possible effects and to assure that we find needed energy substitutes before petroleum supplies are exhausted." Environmental litigation has become, he concluded, "a means to buy time."

## Trans-Alaskan Pipeline

One of the issues which most starkly reveals the Administration's duplicity in the fuels/environment arena is the Trans-Alaskan Pipeline System (TAPS). A consortium of eight oil companies under the corporate name Alyeska has proposed to build the world's largest pipeline—a 789-mile 48-inch pipeline—to bring oil from the Alaskan North Slope to the port of Valdez in Prudhoe Bay.

There is every reason why the pipeline should not be built over this route. For one, the oil is most needed in the Mid-West, but the Prudhoe Bay route would take it via tanker to ports along the West Coast. Secondly, a trans-Canadian energy corridor is already being developed by

Canadian gas companies. It would be a logical and considerably more economical undertaking to lay the gas and oil lines along the same route. Such a route could circumvent earthquake prone areas and wildlife preserves, thus impacting less significantly on the environment. In addition, transport over the land route would eliminate the most disastrous environmental consequence—oil spills at sea. Despite all this, the Nixon Administration has made a commitment to the trans-Alaskan rather than the trans-Canadian route.

In its attempts to build a legitimate case for the Trans-Alaskan route, according to Rep. Les Aspin (D-Wis.), in a July, 1971, *Congressional Record,* the Interior Department deliberately omitted a number of statements from the reports of various U.S. and Alaskan officials which it published with the draft environmental impact statement. Furthermore, according to Rep. Aspin, the Interior Dept. totally withheld four reports: one from an Interior Department official critical of the pipeline; one from the Alaska Corps of Engineers, also critical of the pipeline; one from the Alaska State Housing Authority, which concluded that the Alaska pipeline could hurt the economy of Alaska more than it would help; and a report from the Alaskan Department of Economic Development that a Canadian pipeline would benefit the economy of Alaska more than would the Alaska pipeline.

The oil industries involved apparently plan to export a substantial portion of the Alaskan North Slope oil to Japan, and the Port of Valdez in Prudhoe Bay constitutes a convenient point of embarkation. (This view was reinforced in January, 1972, when Japanese Prime Minister Sato, after meeting with President Nixon in San Clemente, California, said, "We will, of course, be purchasing oil in the event that the pipeline is completely laid.") A pipeline to Chicago, on the other hand, would be no help at all. Thus, while the U.S. is bringing imported oil in under quotas in the name of national defense, it is exporting oil simultaneously out of the back door in the name of good business.

## Natural Gas Policy

The Nixon Administration has been persistently bent on unleashing a series of price boosts for the natural gas industry that promise to evolve as one of the most gigantic subsidies ever awarded to any industry in American history.

Natural gas, whose regulation was initiated in the 1950's to protect the public against wanton exploitation by a monopoly industry, has become a highly sought-after fuel. There are several reasons for this. Most importantly, it is the cleanest fuel available and thus is highly desirable from an environmental point of view.

The normal supply-demand equation has been knocked further awry by the artificially high prices of oil and other petroleum products as a result of the disastrous oil imports program. Had other petroleum products been more realistically priced, so that they were more competitive with natural gas, the demand for natural gas would not have risen to the point where existing available supplies are insufficient to meet demands.

In the meantime, the natural gas industry has untiringly lobbied for higher gas prices at the wellhead source. One of President Nixon's major energy goals is to help the industry accomplish this, a fact which has been made clear by pronouncements from various Administration officials, most notably John Nassikas, chairman of the Federal Power Commission, which regulates the gas industry.

Prices have already been increased in small increments, and in early April, 1972, the FPC announced its plans to raise wellhead gas prices substantially on all new supplies of gas.

On the grounds of a severe gas shortage, the Nixon Administration is also calling for increased research and development of coal gasification. At the same time, the FPC is being besieged with requests to permit imports of liquified natural gas (LNG) from Algeria and other foreign nations for conversion to natural gas for pipeline use. The catch is that synthetic natural gas made from imported LNG, delivered to East Coast distributors, would be about $1.50 per thousand cubic feet. Pipeline quality gas from coal is likewise estimated to cost from $1 per thousand cubic feet on up. (Coal gasification is an enormously inefficient use of coal, and inherently implies the strip mining of millions of acres for additional coal from many Western states.) The plan is to come in with pipeline quality synthetic gas at four to six times the price of natural gas. The obvious disparity will result in mammoth, and seemingly legitimate, pressures from the gas industry, so that in a very short period of time the gas consumer will be paying roughly twice what his monthly bill is now. And a handful of natural gas companies will be richer by billions of dollars.

If the imports of both synthetic and natural gas are from such trading partners as Algeria, or the Soviet Union, the Administration's solemn and steadfast insistence that we cannot import more oil because it might jeopardize national security will be put into an even more ingenious context.

## Coal Gasification and Oil Shale Development

A primary goal of the President's energy policy is to exploit massive fossil fuel resource reserves in the western United States.

What this means is that a combination of new technologies for squeezing high-grade fuels out of low-energy content coal and oil shale deposits, and a new federal give-away program to industry, will be initiated in an attempt to meet additional energy demands.

Technologies for making gas out of coal have been used in Europe for decades, where gas prices have traditionally been higher than in the U.S. Responsibility for developing coal gasification in the Administration is split between the Interior Department and the Environmental Protection Agency (EPA). EPA is working on advanced power cycles designed to use synthetic gas and is considering the environmental impact of coal gasification. The Interior Department is responsible for research overview on possible processes of gasifying Western coal deposits. Interior will spend about $45 million in fiscal 1973 to develop gasification methods according to the Administration budget.

Oil shale exploitation is viewed by the Administration as the next best answer to coal gasification, though not mutually exclusive. Oil shale is a sedimentary rock which must be heated by special refining methods to produce usable oil. Oil shale deposits represent a petroleum energy source worth more than 300 billion dollars. The deposits, located for the most part on federal land in Colorado, Utah, and Wyoming, are at present untappable due to the diluted nature of the energy source.

The Administration has proposed a leasing program scheduled to start just after the '72 elections to assist oil companies in the exploitation of this source. Strip mining, the extraction process by which most of the shale would be mined, would produce enormous, unsightly residue.

In a May, 1971, interview in *U.S. News and World Report*, the president of the Atlantic Richfield Oil Co., a participant in existing oil shale prototype operations, said: "Some of the [shale residue] can be used to fill up a few of the canyons and valleys of the rather desolate parts of Utah, Colorado and Wyoming in which oil shale is found." But the Interior Department's M. King Hubbert, one of the world's foremost petroleum geologists, warns, "I'd just as soon leave it [oil shale] alone. If you want to imagine one hell of a mess, imagine mining that shale and discharging the acid wastes into the Colorado River. I guarantee you'd kill the river."

## Strip Mining

Since World War II a massive shift has occurred within the coal industry from deep mining to strip mining. By 1970, 44 percent of the total coal produced was strip mined, and in one year, between 1969 and 1970, strip mined coal production jumped by 23 percent.

The extent of the devastation wrought by strip mining is staggering and unknown to most Americans living outside strip mined areas. By 1970 more than 3 million acres (one and a half times the state of Delaware) of the United States had been gouged by strip mining for coal. More than two-thirds of that area, or two million acres, was officially classified as unreclaimed by the Department of Interior. Thousands of additional acres remain unrestored, but have been classified "reclaimed" based on subsequent superficial revegetation procedures, not on actual restoration of the land to anything approaching its natural state.

And the stripping is just beginning. A 1972 study by the COALition Against Strip Mining projects that if stripping is allowed to continue at current rates of escalation, in the fifteen states surveyed, 36 billion tons of coal will be strip mined at the expense of 8455.1 square miles of land—equivalent to a path two-and-a-half miles wide from New York City to San Francisco. This projection reflects only the estimated on-site damage and does not include off-site damage to streams and rivers. Nor does it reflect the inevitable off-site damage caused by access roads and spoil banks.

Damage from strip mining is rarely limited to the mining site. It brings to an area acid mine drainage contaminating streams, rivers and subsurface waters. It brings blasting, erosion, landslides, siltation, loss of aquatic life, flash floods, unstable and barren soils, and desolation. Reclamation efforts in twenty-eight states with regulatory laws for the most part range from non-existent to inadequate. Even in those states with reasonably stringent laws, inadequate funding and manpower have diminished serious attempts to regulate strip mining except on a spotty basis. Reclamation, even in states with specific requirements, is typically an exercise in vegetative camouflage, not the actual restoration of the stripped land to the original use or original potential use. When land is "reclaimed" by strippers, they seldom spend more than $300 an acre, though a recent Elkins, West Virginia, demonstration project indicated that the cost of properly reclaimed land, not including clearing and revegetation, was nearly $1,700 per acre. State legislatures have been crippled by the quiet but overwhelming presence of the coal industry.

The coal industry and the Nixon Administration have been conducting a subtle but massive campaign in the halls of Congress to justify a coal policy of accelerated strip mining by warnings of looming shortages in other fossil fuels—namely oil and gas. Congressmen are being advised that the only way to maintain our supply of fossil fuels for electric power generation, or more simply the only way "to keep the lights on," is to strip mine coal. Indeed, one is even left with the impression that stripping must be escalated to compensate for a shortage of easily obtainable deep mine reserves.

Just the opposite happens to be the case. The Administration's national coal policy totally ignores the six-to-one ratio of deep mine reserves to strippable reserves. Total U.S. coal resources are estimated between 1.5 and 1.6 trillion tons "in place" by the U.S. Bureau of Mines and the U.S. Geological Survey. Approximately 57 percent, or conservatively 750 billion tons, are considered to be economically recoverable—and that assumes only the use of present-day technology. The Bureau of Mines estimates, in a recent open file report (June, 1971), that all strippable coal resources total 119 billion tons, while strippable reserves total only 45 billion tons. (Strippable reserves are those considered economically strippable using present-day technology.)

To be sure, strip mined coal is even cheaper than "cheap" deep mined coal—typically several dollars per ton cheaper. Stripping is highly mechanized, employing only a fraction of those people required to deep mine an equal amount of deep mined coal. And while the coal industry is beginning to acknowledge that environmental damage has been caused by stripping, the industry disclaims any corporate responsibility for the clean-up of unreclaimed lands which were mined before state laws were enacted. Carl E. Bagge, president of the National Coal Association, testified before the Senate Interior Committee in November, 1971, that environmental damage caused by these so-called "orphan" unreclaimed lands is a social or public responsibility: "Since the American public benefited in a period of time when we were not environmentally sensitive, the adverse environmental results are a public responsibility."

The Nixon Administration's strip mine coal policy has one priority: increased coal production. While opposing strict federal regulation (to say nothing of a total ban) of strip mining, and attempting to toss strip mine legislation back to the states, it ignores the fact that strip mining has become a national issue because those twenty-eight states with regulatory legislation have been impotent in enforcement.

By placing the primary burden of regulation on the states, the Administration is charting a course which maximizes the bill the public will have to pay, and which does most to encourage environmental blackmail, or the shopping around from state to state by coal companies to find the best deal on lenient strip mine regulation. In the name of good business and free enterprise, giant coal companies, most of which are controlled by oil companies, have not only ravaged the land at enormous profits and cost to the public, but often have not even paid taxes to the communities whose acres they have ruined. The Conservation Foundation reported that, "in Perry County, Kentucky, the largest stripper mined 900,000 tons of coal in 1970, but paid a total of $2,320 in county taxes. Six mineral holding companies owned by large absentee corporations hold approximately 80 percent of the minerals of one heavily stripped Eastern Kentucky county, but paid only $30,000 in taxes in 1970."

The Administration's strip mine legislation would

apply to all minerals, not just coal, a reasonable assurance to the coal industry that requirements will be as broad (and unenforceable) as possible. While the Secretary of the Interior would establish general criteria, the states would be given at least two years to submit state regulatory plans to Interior, another assurance that strip mining will be accelerated, not reduced, in the next two to four years. The impact of the Administration legislation would be to encourage the acceleration of strip mining, at the expense of the environment, the taxpayer, the consumer, and the health and safety of the deep coal miner, whose employers will have an even greater incentive to avoid making deep mines safe workplaces.

It is no surprise that the Administration strip mine legislation has received the substantial endorsement of the American Mining Congress and the National Coal Association. The coal industry has been quick to concur with the White House that the public is sufficiently aware of the environmental and social costs of strip mining to make some federal regulation, to be enforced by the states, a necessity—so long as it in no way interferes with the accelerated production of "cheap" strip mined coal. The debate is not whether coal will be produced, but how it will be extracted. Environmentalists argue that the Nixon Administration can and must endorse a national coal policy which will save the land for future generations while maintaining short-term energy requirements from fossil fuels produced from deep mining coal.

## Energy Growth and Electricity

According to a January, 1972, document issued by the U.S. Department of the Interior (*United States Energy: A Summary Review*), energy studies commissioned for the government indicate that energy needs will grow at 3.5 percent annually between now and the year 2000. This indicates that three times as much consumption of *all* sources of energy will occur in this period.

However, demand for electricity is growing much faster than demand for certain other forms of energy. Presently it is doubling every decade. (In 1970 electric transmission lines covered 4 million acres, an area larger than the state of Connecticut.) This means the construction of hundreds of massive electrical power plants, fueled conventionally (oil, coal, gas) or with nuclear material. In the next ten years alone it is estimated that the U.S. will need 300 large new power plants.

In 1970, Dr. Malcolm Peterson of the St. Louis Committee on Environmental Information warned the Joint Congressional Committee on Atomic Energy of the consequences of this accelerated electrical demand. He told the Committee that, "at some point, we must stop increasing power production. Suppose, for instance, that all electric power is to be produced by modern, 1,000 megawatt (1 million kilowatt) power plants and that each requires an area of only 1,000 feet on a side. If all the country's power needs were presently being met by 300 such large power plants, in less than twenty doublings—that is, in less than two centuries—all of the available land space in the U.S. would be taken up by such plants."

Meeting this problem of rapid energy growth is essential to ameliorate disastrous future environmental consequences. At least one former advisor to President Nixon has been cognizant of the dilemma. Dr. S. David Freeman, former director of the Energy Policy Staff in the White House Office of Science and Technology (OST), declared in 1970 that the country needed to wage "a war on waste in the use of energy and [initiate] the beginning of an era of conservation in its use." Freeman's proposals included redesigning electrical utility rates to cut down on misuse by large consumers and to give small customers a price break, increasing the amount of research and development on clean sources of energy, and developing mass transit.

Since Freeman left the White House in the summer of 1971, hardly a word has been spoken of these concepts, excepting the development of newer technologies (not all of which are so clean). In fact, Freeman's White House "Energy Policy Staff" has been disbanded.

## Power Plant Siting

One of the cornerstones of President Nixon's energy policy has been proposals for legislation to facilitate long-range planning of large electrical power plants. In 1971, the White House sent proposed power plant siting legislation to Congress. Essentially, the legislation would simplify long-range planning by streamlining steps in state and federal certification of power company plans. In addition, the White House has strongly supported legislation which would eliminate some of the public hearings currently required by the Atomic Energy Act of 1954 for nuclear power plants.

Under the guise of "power crises" in 1971 and 1972, the Administration has tried to pass legislative measures to license nuclear power plants without subjecting the plants to full environmental review, as required by the National Environmental Policy Act (NEPA). Legislation proposed by the White House would allow "emergency licensing" of the plants. In effect, such measures totally ignore vital questions of nuclear safety and undermine NEPA.

In March, 1972, Rep. Bob Eckhardt (D-Tex.) submitted a siting bill which would allow for greater citizen and local participation in the bureaucratic process. The national office of Environmental Action endorsed the bill, noting that it marked "the first time that proposed legislation on the subject gives environment more than a superficial nod."

The White House did not back down from its original position, however. Administration efforts in behalf of the legislation it had introduced increased as utilities screamed about power shortages, and more jobs. In March, 1972, hearings before the Joint Committee on Atomic Energy on "emergency" siting legislation for nuclear plants, the

Environmental Policy Center stated that Administration officials (Russell Train, Council on Environmetal Quality; William Ruckelshaus, Environmental Protection Agency; and James Schlesinger, Atomic Energy Commission) had "arrogantly repudiated" environmental law and environmental concern in the rush to build new nuclear plants.

## Nuclear Power

Today, less than 4 percent of U.S. electricity consumption is provided by nuclear reactors, yet this means of producing electrical power is the fastest growing in the U.S. There are only twenty nuclear power plants operating in the U.S. today, but 200 have been projected for 1980 and 400 may be operating by 1990. Nuclear power plants operate somewhat like conventional fossil fueled power plants, the major difference being the use of specially processed uranium as fuel for nuclear fission. This "burning" of uranium produces electrical power as well as deadly radioactive residue.

The policy of the Nixon Administration in regard to nuclear power is one of wholehearted promotion. President Nixon commented in his June, 1971, Energy Message to the Congress that ". . . the safety record of civilian power reactors in this country is extraordinary in the history of technological advances. For more than a quarter century, since the first nuclear chain reaction took place, no member of the public has been injured by the failure of a reactor or by an accidental release of radioactivity. I am confident this record can be maintained."

This safety record is somewhat misleading. Although no deaths among members of the general public can be directly related to malfunctions of reactors or emissions of radioactive materials, there have been a number of deaths of workers in nuclear installations from accidents. In addition, no one knows how many deaths have been caused by the slow dispersion of radioactivity in the environment, including such diversified events as weapons tests and reactor emissions.

The health effects of radiation at low levels are not well known, and a number of distinguished health scientists (led by two AEC health specialists, Drs. John Gofman and Arthur Tamplin) have argued that no new nuclear plants be built until the public can be apprised of this potential danger.

Currently, a series of heated arguments are taking place within the AEC over the effects of nuclear power on public safety as well as health. In 1971, the AEC decided to hold hearings on new agency criteria designed to establish reactor engineering codes for safety devices and codes for the "routine" radioactive pollution of the environment by nuclear reactors and other installations.

The most important hearings are concerned with critical reactor safety devices called Emergency Core Cooling Systems (ECCS). These devices are fitted into nuclear power plant water cooling systems to prevent the possible loss of cooling water in event of an accident. The emergency system is designed to keep the hot radioactive core of the reactor from overheating. Were the core of the reactor to overheat, a major disaster would probably ensue, since the core would melt through the massive power plant, releasing lethal amounts of radiation into the environment.

The National Intervenors, an environmental coalition represented at the reactor safety hearings, has released a number of vital "in-house" documents from various AEC and industry scientists which dispute the adequacy of the AEC's interim criteria for the reactor safety devices. Some of these documents are from scientists working on reactor safety at the Oak Ridge National Laboratory, operated for the AEC by the Union Carbide Corporation. These key nuclear scientists were not invited by AEC to help develop the official reactor safety codes. When the Oak Ridge scientists finally got a chance to testify about their fears at the AEC hearing in March, 1972, AEC officials from the national office in Washington, D.C. tried to disqualify them from speaking. However, they were permitted to testify, and their dissenting opinions are now on record.

Almost all the faith in the emergency cooling systems is based on elaborate computer calculations (called codes) of how the giant reactors might perform in an accident. One of the documents released in the AEC hearing is a letter from the Director of the Oak Ridge National Laboratory, Dr. Alvin Weinberg, to Dr. James Schlesinger, AEC Chairman. Dr. Weinberg wrote: "As an old-timer who grew up in this business before the computing machine dominated it so completely, I have a basic distrust of very elaborate calculations of complex situations, especially where the calculations have not been checked by full-scale experiments. . . ." Dr. Weinberg went on to advocate that the AEC test the safety systems on a large scale.

The AEC, however, is not inclined to initiate large-scale tests of these vital systems because it would cost millions of dollars. Instead, computer codes are relied upon. The only actual tests held so far have indicated that the emergency systems do not work. As for the experiments held so far at the Oak Ridge National Laboratory, the future is dim. The AEC has cancelled funding for these programs, shifting responsibility to the industries who build the reactors.

The true test of a rational nuclear power policy is this very issue. The AEC, itself responsible for the conflicting roles of promotion and regulation, is inclined to shift the burden of work on nuclear safety to the very industries which thrive on nuclear trade. The stakes are high, both monetarily, since reactor construction and maintenance is a multibillion dollar industry, and in terms of public health, since the results of a single major reactor disaster could well be the civilian equivalent of warfare. AEC estimates of the consequences of such a major accident (on a nuclear plant about one-fifth the size of those being routinely built today) indicate that thousands of people would be killed and injured, in addition to billions of dollars in property damage.

In addition to the AEC's lack of concern for issues of nuclear safety, the Commission has had constant problems with adequate environmental review for nuclear power plants. Even though the effective date for implementation of the National Environmental Policy Act (NEPA) was January 1, 1970, the AEC did not require electric utilities planning to build nuclear reactors to consider a broad range of environmental issues required under NEPA until March, 1971.

The U.S. Court of Appeals for the District of Columbia ruled in July, 1971, in the "Calvert Cliffs" decision, that the AEC had failed to implement NEPA, and would have to make more thorough reviews of environmental effects. The Court's decision, which affected no less than ninety-seven nuclear power plants, severely chastized the AEC. "We believe that the Commission's crabbed interpretation of NEPA makes a mockery of the Act," the Court said.

Shortly after the stunning decision of the Appeals Court was announced, President Nixon appointed a new AEC Chairman, Dr. James Schlesinger, a Harvard-trained economist. Schlesinger promptly announced that the AEC would accept the Court's ruling and stated that the Commission would show more concern for the environment. In contrast to this fine rhetoric, however, the Commission under Schlesinger's direction has continued to press for "emergency" legislation to license nuclear plants without full environmental review.

The precipitous rush to nuclear power is laden with the possibility of disaster. Even if perfect safety and radioactive emission control systems for reactors can somehow be developed, the problem of controlling radioactive wastes (left after the reactors' uranium fuel is fissioned) would remain. The AEC calculates that U.S. nuclear power plants will have produced about 38,000 tons of high-level waste by the year 2000. Nuclear wastes remain highly dangerous, in some cases for hundreds of thousands of years. No method to store these wastes safely is yet known, and the AEC is seriously considering shipping them off into space.

## Breeder Reactor

President Nixon's 1971 Energy Message called for rapid acceleration of development on the so-called "fast-breeder" reactor. The fast breeder nuclear reactor uses fuel so much more efficiently than conventional reactors (which use about one percent of the energy content of the uranium raw material) that the reactor is said to "breed" more fuel. In addition, it breeds the most concentrated poison known to man, plutonium, a radioactive element 35,000 times more lethal than sodium cyanide—and it remains lethally active for half a million years. Due to this exceptional threat to the environment, widespread opposition is developing to the construction of prototype reactors proposed by President Nixon. Dr. John Gofman argues that development of the breeder "is the most disastrous mistake the United States has ever made because it's irrevocable. Once we go down the plutonium road and accidents occur, human life on the planet is doomed."

Accompanied by Atomic Energy Commission officials, the President flew to Hanford, Washington, in September, 1971, to announce that a breedor reactor pilot plant would be built there. His enthusiasm over the new nuclear era may be gauged by his speech: "Don't ask me what a breeder reactor is; ask Dr. Schlesinger [AEC Chairman]. But tell him not to tell you, because unless you are cne of those Ph.D.'s you wouldn't understand it either. But I do know that here we have the potentiality of a whole new breakthrough in the development of power for peace. That means jobs—jobs for this area, and jobs and power for hundreds of millions of people all over the world." President Nixon added that although the Western White House is near a large nuclear power plant, he wasn't afraid of nuclear pollution or accidents. "I am not afraid," he said, "not because I know much about it, but because what I do know tells me that here we have a new source of energy . . . that is absolutely important to the future of the world."

President Nixon neglected to mention that the development of breeder reactors has not been easy. The only breeder reactor built to produce commercial electrical power in the U.S. had to be shut down shortly after it went into operation, due to a nearly disastrous accident. The incident occurred at the Fermi fast breeder reactor (near Detroit, Michigan) in October, 1966. Undaunted by this close call, the AEC has relicensed the repaired Fermi plant to operate at low power levels as a "test facility."

As is the case with conventional nuclear reactors, little is known about the efficacy of safety systems in the proposed new breed of reactors. The only available information is scanty data from computer calculations. Additionally, the problem of disposing of breeder wastes is even more difficult than with today's nuclear plants. Yet Nixon has committed the nation to the construction of two breeder pilot plants by 1980. The AEC expects the breeder to then replace the current type of reactor, and has issued one document projecting 2,600 breeder reactors by the year 2020. Each breeder reactor core would contain about 3,500 pounds of plutonium.

The Scientists' Institute for Public Information (SIPI) filed suit in U.S. District Court to force the AEC to submit an environmental impact statement (as required by the National Environmental Policy Act) on the entire breeder program, rather than merely on individual demonstration plants. The District Court ruled against SIPI in March, 1972, and the case is being appealed. SIPI is asking for a detailed assessment of the program in order to evaluate fully the environmental risks as well as other options for supplying power in the future.

## Nuclear Fusion

In addition to the tremendous priority the Administration places on the breeder reactor as a future technology for supplying electricity, the development of power through the nuclear fusion reaction is being pushed. As opposed to the nuclear fission reaction, which splits heavy atoms (uranium), the nuclear fusion reaction combines light atoms (hydrogen) at extremely high temperatures. The hoped-for, but as yet unobtained, controlled fusion reaction would duplicate the energy process of the sun itself. To date, fusion has been attained by explosion of the hydrogen bomb, but not controlled for power.

Fusion research is being funded at approximately the same level as coal gasification. The new Nixon budget calls for spending $40 million on fusion research in Fiscal 1973. Research scientists in the field would like more funding to demonstrate the possibility of the fusion reaction, but generally seem pleased that the new budget has boosted spending from a former level of less than $30 million per year.

The Administration places some priority on the development of fusion research, but not enough. Proposed fusion reactors could potentially be far safer than the breeder program.

## Clean Energy Sources

Other than the Administration's ill-considered development of breeder reactors, coal gasification, and strip mining massive areas to provide low-energy-content fossil fuels, a number of key technologies do exist to provide clean energy sources. These technologies include solar energy, fuel cells, MHD, energy storage systems, geothermal power, and wind power. In addition, a number of technologies exist to provide "new" clean fuels, such as pure hydrogen, which could supplant the use of existing fossil and nuclear fuels for use in transportation, electricity production, and building heating and cooling.

Although officials in the Nixon Administration recognize the value of these new energy sources, they are reluctant to spend much money to develop or implement them. President Nixon commented in his 1971 Energy Message that solar energy "offers an almost unlimited supply of energy if we can learn to use it economically...," but he offered no hope for funding to do just that.

In fact, solar energy technology for heating and cooling buildings is well understood and could be immediately developed for use in all parts of the United States. As for its economic value, a 1971 report of Resources for the Future, Inc. to the National Science Foundation states: "Reliance on partial solar house-heating is economically sound today.... That body of individuals, of increasing number, who think the higher cost of electric heating is more than offset by its cleanliness and reliability should constitute a market for solar house-heating, provided they are advantageously located." Understated though the report is, it does point out that immediate adoption of solar energy technology for home heating is both possible and economic.

Other uses of solar energy technology involve special materials, such as silicon solar "cells" which convert sunlight directly into electricity. The price of electricity from silicon is far too high to compare with conventional electrical power costs, but the silicon cells are currently made by hand and modern mass production techniques could reduce the high cost of this form of power.

Solar energy can be harnessed to produce electricity in other ways. Researchers at the University of Arizona have proposed solar power plants for the sun-rich Southwestern United States which would produce all the electricity the U.S. needs in the 21st Century as cheaply as conventional power plants. Numerous other technologies have been proposed for the conversion of the sun's rays into useful forms of power, including the production of gaseous fuels.

Administration officials charged with overseeing the development of U.S. energy sources have not chosen to develop solar energy. Interior Secretary Morton told a Congressional Committee in April, 1972, that solar energy is still on "the technological frontier," indicating a great ignorance of available techniques for converting this great energy source.

Needless to say, the use of solar energy is virtually pollution-free. Solar power plants, whether on the desert or on roof-tops, give off no noxious pollutants, nor do these facilities require mining any natural energy resources. At most, certain types of solar plants would require cooling water or the use of land. Even in the case of land use, solar plants would use up about the same amount of land for the power produced as a coal plant uses for strip mining. And the land used would not be despoiled, as is the case with mining.

The rapid development of solar energy should be a major national energy priority, but the Nixon Administration is hardly taking it seriously. In 1972, the Administration is spending only about $2 million to explore the idea of solar power, while it is spending hundreds of millions of dollars on the development of new nuclear reactors.

Other advanced energy technologies include special types of power plants which use fossil fuels efficiently and with a minimum of environmental degradation. Two such power systems are fuel cells and MHD (magnetohydrodynamic) plants.

Fuel cells are similar to batteries but can operate with a constantly rechargeable fuel supply. Fuel cells in operation today supply power on a trial basis to homes and businesses. Burning natural gas, they supply power quietly and with high efficiency, which results in the use of less fuel than conventional power plants need to supply electrical power. An association of gas utilities working with the Pratt & Whitney Company has spent over $50 million to produce the fuel cell power plants in use today.

The Nixon Administration has adopted a *laissez-faire* attitude toward these remarkable power devices, spending practically nothing towards their implementation. The Interior Department's 1972 energy summary said that fuel cell development for electrical power use was "remote," notwithstanding the fact that they are already in use. Interior's budget for 1972 indicates that nothing will be spent by the government for further development.

Likewise for MHD. The Interior Department has budgeted only $3 million for the development of this electrical power system, which would burn fossil fuels half again as efficiently and trap more of the combustion by-products than conventional power plants.

Geothermal energy, the natural heat trapped under the earth's crust, is yet another remarkably clean source of power for electricity. In December 1971, Dr. Tsvi Meidav, an energy consultant to the United Nations, speaking at the annual meeting of the American Association for the Advancement of Science, told delegates that "the geothermal energy reserves of the world are orders of magnitude greater than the total reserves of any other form of energy." Much of this clean energy is found in the Western United States, Canada, and Mexico. Dr. Meidav noted that countries which have tapped geothermal power have found that costs average one-half to three-fourths that of conventional power.

Yet the Interior Department plans to spend only $2.5 million investigating ways to implement this energy source. Interior Secretary Morton has called it another source on the "technological frontier," in ignorance of the fact that geothermal heat has been successfully harnessed for power production in such countries as Iceland, Italy and Mexico for decades.

The development of modern energy storage systems is another vital technology which could be implemented on a large scale to cut down on power needs. Today, electrical power plants are built to meet *peak* power needs, not to meet an *average* load. Were large-scale storage systems to be used to store electricity during off-peak hours (at night, for example) and then "feed" this power into the electrical transmission grids during peak use periods, many new power plants would not have to be built at all.

One way of storing power for peak periods is the environmentally undesirable method of "pumped-storage," a system of storing water in reservoirs at night, then using the water to drive turbines for electricity production during the day. Several technologies appear feasible to supplant the pumped-storage system, including the use of modern batteries and air storage systems. Air storage is used in connection with gas turbines, where air is stored in underground caverns as well as in the ground itself. Such systems are in use in Sweden and Germany, but not in the U.S. These systems offer greater efficiency and far less environmental damage than either building new plants or using unsightly water reservoirs. Yet the Nixon Administration is spending nothing to develop air storage systems, and very little for the development of new batteries for commercial electrical energy storage.

Considerable interest has developed in the U.S. Senate in the problems of energy research and development. In March, 1972, the Senate Commerce Committee held hearings on legislation to accelerate energy research with federal funds, proposed by Senator Warren Magnuson (D-Wash.), Chairman of the Committee. President Nixon's key science advisor, Dr. Edward David, Director of the Office of Science and Technology, opposed the legislation, arguing that private electric utilities should fund energy research without federal interference.

President Nixon's former energy advisor, Dr. S. David Freeman, said that passage of the legislation would "assure that the public's concerns dominate the planning and execution of the R & D program," whereas "they would not be present in an all-industry program." Freeman added that if the electric utilities were responsible for research, key programs might not get funding. "The technology which would seem most attractive to the electric power industry could well be different from the technological innovations which would be funded pursuant to [Senator Magnuson's proposed legislation]." "I think it would be too much to expect of an electric power industry group to go all out for a technology such as the fuel cell, for example, which, if it were successful, could provide consumers with a source of electricity in their home that would compete with the services of the local power company...."

Dr. David's presentation apparently ended President Nixon's brief enthusiasm for wide-scale development of necessary clean energy sources. Although Dr. David realized the pathetic state of energy R & D funding by the electric utilities, which spend far more for advertising than for research, he appeared before the Senate and endorsed the industry's approach.

The energy policies of the Nixon Administration have been industry-oriented, tending with care the vested interests of oil, coal and gas companies. Only in the case of development of nuclear power can federal energy policy truly be said to be federal. And even in this instance, the environment takes second place to the boosters of untrammeled power growth.

Solutions to the energy-environment dilemma can be found in the implementation of policies to decrease the demand for power growth, as well as the logical application of technologies, such as solar energy and energy storage systems, to supply truly clean energy. But the Nixon Administration has shown neither the foresight nor the desire to investigate the necessary solutions.

# THE PUBLIC LANDS

## GEORGE ALDERSON

The public lands put every administration to a test, because the laws concerning them leave so much to the discretion of the Executive Branch. The laws governing the national forests, for example, give only general instructions to the Secretary of Agriculture. It is up to him and his department's Forest Service to translate the extremely general laws into the specifics of whether or not to clearcut timberland, and how high a priority to give protection of wilderness.

This freedom is tempered by two countervailing influences. First, the agencies themselves prove highly resistant toward any significant change in policy. The National Park Service, for example, has been slow to carry out the Wilderness Act of 1964 even after Secretary of the Interior Walter Hickel made a speed-up of its implementation one of his top priorities. The reasons involve bureaucratic inertia, as well as outright hostility. Second, every agency has traditional clients resisting reform. The

---

*George Alderson has been Legislative Director of Friends of the Earth since 1969. During this time, he also served as the Coordinator for the Coalition Against the SST. Alderson is a monthly columnist for* Not Man Apart, *and the author of "How to Influence Your Congressman," which first appeared in the* Voter's Guide to Environmental Politics, *a Friends of the Earth-Ballantine Book. Alderson is a veteran lobbyist on public land and other environmental issues.*

## The Public Lands

One-third of the Nation's land belongs to the public. Owned by the federal government, it is managed by a number of agencies, predominantly by the Interior and Agriculture Departments. In the East, Midwest and South, early land policies favored the disposal of government land into private hands. In the West, however, conservationists have succeeded in keeping much of the land under government control. The disposition of these public lands is a never-ending fight between conservationists and developers.

|  | Acres | Percent |
|---|---|---|
| *Department of Interior* | | |
| Bureau of Land Management | 470.4 million | 62% |
| Fish & Wildlife Service | 26.6 | 4 |
| National Park Service | 23.3 | 3 |
| *Department of Agriculture* | | |
| Forest Service | 186.9 | 25 |
| Other Agencies | 48.2 | 6 |
| TOTAL | 755.4 million | 100% |

SOURCE: *One-Third of the Nation's Land,* the report of the Public Land Law Review Commission, June 1970.

---

Forest Service has the timber industry. The Bureau of Land Management has ranchers. The National Park Service has the tourist industry. These interests restrict the Administration's initiatives, as happened in January, 1972, when the Council on Environmental Quality (CEQ) proposed an executive order to restrict clearcutting. When word of this leaked, pressures from the timber industry won a swift rejection of the proposal by White House staffers.

Seldom can an Administration make major reforms simply by issuing an order. But if it is serious about changing policy, it can overcome countervailing influences by devoting time and effort to the issue. This was the case with the Nixon Administration's decision against the Everglades jetport, and its proposal to acquire Florida's Big Cypress Swamp. In such instances, some of the Administration staff must learn the issue thoroughly and spend time piloting the proposal through obstacles erected by the bureaucracies and commercial interests.

Senators and Congressmen must also be mollified. In the case of public lands, four Congressional committees reflect the exploitative views of public land industries. Besides the House and Senate Interior Committees, industry views are largely reflected in the two Subcommittees on Interior and Related Agencies of the House and Senate Appropriations Committees.

## The Mining Law of 1872

The single most outdated policy on the public lands is the Mining Law of 1872. It covers hardrock minerals and gives mining first priority over all other land uses. If a miner stakes a claim containing enough minerals to be extracted at a profit, there is no way to prevent him from mining it except by buying up his claim, and the cost of doing this is usually prohibitive. The miner not only gets the minerals, he receives patent to the land itself. Under this "location-patent" system, there is no chance for any government agency to weigh the merits of the proposed mine against other uses which might be more important to the national interest. Watersheds, timber, grazing, scenic values—all yield to mining under the 1872 Mining Law.

Oregon's Three Sisters Wilderness, for example, has mining claims dating from 1961 and is about to be mined for pumice, a volcanic rock common to the Cascade Range in Oregon and California. Oregon legislators, and even the local chamber of commerce, are aghast that a pumice mine cannot be stopped from impairing the scenic and recreational value of the wilderness, but there appears to be no way of stopping it save by buying the claim.

The 1872 Mining Law applies throughout the national forests and the lands administered by the Bureau of Land Management, except where specific areas have been withdrawn by secretarial order. Attempts to reform the old law have been made for many years, but with small gains. The law was amended some twenty years ago to bar new claims for common minerals such as sand and gravel, but otherwise it is essentially unchanged.

Conservationists have long sought to repeal the 1872 law and to replace it with a mineral leasing system similar in principle to the mineral leasing already applied to oil and gas. In January, 1969, just before leaving office, Secretary of Interior Stewart L. Udall told the Public Land Law Review Commission that he favored this proposal. He termed the mining law "the major obstacle to the wise conservation and effective management of the natural resources of our public lands."

The Nixon Administration took no action on Secretary Udall's proposal. Almost all legislation dealing with the public lands was held up until 1971 because the chairman of the House Interior Committee, Wayne Aspinall (D-Colo.), wanted to await the final report of the Public Land Law Review Commission (PLLRC), which he chaired. (The Public Land Law Review Commission was established by Congress in 1964 to review the Federal policies and laws governing use of public lands. The Commission's report, *One-Third of the Nation's Land*, was published in June, 1970.) The Commission came out for retention of the basic "location-patent" system, with some changes: miners could patent only the minerals, not the land (although miners would have preferential rights to buy the land on their claims), and the land-managing agencies would have authority to regulate miners' surface activities.

In February, 1971, Senator Henry M. Jackson (D-Wash.), chairman of the Senate Interior Committee, introduced a bill to replace the 1872 law with a mineral leasing system as part of his Public Lands Organic Act.

Reps. John P. Saylor (R-Pa.) and Morris K. Udall (D-Ariz.) introduced similar bills in the House.

It was not until November 18, 1971, that Secretary of the Interior Rogers Morton offered the Nixon Administration's proposal to change the mining law. Instead of abolishing the 1872 law, he would merely modify it, generally along the lines suggested by the PLLRC. A minor improvement over the PLLRC proposal, Morton's plan would only let miners lease the land on their development claims. Otherwise, the measure is essentially what the PLLRC mining advocates wanted. It retains the historic domination of mining over other land uses, and it provides no mechanism for weighing the alternative public values against mining.

Very little action has been taken within the Congress on any of this legislation. The Administration's position, however, played into the hands of mining interests and weakened the opportunities for reform.

## Public Domain Lands

The Bureau of Land Management, in the Department of Interior, administers 470.4 million acres of land—the largest holding of any federal agency. Unlike the Forest Service and the National Park Service, the BLM was originally established as an interim agency, to manage public domain lands until the federal government could dispose of them. During the past twenty years, however, it has been accepted by almost all that very little disposal should take place. Lands of the public domain are largely of such low productivity for agriculture and commercial purposes that the government should keep them and carry out a stewardship role. The real values of these lands are their watersheds and wildlife populations. Unfortunately, the BLM still languishes without a permanent congressional directive.

Senator Henry Jackson thus introduced in February, 1971, his Public Domain Lands Organic Act to give BLM a permanent charter, to establish a policy of retaining most of the land, and to direct that the land be managed under multiple use and sustained yield principles. An Administration bill with similar provisions was proposed in July, 1971.

These proposals have yet to pass Congress. Meanwhile, the major commercial users of the public domain lands, the livestock grazers, have got a handout from the Administration. The Johnson Administration had initiated a ten-year program, to begin in 1969, bringing grazing fees up to the fair market value instead of charging stockmen a fraction of what they would pay on equivalent private land. But in 1970, the Administration called a moratorium on fee increases. In 1972, it proposed only a 2-cent increase, from 64 cents to 66 cents per animal-unit month, instead of the 10-cent raise projected in the ten-year program. The net effect is a continuing subsidy to stockmen who graze their cattle or sheep on public lands.

Computations by the Wildlife Management Institute show that the loss to the U.S. Treasury resulting from the 1970 moratorium will amount to $12.5 million over the ten-year period, and that the loss from the partial increase in 1972 will be $11.2 million. These sums assume that the scheduled increases will be made in 1980 and 1981 to compensate for the lapses. If there is further delay, the loss will be greater.

## National Forests

The national forests, occupying almost one-tenth of our total land area, supposedly operate under the principle of multiple use and sustained yield, as directed in the Multiple Use-Sustained Yield Act of 1960. But a gross imbalance in the treatment of the several uses (timber, water, wildlife, grazing, and recreation) has arisen through the years, so that even the Forest Service itself admits that timber production has been enthroned as its chief concern.

The Nixon Administration has, in fact, taken steps to make this imbalance worse. In 1970, the Administration and the timber industry were pushing the "National Timber Supply Bill" (HR 12025) designed to allow an immediate increase of 60 percent in the annual cut from the national forests. The House of Representatives, responding to conservationists' concern, defeated the bill. Shortly thereafter, Bryce Harlow, then counselor to the President, told a loggers' convention: "In your vigorous struggle for HR 12025, I hope it is not news to you that you had as your ally every element of the Nixon Administration. The opponents of the bill were a host of grumpy citizens."

Four months later, on June 20, 1970, President Nixon told the Forest Service to increase their cut by the same amount called for in the defeated bill. Rep. Saylor (R-Pa.) said: "The effect of President Nixon's 'directions' to the Agriculture, Housing, and Interior Secretaries was to do by executive fiat what could not be done legislatively."

The over-cutting question has been overshadowed by growing challenges to the Forest Service's policy of clearcutting—logging off whole tracts of forest land so that no trees are left standing. The method is being used both in the western forests and in the Appalachians, and has replaced selective cutting, by which individual trees or small groups were cut without a massive disturbance of the soil. Senate Interior hearings in 1971, in Washington, D.C., Atlanta, Ga., Portland, Ore. and Syracuse, N.Y., documented the devastation and permanent damage to the forests caused by clearcutting.

One of the critics was Arnold Bolle, Dean of the Forestry School at the University of Montana. Bolle chaired a faculty study of the Forest Service's management of Bitterroot National Forest, and his task force concluded that "clearcutting . . . cannot be justified as an investment for producing timber on the Bitterroot National Forest." One of the most damaging consequences of clearcutting was noted by a University of Montana geologist, Dr. Robert Curry, whose studies show that the nutrient balance in the soil takes thousands of years to evolve. Dr. Curry testified that clearcutting so depletes the soil of nitrogen and other nutrients that two or three crops of timber may exhaust the soil altogether. Hurlon C. Ray, of the Environmental Protection Agency's Water Quality Office testified that water supplies are likewise damaged by clearcutting. Sediment in streams, he said, increases 7,000 times in some clearcutting areas, causing loss of natural stream vegetation and a destruction of fish habitat miles downstream from the logging site.

In response to this growing public concern, the White House Council on Environmental Quality (CEQ) drafted an executive order to limit clearcutting in sensitive areas, such as on steep slopes, along streams, in unstable soils, and in areas of special scenic value. CEQ's proposal merely reiterated the Forest Service's own rules, but Edward P. Cliff, then chief of the Forest Service, admitted that the rules were not being followed. When word of the new proposal got out in January, 1972, the lumber industry succeeded, with the help of Agriculture Secretary Earl L. Butz and Interior Secretary Morton, in blocking it. According to the *Wall Street Journal*, sources within the Administration "said the order to scrap the council's plan came from top Nixon aides concerned about its possible impact on timber company profits, timber supplies, and support for GOP candidates, like Mr. Nixon, in an election year."

Another area of the Nixon Administration's intransigence has been the lack of protection of wild lands in many forests in all parts of the country. In the West, many small areas have never been logged, generally because of poor access, but have no protective designation by the Forest Service. In the East, Midwest, and South, roadless tracts exist which were logged decades ago and have grown back to typical hardwood forest; some even contain small areas of virgin forest. Citizen conservation groups are proposing that these areas of *de facto* wilderness throughout the country be designated by Congress as official wilderness areas. But the Forest Service has responded unsympathetically. In some cases it has actually proceeded to build roads and begin logging, thus disqualifying these areas from being considered as wilderness. An executive order to ban new roading in *de facto* wilderness was considered by the White House in 1971. The proposed order had the backing of Secretary Morton and the Council on Environmental Quality. But the loggers gained the support of Clifford Hardin, then Secretary of Agriculture, and the resulting fracas at the White House put an indefinite hold on the proposal.

## National Parks

The Administration's record on National Parks must be judged on two criteria: whether existing parks were protected, and whether new ones were established. The lengthy list of new historic sites or small parks is of minor importance because many of these are any administration's "park barrel," designed to bring credit to the Congressmen in whose districts the areas are located. The real test concerns parks established over the objections of miners, loggers, and dam-builders, as well as old parks from which road-builders and other developers are told to stay out. It also concerns parks that involve substantial federal spending.

The Nixon Administration's showcase park has been Everglades National Park in Florida. It was here that Secretary Hickel made his maiden publicity voyage as a conservationist, announcing a war on alligator poaching. In 1969 President Nixon and Secretary Hickel ruled out the proposed jetport over the objections from the South Florida business community and local politicians. And in late 1971, the Administration proposed the acquisition of the Big Cypress Swamp, a watershed vital to the Everglades, at a cost of $156 million.

As with most positive Administration initiatives, this resulted from political and conservationist pressure, but the White House put substantial effort into its Everglades actions, including expert staff work in the White House and behind-the-scenes maneuvering to cope with the opposition. The White House was offered an easy way out, for example, when the National Park Service proposed a complex management system that would have left the Big

Cypress in private ownership, while compensating those landowners who objected to loss of their development rights. The compensable management plan was pleasing to the Office of Management and Budget, which objected to the high cost of outright acquisition. But White House advisors, and Interior Secretary Rogers Morton, convinced President Nixon that buying the Big Cypress was the only sure way to protect the National Park's watershed.

President Nixon has continued the trend of proposing new parks near major cities. He has supported the Gateway National Recreation Area, composed largely of federal properties around the entrance to the New York harbor, plus $27 million worth of private land; and the Golden Gate National Recreation Area, occupying a similar position at the entrance of San Francisco Bay. These proposals were actually formulated earlier by Senators and Congressmen from the affected areas, but President Nixon picked up the issues and publicized them through personal appearances and speeches. However, the President's proposals omit some key areas proposed for inclusion by local conservationists and members of Congress.

The Administration's widely touted "Legacy of Parks" program consists largely of granting small parcels of unused federal land to local park agencies. Of more importance is President Nixon's full funding for the Land and Water Conservation Fund, which is used by federal, state, and local governments to acquire new park lands. After cutting the 1970 budget request from LBJ's $154 million to $124 million, President Nixon changed his policy, after vigorous lobbying from conservationists, and since fiscal year 1971 has been spending the full amounts authorized, $300 million a year.

On some of the other major parks, the Administration has been the spoiler rather than the advocate. Longstanding citizen efforts in Idaho to establish a Sawtooth National Park and an adjacent national recreation area in a location threatened by an open-pit copper mine were rewarded with the opposition of the Nixon Administration.

As a result, consideration of the park is put off at least until 1974. Instead, legislation is being enacted which favors the worst opponents of the park—the mining industry. The bill creates a national recreation area, with only a five-year ban on new mining claims, and with provisions giving the miners rights to build processing mills and tailing ponds within the recreation area. The conservationists' proposal, by putting the threatened area in a national park, would have prevented these intrusions, and, by requiring miners to truck the ore out of the park, could have made mining unfeasible.

The Nixon Administration also failed to pick up on the Johnson Administration's proposal to protect the Potomac River by federal acquisition of its banks and establishment of a Potomac National River. The measure was ditched; and, instead, the C & O Canal on the north bank of the river, with the Administration's support, was converted in 1970 from a national monument to a national historic park. The National River, involving major federal expenditures to buy private lands on both banks, would have enclosed the river in a "green sheath" of land protected from despoilation and open to public enjoyment. The Administration's bill merely provided for federal purchase of key areas along the C & O Canal. The result of the 1970 law will be partial protection for one bank of the River, but the opposite bank and many areas on the north bank will still be wide open to destructive private developments that could have been prevented by a National River.

Protection for existing parks has been minimal. The basic law in this field is the Wilderness Act of 1964, which set aside 9 million acres as wilderness. It also prescribed a 10-year review procedure, involving studies by the National Park Service, the Forest Service and Bureau of Sport Fisheries and Wildlife, and a recommendation to Congress by the President, during which additional areas within these federal lands could be designated as wilderness. When Walter Hickel took office, the review was far behind, mainly because the National Park Service had insisted on going into unnecessary detail on its proposed developments. The Wilderness Act was being used as a stimulus to Park Service developers to plan additional developments. Secretary Hickel issued a speed-up order, and publicized this as one of the top priorities of the Interior Department. But this had little effect on the National Park Service until Nathaniel Reed took office as Assistant Secretary of Interior for fish, wildlife and parks in 1971. As a result of Reed's effort, the work got back on schedule. Still, with two-thirds of the ten-year review period already elapsed, only 1.2 million acres of a potential 40 million acres in national parks, forests and wildlife refuges, have been added to the system. President Nixon has submitted proposals for an additional 4.9 million acres.

The Nixon Administration has vetoed the "wilderness enclaves" concept pushed by National Park Service Director George B. Hartzog, Jr. The Park Service argued that areas in the middle of wilderness land, ranging in size from three acres to 400 acres, should be left open to development of commercial concessions and other developments at Park Service discretion. Such proposals existed for North Cascades, Sequoia-Kings Canyon and other national parks. Repeated protests by conservationists brought a resolution of the issue on May 5, 1972, when Assistant Secretary Reed agreed to revise all the wilderness proposals, removing the enclaves.

## Alaska

The State of Alaska, still largely untouched by the heavy hand of exploitation, is, as lobbyist Bob Waldrop has said, "our last chance to do it right the first time." Most of Alaska remains for our generation either to protect or to devastate, and the most far-reaching decisions affecting the state's future are taking place during the tenure of President Nixon.

Of Alaska's total area, 365 million acres—as large as Texas, California, Oregon and Idaho combined—95 percent is federal land. Because most of this is not readily accessible for commercial purposes, little has been done to hurt the land—some mining here and there, oil drilling in Cook Inlet, heavy logging along the coast of Southeast Alaska. The terms of settlement of Native land claims, and the final decision on the Trans-Alaskan Pipeline, will influence the future of the land more profoundly than any other Alaska action taken by the government. The issue is nothing less than the opening of Alaska.

Out of the remaining federal land, the Alaska Statehood Act of 1958 entitles the State to select 103 million acres, supposedly as a sort of patrimony, to be disposed of as the state sees fit. Most of this will presumably be sold off to finance the state government, although some will be used for state parks. So far, the state has completed the selection process on some 25 million acres.

When President Nixon took office, however, all federal land in Alaska had been withdrawn from disposal by a "land freeze" order of Secretary Udall, who intended to hold the land in status quo until the land claims of many groups of Alaskan Natives—60,000 Eskimos, Indians, and Aleuts—had been settled. The claims, then pending in court, and being considered in Congress as well, represented the assertion by Natives that they were being dispossessed of their land without compensation. Unlike Indian tribes in the "lower 48" states, the Alaskan Natives never gave up their land through treaties with the government. They still had "aboriginal title" to the land, as several Acts of Congress had confirmed through the years. The claims covered practically all of the state, and many areas were claimed by more than one Native group. The "land freeze" insured that these knotty problems would be solved before the new problems of state selection and private ownership were added.

Although Mr. Nixon's first Interior Secretary, Walter J. Hickel, initially said of the freeze, "What Udall did, I can undo," he agreed during his confirmation hearings before the Senate Interior Committee to extend the freeze.

But the Native Claims bill came to a head gradually over several years. The clincher that put it through in 1971 was oil. Edward Weinberg, an attorney for the Natives, and former Solicitor of the Interior Department, told the *National Journal*: "The justice of our cause, mixed with oil—that's what did it." The oil companies seeking to bring the oil out from Prudhoe Bay had been challenged by Native villages claiming land over which parts of the Trans-Alaskan Pipeline would pass. In addition, many oil fields were tied up as long as the Native claims were not settled. From the oilmen's standpoint, settlement of the Native claims would get the Natives out of the way in most places the oilmen wanted to seek or extract oil. Most of the talk on Capitol Hill centered on a combination of land and money that would largely limit Native land holdings to the areas near existing Native villages and leave most of the state free for oilmen.

The Natives themselves were represented in Washington by the Alaska Federation of Natives, and by exceptionally able Washington lawyers, including Weinberg and former Attorney General Ramsey Clark. The Natives' proposal called for 60 million acres of land, one billion dollars in cash, and a perpetual royalty on Alaskan minerals and timber. A just settlement of the Native claims was needed to alleviate the poverty and ill health of Natives still living in villages.

The intercession of the oil interests was generally given credit for the policies of the Nixon Administration. Until 1971, the Administration had backed a bill allotting to the Natives only 15 million acres and one billion dollars. On March 31, 1971, the Administration unveiled a new proposal basically allotting 40 million acres of land and one billion dollars.

A major problem remained: how to balance the national interest against the specific interests of Alaskan Natives and the State of Alaska? Until the closing months of debate on the Native Claims Bill, no significant attention was devoted to this question.

Under the Administration and other principal versions of the legislation, the lands would be selected by the State and by the Natives without any opportunity for the federal government to consider whether the areas selected might best be kept in federal hands. Potential national parks, wilderness areas, or wild rivers would have gone to the first claimant.

The Wilderness Society and Friends of the Earth first raised the issue at House hearings in May, 1971, proposing that further State and Native selections await completion of a joint federal-state-Natives land use plan with the exception that Native villages would obtain their land immediately. Later augmented by the Sierra Club and other organizations, conservationists attempted to have the House Interior Committee adopt the Saylor-Udall amendment, providing for the land planning requirement. The Administration opposed the amendment, and covertly backed a substitute, the Kyl Amendment, which would have set aside all federal land in Alaska, but gave carte blanche authority to the Secretary to reopen the land. Under the Kyl Amendment, the Secretary could even permit exceptions from the withdrawal. The Kyl amendment was adopted by substitution for the Saylor-Udall amendment, 26-10.

The bill next went to the House floor, where a new amendment (known as the Udall-Saylor amendment) was proposed by conservation groups. It provided for 60 million acres of federal land to be set aside by the Interior Secretary as national interest study areas. Lobbying was intense on both sides. The Natives opposed the measure as part of their deal with Chairman Aspinall to fight all amendments in exchange for his support for the bill. The Administration also opposed it; every Congressman received a letter from President Nixon endorsing the committee bill. The amendment was defeated 217-177.

Nevertheless, the "National Interest" provisions were adopted on the Senate side, the Natives accepted them, and they were sustained in the final law. Under these provisions, enacted over the Administration's opposition, Secretary Morton, on March 15, 1972, announced his withdrawal of 125 million acres of federal land for study as potential national parks, national forests, national wildlife refuges, wild and scenic rivers and other national categories. Conservationists praised these withdrawals, which covered most of the areas which they had asked Morton to protect. But Morton's action also involved a concession to mining interests by leaving part of the Wrangell Mountains and areas in the proposed Gates of the Arctic National Park open to mining.

## Trans-Alaskan Pipeline

If the Nixon Administration had got its way, the Trans-Alaskan Pipeline would have been almost completed by 1972. As U.S. District Court Judge George L. Hart concluded, the government appeared ready in May, 1970, to issue the permit for construction of the haul road. Only the injunction imposed by Judge Hart, responding to a lawsuit by The Wilderness Society, Friends of the Earth, and the Environmental Defense Fund, stopped the project and permitted the debate that is still going on. The injunction was based on the failure of the Interior Department to prepare an adequate environmental impact statement, as required by the National Environmental Policy Act.

Unlike oil pipelines in the "lower 48," the Alaskan Pipeline from the North Slope oil fields to the port of Valdez would lead to major damage of the last and greatest wilderness in the United States. Besides disturbing the wildlife, much of the pipeline would be routed over permafrost (permanently frozen ground), and its construction would leave open scars imprinted on the land surface for years. Oil spills would pollute the rivers along its course which still bear a rich harvest of fish. One mile of the 800-mile pipeline would contain 500,000 gallons of oil. Shipment of the oil to the West Coast of the country would certainly lead to ocean pollution along the tanker route—a problem that has elicited concern from Canadian officials as well as from fishermen, both in Alaska and in Puget Sound.

Eight months after the injunction was imposed, the Interior Department released its draft impact statement, and public hearings by the Interior Department were held in Washington, D.C., and in Anchorage, Alaska, in February, 1971. The impact statement was roundly drubbed for significant omissions, such as the failure to consider alternative routes through Canada, and the impact of tanker shipment of the oil south to the "lower 48." The public attention drawn by the hearings apparently led Morton to announce shortly afterward, as one of his first major pronouncements as Secretary, that no action would be taken in 1971 on the pipeline.

It was a different story, however, when the final impact statement was released in 1972. The new statement was notable for its sheer bulk—six volumes, weighing twenty-five pounds. Conservationists and numerous Senators and Congressmen called for public hearings on the statement, to cover the voluminous new information presented in the documents. But Undersecretary of Interior William T. Pecora said: "The Secretary has ruled out public hearings." Hearings would be a "circus," and "would interfere with a more thoughtful, rational analysis." By limiting himself to a single television appearance on the issue, and by having Pecora release the impact statement, Secretary Morton seemed to be dissociating himself from the issue, in contrast to his 1971 role as champion of the conservation viewpoint. Insiders reported that Morton was set on issuing the construction permit in 1972, and that the Administration would do its best to keep the issue quiet.

Indeed, on May 11, 1972, the Secretary released a statement, without any press conference or TV appearance, that he had decided to issue a construction permit "as soon as that can be done without violating any court order." Rejecting the alternative route through Canada and the alternative of leaving the oil in the ground for future use, he said, "I am convinced that it is in our best national interest to avoid all further delays and uncertainties in planning the development of Alaska North Slope oil reserves by having a secure pipeline located under the total jurisdiction and for the exclusive use of the United States."

"Although Mr. Morton frequently used 'I' in his statement," reported the *Wall Street Journal*, "one administration source involved in oil policy planning said the decision was intensively discussed at White House meetings, including ones at the Cabinet level. . . . Administration sources also suggest that Mr. Nixon, heeding the urgings of Treasury Secretary John B. Connally, was anxious to end the uncertainty that has confronted U.S. oil companies since they initially approached Washington with the pipeline proposal in 1969."

The oil companies, of course, were delighted by Morton's announcement. Robert O. Anderson, chairman of Atlantic Richfield, said his company is convinced the pipeline can and will be built "with minimal effect on the environment." Charles E. Spahr, chairman of Standard Oil (Ohio), called Morton's action "a major step forward." "The benefits that will result," he said, "from completion of the pipeline are potentially greater for Sohio than for any other company. Our leases on the North Slope of Alaska hold in excess of 50 percent of the proved recoverable reserves of crude oil in the Prudhoe Bay field. We also have a 27.5 percent interest in the pipeline."

Morton can't issue the permit, however, until the injunction won by the conservationists is dissolved. The conservationists plan to continue fighting the decision in court, and the dispute may go all the way to the Supreme Court. David Brower, president of Friends of the Earth, said, "Building a pipeline now, and quickly using up all the Prudhoe Bay oil as a national security measure, is about as rational as burning up all your firewood before winter." Brower urged that the oil be kept as an energy reserve. "We should do with the Prudhoe Bay oil what the Navy Department has done with its Naval petroleum reserves—leave the oil in the ground. It will keep until we really need it."

Morton's action followed the pattern of keeping the issue quiet. The statement was released during a week when the headlines were occupied by news of the bombing and mining of North Vietnam. It was also evidently designed to get the issue settled as early as possible before the November election, in hopes that public concern would by then subside.

The Nixon Administration's term in office has been a time of frustration for defenders of the public lands. The Administration's persistent habit has been to take an issue away from the original advocates through sheer publicity, and then let it die of neglect.

Such was the case with mining. After months of waiting, Secretary Morton announced his proposal to revise the 1872 mining law. The weight of his entry on the issue overpowered the environmental advocates and dominated the media coverage, resulting in news stories and editorials about the Administration's attack on an antiquated law, although his proposal basically favored the miners and continued the concept on which the 1872 law was based. Then nothing happened. The Everglades is the notable exception. In that case, the Administration's follow-up was effective and continuous. But by and large, there has been much talk and little action.

On issues involving big public land industries, on the other hand, the Administration has been active. But in these cases it is on the side of the industries. One has only to review the Administration's record on the national forests, or on Alaska, to see the highly effective work done to benefit the timber and oil industries.

The history of the public lands has traditionally been one of exploitation by private interests. But in these years of growing public concern for these lands, the Nixon Administration's failure to defend consistently and actively the national interest is one more example of the disparity between rhetoric and action.

# WILDLIFE

## TOM GARRETT

"The Nixon Administration has been far more favorably disposed, by and large, toward wildlife and animal protection legislation than any previous administration. The Department of Interior has used administrative discretion in a number of cases to help the animals. This was unheard of before 1969. So, whatever we think of Nixon's policies on issues affecting wildlife habitat, in the narrow area of direct wildlife protection they could have been much worse."

So speaks Christine Stevens, the secretary of the Society for Animal Protection Legislation. Mrs. Stevens was the first wildlife lobbyist in Washington, and she's witnessed a gradual improvement in the government's attitude toward animals ever since the dark days of the Eisenhower Administration. Her assessment is correct. The Nixon Administration has pursued a more enlightened wildlife policy than any of its predecessors, but the urgency of the wild-

---

*Tom Garrett came to Washington from a ranch in Garrett, Wyoming, in June, 1971. He had come to spend one week lobbying on behalf of the beleaguered whale, but, without really planning to, he has extended his visit. Garrett is now the wildlife conservation director for Friends of the Earth. He has written articles for the* New York Times *and the* Washington Post, *and has submitted numerous testimonies to Congressional committees. Anne Wickham and Pat LeDonne assisted Garrett in researching and writing this chapter.*

life crisis is greater than ever before, and in certain critical areas the Administration has not made the needed difficult decisions.

Before hurrying forward with plaudits, one should examine the political anatomy of the Administration's more dramatic decisions. Some of them, like Walter Hickel's move to protect the whales, were not made at the President's initiative, and appear to have run against the general direction of Administration policy.

Since different federal agencies are often in drastic conflict, it is sometimes difficult to determine President Nixon's personal position. The Departments of Interior and Commerce, for example, have struggled fiercely for jurisdiction over ocean mammals. The Commerce Department is far more friendly to industry, and less responsive to conservationists, than the Interior Department. But despite its professed concern about wildlife, the White House has consistently backed the Commerce Department's struggle to grab this jurisdiction. President Nixon himself triggered the battle in 1970 by putting the new National Oceanic and Atmospheric Administration (NOAA) into the Commerce Department, taking away from the Department of Interior many of NOAA's functions.

The Nixon Administration's increased concern about wildlife reflects the enormously heightened level of public consciousness. Many new animal protection groups, such as Friends of Animals, Fund for Animals, and the Committee for Humane Legislation, have, with their rapidly growing memberships, entered the political arena. Wildlife protection, now popular with the press, has become a richly rewarding political issue, and since one does not necessarily have to combat vested economic interests, some politicians use the issue to parade themselves as environmentalists knowing they will not seriously offend corporate interests. The advantages of this approach have not been overlooked by the men shaping decisions in the Nixon Administration.

Unfortunately, this approach has definite limitations:

most of the species recently given protection by the federal government are already rare and therefore of declining commercial importance. It is one thing to provide protection to wild horses, when most of them have already disappeared into pet-food cans, but quite another to stop the tuna industry from killing a quarter-of-a-million dolphins each year.

## Endangered Species

The Endangered Species Act of 1969 required the Secretary of Interior to publish a list of endangered species, and once an animal was placed on the list its products would be banned from import from any foreign country. Unfortunately, major loopholes weaken the law. Before putting any species on the list, the Secretary must have evidence of "world-wide extinction." Reluctant administrators in the Office of Endangered Species have used this provision as an excuse to keep geographically isolated subspecies off the list, even though the subspecies may be thousands of miles from their nearest relatives and certainly threatened with extinction. No federal penalties exist for killing domestic endangered species. Even after a species is placed on the list, its products may be imported for another full year under "hardship" permits routinely granted to importers.

The Secretary has substantial discretion. If sufficiently determined he can use the law to protect many species, as Walter Hickel did for the great whales. But the Interior Department finds it more politically expedient to ignore the plight of commercially valuable species. Spotted cats and polar bears are only two of the animals which have suffered from the loopholes and administrative delays. Between 1968 and 1970, U.S. furriers alone imported 18,456 leopard skins from Africa, and 31,105 jaguar skins and 249,680 ocelot skins from South America. In one year alone, 1969, the value of imported skins was $10.6 million. Cheetahs and some subspecies of leopard and tiger have become critically rare in Asia and Africa. Snow leopards, clouded leopards, and Siberian tigers are near extinction.

The Office of Endangered Species has consistently resisted pressures from the Congress, conservationists, the press, the public, the scientific community and even their own superiors to list certain species as endangered. The former head of the Office, Harry Goodwin, adamantly opposed the listing of spotted cats. His assistant, Eley Denson, said he wanted to buy his wife a leopard-skin coat. Earl Baysinger, who replaced Goodwin as head of the Office in June, 1971, was equally intransigent. All were strongly supported by Brewster Chapman, Associate Solicitor for Territories, Wildlife, and Claims in the Department of Interior. Assistant Secretary Bohlen, embarrassed by prodding from the conservation groups, finally brought Baysinger into his office for a meeting with some of the Department's biologists who favored putting the cats on the protected list. Baysinger's use of the "world-wide extinction" argument was cut to pieces. On March 30, 1972, Secretary Morton put eight spotted cats on the Endangered Species List: ocelots, jaguars, cheetahs, margays, leopards, snow leopards, tigers and tiger cats. Baysinger's performance in the spotted cat controversy may or may not have led to his replacement as chief of the Endangered Species Office by Keith Schreiner in May 1972.

Much of the credit for this action goes to Lewis Regenstein, the Washington Representative for the Fund for Animals. When Regenstein learned that Morton was to appear on the Dick Cavett Show in January, 1972, he arranged to have some questions about the cats. Secretary Morton, caught off-guard, said that he would put some of the cats on the list. When the listing was delayed, Regenstein contacted Congresswoman Julia Butler Hansen, Chairwoman of the House Appropriations Subcommittee on the Interior and related agencies, urging her to investigate the matter in forthcoming hearings. Finally, Baysinger was forced to list the cats.

Polar bears have not been so lucky. Despite a lawsuit by several environmental groups and considerable evidence that the bears are extremely scarce, Secretary Morton claims there is no "world-wide extinction." Meanwhile, "sport" hunting, largely from airplanes, continues to reduce the species. There are virtually no polar bears left off the Alaska coast, and the total Arctic population is now down to about 10,000 animals. The species, spread over the entire Arctic region, will have trouble surviving. Even so, about 1,200 are killed each year, 300 by Americans. Brochures from World-Wide Trophy Outfitters describe the big "trophy" bear as a "no longer productive type of animal" and urge customers to hurry since hunting of "this beautiful, impressive animal" may be banned entirely.

In February, 1972, President Nixon proposed new legislation which would fill the major loopholes in the existing Endangered Species Act. Evidence of "world-wide extinction" would no longer be required before a species could be added to the endangered list, and the killing of domestic endangered species would become a federal offense. These reforms were long overdue, and the President deserves much credit for proposing them, but there is one significant problem with his proposal: the White House is insisting that the Secretary of Commerce have jurisdiction over protection (or nonprotection) of most endangered marine species. The Commerce Department fears that, should reformers in the Department of Interior gain control, certain species of commercial fish might be listed as endangered species; conservationists fear that, if the Commerce Department gains the jurisdiction, NOAA would remove the eight great whales from the endangered species list. Representative John Dingell (D-Mich.), Chairman of the House Subcommittee on Fisheries and Wildlife Conservation, and conservationists are strongly resisting any expansion of the Commerce Department's authority.

## The Great Whales

In our time, the great whales may disappear. Man is feverishly engaged in efforts to exterminate these species, which are perhaps more intelligent and certainly more gentle than man himself.

Seventeen nations signed a convention in 1946 establishing the International Whaling Commission which was charged with "conservation and rational utilization" of the world's whale resources. What followed was not a reduction but a dramatic acceleration of the massacre. During the 1960's, new killing records were set, reaching the all-time high of 67,000 in 1962.

### Estimated Populations of the Great Whales

|  | 1930–1940 | 1970 |
|---|---|---|
| Blue | 100,000 | 600 to 3,000 |
| Finback | 400,000 | 100,000 |
| Sei | 150,000 | 75,000 |
| Sperm | 600,000 | 250,000 |
| Humpback | 100,000 | 2,000 |
| Right | unknown | 500 to 1,000 |
| Grey | unknown | 5,000 to 12,000 |
| Bowhead | unknown | 500 to 1,000 |

Since 1960, nation after nation has been forced to stop whaling because of the scarcity of whales. Today, only the Japanese and the Russians, accounting for 85 percent of the reported 42,266 whale killings in 1970, are still engaged in large-scale operations using spotter helicopters, radar, and sonar. The Japanese and Russian industries are quite deliberately "whaling themselves out of business," because the men involved have decided it is more profitable to whale on a very large scale for a few years, until the whales are gone, than to whale indefinitely on a limited but sustained yield basis.

Until fairly recently, the United States imported one-third of the world take from whales. Walter Hickel's last act as Secretary was to place the finback, sei, sperm, grey, blue, right, humpback and bowhead whales on the endangered list. Hickel, who probably suspected his impending dismissal, sent the whale listings to the *Federal Register* on Wednesday before Thanksgiving Day, 1970. On Friday, he was fired.

After Hickel's departure, the Interior Department, reportedly because of pressure from Secretary of Commerce Maurice Stans and an order directly from President Nixon, decided to recall the proposal to put the whales on the list before it could be published in the *Federal Register*. But when this decision was leaked to the press, the uproar of protest and indignation was so great the Administration backed down. Almost miraculously, the eight great whales appeared on the endangered species list effective December 1, 1970.

The section of the Endangered Species Act of 1969 permitting one-year extensions for "hardship" cases was immediately invoked by the importers. Kal Kan, the dog food manufacturer which sponsors "Animal World," secured a permit to import 11.5 million pounds of sperm and baleen whale meat to use in pet food. Over 30,000 tons of sperm oil were imported under thirty-seven endangered species permits. The claims of "hardship" were not investigated, but permits were issued as a matter of course upon proof of previous importation.

In December, 1971, the Endangered Species permits expired, and despite pressure for de-listing of the whales, the Administration announced that U.S. whaling and whale imports would be banned.

The United States has attended twenty-three meetings of the International Whaling Commission since it was established in 1946. The U.S. delegates have attended these conferences with instructions to ameliorate the "overharvesting" of whales, but their rather timid requests have been largely ignored. They have no mandate, and apparently no inclination, to take a firm or meaningful position. In 1972, however, there are some hopes for change.

Mr. Fujita, a Japanese whaler, is being replaced as Chairman of the Whaling Commission by the U.S. Commissioner, Dr. J. M. McHugh.

International treaties and conferences concerning marine wildlife are normally handled by the Office of Oceanic Affairs in the State Department, and coordinated by Ambassador Donald McKernan. McKernan has shown little sympathy in the past for the fate of the whales. Until recently, his office was relatively immune to outside pressure; its policies were either subordinate to the "larger considerations" of the State Department or left to the discretion of McKernan or his associates. Recently, however, the pressure on McKernan has been quite strong. Both Houses of Congress passed resolutions in 1971 calling on the State Department to push for a ten-year moratorium on whale killing.

McKernan gave assurances in April, 1972, that the State Department would indeed pursue the moratorium at the International Whaling Commission meeting in London scheduled for June, 1972. As of this writing there is little hope that the whaling nations will take it seriously unless the State Department gets tough, which is unlikely. But conservationists are encouraged by President Nixon's April 27, 1972, appointment of Russell Train as his special representative at the London negotiations.

## Antarctic Seals

In late January, 1972, a minor tempest arose in Congress and among conservationists when it was learned that the State Department's Donald McKernan was scheduled to attend a meeting in London on the "conservation" of Antarctic seals. The circulated draft convention would have set commercial quotas for the killing of three of the four species of seals unique to the area south of latitude 60°. The seals to be "conserved," crabeaters, weddels, leopards, and Ross seals, are the only pinnipeds remaining which have never been subjected to commercial massacre.

It came out at the conference that the Norwegians were

openly preparing to seal, the Russians and Japanese were "interested," and the British were pushing for a commercially favorable treaty. The British attitude was based on the fact that the British fur industry processes the bulk of the world's hair seal kill, and that this industry is now threatened by the "overharvesting" of the northern seal. The Reba Fur Company of Bergen, Norway, and its Canadian subsidiary, which does the bulk of the killing, have already virtually extirpated the harp seal herds off Canada and north of Jan Mayen Island. The Antarctic seals are the last untapped "supply" of victims. The problem for conservationists is not just one of overkill but also one of inhumane killing.

McKernan, under instructions to work for a treaty with control and inspection safeguards to shield the seals from an unrestricted massacre like Japan, Russia and Norway have already inflicted on the Antarctic whales, performed creditably. He extracted every concession possible from the other nations, but in the end he agreed to a treaty which provides only for eventual consideration of inspection and enforcement. The American delegation considered it better to be a part of a weak treaty, and work to strengthen it from within, than to remain outside, presumably with little influence. The quota for all countries combined was set at 175,000 crabeaters, 12,000 leopard seals, and 5,000 weddel seals a year.

If seven of the twelve nations attending the conference ratify the convention, it will go into effect as an international treaty. The United States Senate will probably decide the issue sometime in 1972. Whether or not the Senate accepts the State Department's philosophy that we can best ameliorate the massacre from within the treaty, there seems little doubt that a new slaughter is in the offing, and that the earth's last "living laboratory" is faced with new desecration.

As in the case of the great whales, the Nixon Administration negotiators at the international conferences on seals have recently taken a generally conservationist position. But in terms of taking the steps necessary for effective results, the Administration has failed because it has not gone beyond the conferences and used its political leverage at higher levels to persuade foreign governments to stop the commercial slaughter.

## Predator Control

> "Americans today set a high value on the preservation of wildlife. The old notion that 'the only good predator is a dead one' is no longer acceptable as we understand that even animals and birds which sometimes prey on domesticated animals have their own value in maintaining the balance of nature.... Certainly, predators can represent a threat to sheep and some other domesticated animals. But we must use more selective methods of control that will preserve ecological values while continuing to protect livestock."
>
> President Nixon,
> *Environmental Message,* February 8, 1972.

The Division of Wildlife Services (DWS) in the Department of Interior has for forty years waged a massive campaign to poison and "manage" wildlife. Having killed more than 80,000 coyotes, bobcats, bears, wolves and lions in 1971 alone, it is one of the most hated agencies among conservationists.

The Division's major campaign has been the extermination of the coyote. DWS first relied on "coyote getters," capsules of cyanide attached to a pistol cartridge. These were put upright in the ground and smeared with an odoriferous paste. When coyotes or other predators investigated the scent and pulled on the cylinder, the cartridge shot the cyanide into the animal's mouth and killed it. The initial impact of these "getters" was enormous, but by the mid-1950's the coyotes had "gotten wise" and began to make a come-back.

## Known Number of Animals Killed by the Division of Wildlife Services and its Predecessors

| Year | Bears | Bobcats | Coyotes | Red Wolves | Lobo Wolves | Mt. Lions |
|---|---|---|---|---|---|---|
| 1937 | 299 | 7,472 | 80,299 | 980 | 27 | 212 |
| 1938 | 392 | 7,189 | 84,844 | 1,343 | 17 | 255 |
| 1939 | 495 | 9,033 | 93,039 | 1,188 | 26 | 241 |
| 1940 | 608 | 10,566 | 104,072 | 1,246 | 9 | 214 |
| 1941 | 528 | 10,347 | 110,495 | 1,362 | 5 | 204 |
| 1942 | 636 | 10,957 | 111,076 | 781 | 10 | 204 |
| 1943 | 618 | 9,527 | 103,971 | 1,004 | 10 | 147 |
| 1944 | 592 | 8,900 | 108,050 | 1,161 | 9 | 167 |
| 1945 | 619 | 7,325 | 102,979 | 1,354 | 11 | 163 |
| 1946 | 730 | 6,487 | 108,311 | 1,551 | 6 | 113 |
| 1947 | 919 | 6,508 | 103,982 | 1,450 | 10 | 127 |
| 1948 | 744 | 7,223 | 90,270 | 1,053 | 14 | 148 |
| 1949 | 652 | 8,231 | 75,448 | 1,032 | 4 | 131 |
| 1950 | 719 | 10,874 | 66,281 | 1,051 | 108 | 236 |
| 1951 | 733 | 13,343 | 60,455 | 1,244 | 134 | 229 |
| 1952 | 714 | 13,476 | 50,661 | 1,451 | 182 | 197 |
| 1953 | 729 | 18,905 | 55,000 | 1,797 | 65 | 184 |
| 1954 | 860 | 19,559 | 52,636 | 1,589 | 93 | 232 |
| 1955 | 874 | 19,249 | 55,204 | 2,487 | 171 | 195 |
| 1956 | 977 | 19,495 | 55,402 | 1,940 | 96 | 285 |
| 1957 | 1,039 | 22,198 | 62,585 | 2,681 | 109 | 267 |
| 1958 | 1,023 | 23,453 | 62,765 | 2,615 | 172 | 331 |
| 1959 | 978 | 25,079 | 78,714 | 3,393 | 161 | 292 |
| 1960 | 1,023 | 25,808 | 94,769 | 3,830 | 2 | 290 |
| 1961 | 1,039 | 25,177 | 100,363 | 2,532 | 1 | 276 |
| 1962 | 815 | 21,228 | 104,787 | 2,780 | 2 | 254 |
| 1963 | 842 | 20,780 | 89,653 | 2,771 | 8 | 294 |
| 1964 | 711 | 20,918 | 97,096 | 2,617 | 24 | 323 |
| 1965 | 605 | 17,294 | 90,236 | — | 15 | 280 |
| 1966 | 549 | 13,365 | 77,258 | — | 5 | 212 |
| 1967 | 499 | 11,031 | 75,892 | — | 9 | 143 |
| 1968 | 440 | 9,351 | 69,390 | — | 34 | 152 |
| 1969 | 399 | 8,443 | 74,070 | — | 14 | 145 |
| 1970 | 403 | 8,403 | 73,093 | — | 11 | 121 |

SOURCE: Report to the Council on Environmental Quality and the Department of Interior by the Advisory Committee on Predator Control, Stanley A. Cain, Chairman, January, 1972.

The DWS then shifted to still more deadly poisons, notably the dreaded 1080, sodium monofluoroacetate. Since 1080 doesn't dissolve or break down chemically it kills not only the target animal but also the scavengers that feed off the carcass, travelling up the food chain in a devastating fashion. Massive applications of 1080 and other poisons can virtually wipe out all the carnivores in a given area.

1080 is an exceptionally cruel and abominable poison. One night, during the fall of 1965, I awakened in my house in the southern Wyoming mountains to the apocalyptic howling of my border collie. I rushed to the door and let the slavering, terrified dog in. My brother was already melting lard, which will frequently relieve animals poisoned by strychnine. We forced this down his throat, and his howls subsided to occasional whimpers. He rested his chin on my knee, looking at me trustingly. We sat with him through the night, cherishing a faint hope that the poison was strychnine rather than 1080. We poured more melted lard in his mouth when the pain began to recur, until early dawn when the pain could no longer be relieved. He broke loose, flung himself against the wall, and lay writhing in agony until he died. This has happened to thousands of dogs throughout the American West, countless millions of coyotes, prairie dogs, foxes, bears and other animals, and about a score of humans.

Conservationists were therefore delighted when President Nixon issued his executive order in February, 1972, to end the use of poisons on federal lands. The Environmental Protection Agency quickly cancelled the registration of thallium sulfate, and barred 1080 and strychnine from interstate commerce. A proposed bill written by the Interior Department repeats the language of the executive order and provides a $6 million subsidy over three years for states which conduct their own predator control programs without using poisons.

But the battle is far from over. Hearings before Rep. Dingell's Subcommittee on Fisheries and Wildlife in April,

1972, strongly suggested that federal actions taken to date will not be enough to prevent the states from employing 1080 and other dangerous poisons. Livestock interests, having lost a battle at the federal level, are now pressuring the states. Since the subsidy proposed by President Nixon to induce the states away from poisons is modest, it is fairly clear that in many areas poisoning will continue until 1080 and strychnine are completely outlawed, their possession made a felony, and the Bureau of Land Management is authorized to cancel grazing leases of ranchers known to be involved in poisoning activity.

While poisoning has certainly been the most devastating and indiscriminate method of predator control, the real question is whether the Division of Wildlife Services should indulge in massive "predator control" programs at all. Missouri and Kansas long ago dropped out of the federal program. These states respond to complaints from farmers and ranchers by teaching them how to trap the animals doing the damage. Damage from predators was sharply reduced under this system, and the cost for each state is one-tenth what the Federal Predator Control Program costs in the neighboring state of Oklahoma.

But the Division of Wildlife Services seems more concerned about its own bureaucratic growth than about the effectiveness of such modest operations. Now shifting its emphasis to aircraft hunting (in Wyoming, about one fourth of the 4,000 coyotes killed last year by DWS were killed by aircraft shooting), DWS is also encouraging hunting from cars and snowmobiles by ranchers and "sportsmen." It is obvious that DWS is going to continue in the business of killing wildlife. Until the Division of Wildlife Services is disbanded, or the people in it are displaced by others with a different mentality, it will continue to wage war on American wildlife with whatever weapons it has at its disposal, exchanging one mass-killing technique for another.

The bald eagle, as a result of DDT poisoning in much of the U.S., and probably the use of 1080 in the West, for example, has become critically rare. About 2,000 to 4,000 remain. This has been accompanied by a relative increase in the number of golden eagles (there are now about 8,000 to 10,000 golden eagles in North America). This led to complaints (disputed by conservationists) from sheep ranchers that golden eagles are killing lambs.

The thallium poisoning of at least twenty-two eagles by Van Irvine in central Wyoming in the summer of 1971 made national headlines, but drew only the minimum fine of $679. A subsequently discovered massacre of 570 eagles by helicopter gunners reportedly employed by Herman Werner, Irvine's wealthy father-in-law, has resulted in the filing of federal charges. But there had been a protracted and rather inexplicable delay. One of the persons involved in the killing claims "only about five" bald eagles were killed. The bald eagle, of course, is the national bird, and is on the endangered species list. The killing of this bird has been outlawed. It is also illegal to kill the golden eagle without a permit issued under the Federal Predator Control Program. No permit to kill golden eagles has been issued since 1969.

## The Marine Mammal Legislation

The Marine Mammal Protection Bill is one of the most important animal protection measures ever to come before the United States Congress. Originally drafted by lawyers for Alice Herrington, the President of Friends of Animals, the measure was introduced in early 1971 by Senator Fred Harris (D-Okla.) and Rep. David Pryor (D-Ark.). The "Harris-Pryor Bill" was a sweeping measure which would have prohibited the killing of all marine mammals, such as whales, seals, walruses, porpoises, manatees, and sea lions, as well as the import of any product derived from them.

The bill's initial reception was favorable. But before long it suffered a counterattack from the tuna lobby and New York furriers and federal and state agencies. Once again, the Nixon Administration argued that the Commerce Department's National Oceanic and Atmospheric

Administration, rather than the Interior Department, should be given jurisdiction over marine mammals. Rep. Dingell, chairman of the Subcommittee on Fisheries and Wildlife Conservation, and conservationists pushed hard to have all jurisdiction given to Interior, but the Nixon Administration joined those members of the subcommittee wanting it given to the Commerce Department. Eventually, Dingell was overruled by his subcommittee. Pleas that the Commerce Department was commercially oriented, and would use administrative discretion to favor the exploiters, fell on deaf ears. Interior was given jurisdiction only over manatees, polar bears and walruses.

Another key issue during the hearings was the killing of dolphins during tuna catching. The hearings disclosed that more than 250,000 dolphins are killed each year by purse seine net techniques. Tuna and dolphins are often found together, and the giant purse seine nets are circled around dolphin schools in order to catch the tuna underneath. In the process, many of the dolphins are killed or injured in the net. During the House hearings, a well-financed tuna lobby appeared on Capitol Hill, and, along with friends on the committee, it managed to keep out of the bill any meaningful restrictions on the dolphin killing.

When the weakened bill came to the House floor on March 9, 1972, Rep. Dingell deflected much of the conservationist opposition by adding a five-year moratorium on the killing of all marine mammals, other than Pribilof fur seals and dolphins killed by tuna nets, as well as a similar moratorium on imports, excepting the fur-seal pelts. In a conservationist attempt to strengthen the bill, two key amendments were sought: to return jurisdiction to Interior and to establish tougher restrictions on purse seine netting. Both were defeated, with the Nixon Administration actively lobbying against the conservationsts' Interior amendment. Every Republican on the House floor voted against the amendments except for Ogden Reid (N.Y.), who shortly thereafter became a Democrat. Rep. Thomas Pelly (R-Wash.), the ranking Republican on the full Merchant Marine and Fisheries Committee, even threatened the possibility of a Presidential veto if jurisdiction was given back to Interior.

The Senate bill will apparently be stronger in most respects than the House bill. But the Senate deliberations have been marked by the appearance of a hair seal lobby, in the form of one Isadore Bergner of New York, acting on behalf of a number of New York furriers. His efforts are expected to result in some relaxation of the import restrictions on hair seals.

In all probability, the future of those ocean mammals affected by U.S. policies will depend on the way in which NOAA and the Commerce Department exercise administrative discretion on what has all the earmarks of being a weak law. The forbodings of conservationists will soon be put to the test.

Incredible as it may seem, in view of such Administration policies as giving the Commerce Department authority over marine mammals, President Nixon's initiatives to protect wildlife have far exceeded those of any previous administration. But all that has been done is still too little, and, for some species, probably too late. The ultimate threat to most wildlife will come not from direct hunting but from the destruction of their habitat. Whether or not animals are deliberately molested becomes academic if their range is destroyed or their food supplies poisoned.

The protection of habitat creates much more difficult problems for the Nixon Administration because it runs head on into the interests of industrial and agricultural powers. Streams and lakes ruined by industrial wastes or backed up by siltation from strip-mined hills, clear cut forests, insufficiently treated sewage—all destroy the habitat of wildlife and fish. Persistent pesticides like DDT poison the food and water of animals and birds and have already brought several species of birds, such as the peregrine falcon, the bald eagle and the brown pelican, to virtual extinction. The dangers of these pesticides have been known for years, but still they are not completely banned.

DDT decomposes very slowly. It is in the earth and in our waters and will remain there for scores, and perhaps hundreds, of years. Heavy metals such as mercury are dumped into fresh and sea waters, contaminating, in an accumulative way, the fish, and then the animals who live off them (including ourselves).

One of the saddest cases of marine mammal abuse is that of the manatee, commonly known as the sea cow. Found along the Florida coast, this lumbering, helpless animal is being slaughtered to a critical degree. One expert estimates that there are only 1,000 manatees remaining, scattered throughout the state of Florida. The dangers they face come from two directions. Most critically, their food supply is being destroyed by water pollution. Industrial effluent with great quantities of pesticides and other poisons are killing the aquatic plants on which the manatee feeds. Secondly, the manatee is very vulnerable to power boats. The propellers of a boat passing over a feeding manatee slice into his back, either killing him or scarring him permanently. Boaters never realize what they've done, for the manatee often sinks to the bottom quietly and bleeds to death.

The President has increased available parkland and wildlife preserves, but he has been weak in protecting wetlands and salt marshes from being filled in by the Corps of Engineers and private industry. At the same time, the perpetuation of massive dam and canal construction and the continuation of stream channelization negate the effort to preserve wildlife refuges. The problem must be thought of not piece-meal, but as a whole. It is necessary to balance the demands of industry and agriculture against the need to preserve land, air and water for wildlife, birds and fish. Wildlife habitat is sure to be crowded out unless population growth, industrial growth and technology are all brought under control. Yesterday the President could still attempt to please both industry and animal protection groups. Today, this is increasingly difficult. The President must choose.

# PESTICIDES

## HARRISON WELLFORD

At the 1971 annual meeting of the American Association for the Advancement of Science, a symposium attempted to rank nineteen major environmental stresses as to their potential risks for man and the ecosystem. According to Dr. Howard Reiquan of the Battelle Memorial Institute, who devised the rating system, each environmental threat was scored according to the persistence, range, and complexity of its hazards. At the top of the list stood pesticides with a score of 140, followed by heavy metals such as mercury (90), carbon dioxide (75), sulphur dioxide (72), air particulates (72), oil spills (48), waterborne industrial wastes (48), and noise with the lowest rating of 4. The key characteristic of pesticides which earned them their high rating was the persistence and omnipresence of their residues in food, water, and air.

---

*Harrison Wellford is a graduate of Davidson College (B.A.), Cambridge University (M.A.) and Harvard University (Ph.D. candidate). He has been a teaching fellow in government at Harvard University and is presently a research associate of Harvard's Institute of Politics. He was the first Executive Director of the Center for Study of Responsive Law, a research institution established by Ralph Nader in 1969. He is the author of* Sowing the Wind: Food Safety and the Chemical Harvest *(Grossman Publishers and Bantam Books, 1972), and his articles have appeared in* Harpers, the Washington Monthly, The Environmental Handbook, *and* The Voter's Guide to Environmental Politics.

That pesticides should deserve this distinction in 1971 was disheartening. Unlike some other threats discovered in the ecology renaissance of the 1970's, government regulators and environmentalists had an early warning of pesticide hazards. In *Silent Spring* (1962), Rachel Carson documented the destructive effects on birds and wildlife resulting from excessive uses of chemical pesticides heedlessly promoted by the pesticide companies and the Department of Agriculture. Subsequently, tests sponsored by the National Cancer Institute between 1964 and 1969 revealed that some pesticides cause cancer and birth defects in test animals, raising the possibility that pesticide residues might cause similar effects in human beings. But while pesticide use more than doubled between the publication of *Silent Spring* and the advent of the Nixon Administration in 1969, these warnings had gone largely unheeded. In 1969, the Commission on Pesticides and Their Relationship to Environmental Health, a panel of distinguished scientists appointed by the Secretary of Health, Education and Welfare (and the Nixon Administration's first positive step in the pesticide field), surveyed the available data on pesticides and gloomily concluded that too little had been done too late.

The Commission noted that the individual is exposed to pesticide residues in the food he eats, the water he drinks and the air he breathes; that he may be further exposed to contaminants from aerosols and no-pest strips in his home; and that chemical factory and farm workers continually inhale or absorb pesticides through their skin. The Commission found that in many instances pesticides account for the highest level of foreign material present in fatty tissue and perhaps the liver. It concluded, "The field of pesticide toxicology exemplifies the absurdity of a situation in which 200 million Americans are undergoing life-long exposure, yet our knowledge of what is happening to them is at best fragmentary and for the most part indirect and inferential." The Commission strongly recommended that persistent pesticides like DDT and other chlorinated hydrocarbons be phased out, and that pesticides which caused cancer and birth defects in test animals be restricted.

As this 1969 report shows, for all the furor created by *Silent Spring* in 1962, the net effect on federal pesticide policy had been virtually nil at the time President Nixon took office. The promises made by federal regulators at congressional hearings and by science advisory panels since 1962 had not been followed up effectively by environmental and health groups interested in the pesticide problem. In retrospect, these groups appear to have suffered from a rationalist bias. Environmentalists, like foreign affairs analysts, tend to use rational models of decision-making to explain policy outcomes, and just as often they are betrayed by them. In the Sixties they devoted their resources to documenting the harmful effects of pesticides and discussing broad policy questions of control. While this educational approach raised the level of the pesticides debate, the environmentalists tended to forget that most pesticide programs were entrenched in the bureaucratic and organizational politics of the agricultural establishment on Capitol Hill and in the Department of Agriculture where they would not be budged by more facts and scientific testimony.

For example, Rachel Carson and her followers largely ignored the Pesticide Regulation Division (PRD) of the Department of Agriculture, the government agency which had sole responsibility for enforcing the nation's most important pesticide law, the Federal Insecticide, Fungicide and Rodenticide Act of 1947. As the agency which must approve all pesticides before they are released in the market and restrict those pesticides found dangerous after release, PRD was clearly the vital point of leverage upon which environmental activists should have pressed. Unfortunately, PRD was a stepchild of the government's most enthusiastic promoter of pesticides, the Department of Agriculture (USDA). Moreover, its budget was controlled by the agricultural appropriations subcommittees in the

House and Senate whose chairmen, as representatives of the cotton farmers of the Deep South, had little interest in pesticide reform.

With production-oriented politicians and administrators rather than environmentalists or public health officers in control of its authorizations, appropriations, and personnel, pesticide control had become a hostage of agricultural policy. For well over twenty years, this small agency of 270 people, with only a $3 million budget in 1969, presided over, in ways largely unaccountable to the public, a vast proliferation of agricultural chemicals.

As a result, when the Nixon Administration took office in 1969, pesticide regulation was in disarray. In investigations by Richard Chervenak and Morton Myers, two analysts for the General Accounting Office (the watch-dog agency for Congress), and by the House Intergovernmental Relations Subcommittee in the spring of 1969, PRD revealed itself as a classic case of the "captured" regulatory agency. The House hearings brought out the following disclosures:

- Although PRD had the power to recall dangerous products from the market since 1947, it failed to exercise this power until 1967, and did not set up a formal procedure for the recall of faulty products until May 5, 1969, two days before the House Intergovernmental Relations Subcommittee was to begin hearings into PRD's misconduct.

- Only once in twenty-two years did PRD initiate criminal proceedings against violators of the pesticide laws.

- Of an estimated 50,000 pesticide accidents involving human beings each year, PRD investigated less than sixty. It investigated twice as many incidents involving farm animals.

- PRD regularly approved subsequently restricted pesticides, (including mercury treated seeds, alkylmercury compounds, the use of no-pest strips around infants, the aged, and in food areas, and compounds which caused cancer in test animals), over the objections of the Food and Drug Administration and the Public Health Service.

• When PRD seized unsafe products (such as thallium sulfate, which poisoned 400 small childen in 1962–1963) from retail shelves, it did not check with manufacturers to see where else the pesticide was being sold so that it could be seized elsewhere. As a result, thallium, for example, was being sold for over three years after it had been banned by PRD.

Against this background of massive non-enforcement of the pesticide laws, the Nixon Administration's pesticide policy makers had really nowhere to go but up. Nixon's major achievement in this field was the creation, on December 2, 1970, of the Environmental Protection Agency which took pesticide regulation away from the Department of Agriculture.

The creation of EPA did not automatically mean that pesticide control would be taken from the Department of Agriculture. The National Agricultural Chemicals Association protested any shift, as did the farm congressmen on Capitol Hill. At first, it appeared that the President might yield to these pressures and leave pesticide control out of the new agency. When he campaigned in the South in 1968, Nixon promised to maintain federally subsidized pesticide spraying and oppose any restrictions which would hurt farmers.

These political considerations were overturned, however, by the environmentalist tide sweeping the nation in 1970, and by the continuing revelations of incompetence and agribusiness bias in the Pesticide Regulation Division. The Sierra Club, Friends of the Earth, the Environmental Defense Fund, and the Center for Study of Responsive Law focused public attention on this regulatory malfeasance through lawsuits and testimony before congressional hearings. A shift to EPA seemed the best way to relieve the pressure.

The move of PRD to the Environmental Protection Agency ended the conflict of interest inherent in having agencies in the same department regulate and promote pesticides. Citizen access to pesticide decision-making improved as William Ruckelshaus, Administrator of EPA, acknowledged that environmentalists, farm workers, and the like were legitimate constituents of the agency. Government reorganizations, however, are frequently triumphs of form over substance. EPA inherited the pesticide bureaucracy of PRD, as well as the residue-tolerance-setting functions of the Food and Drug Administration. Ruckelshaus has been slow to remake the pesticides division in his own, more aggressive image. Moreover, like his predecessors in USDA, he must go to Jamie Whitten (D-Miss.), Chairman of the House Appropriations Subcommittee on Agriculture, for his funds. Whitten today is as forthright a champion of unrestricted pesticide use as he was when he wrote his book, *That We May Live,* in rebuttal to Rachel Carson. The performance of the Nixon Administration on pesticide problems since the creation of the EPA is mixed and must be judged on a case-by-case basis.

## DDT

The chasm between public promises and official performance on DDT is deep, and surprisingly unknown to the public. It is a paradigm of the federal government's ability to counter public clamor for environmental protection with the gossamer weaponry of the press release. On November 20, 1969, the Nixon Administration, with great fanfare, announced that the Department of Agriculture, in the first step toward a promised total ban, had "cancelled" DDT for use on tobacco, shade trees, in households, and, with certain exceptions, in aquatic areas. (In August, 1970, USDA cancelled fifty additional uses without protest from the DDT manufacturers, but these uses involved only small amounts of DDT.) Compared with the massive inertia of the Johnson Administration on pesticide abuses, this step was a breakthrough of sorts, and reaction in the press was swift and laudatory. The *New York Times* praised the Nixon Administration for "taking a giant step forward in rescuing the menace to all living creatures of the long-lasting poisons that have been used with such careless and ignorant abandon for many years." Thirty days later, with no fanfare, the leading manufacturers and marketers of DDT appealed this ban and set in motion a stately procession of administrative delays. Two-and-a-half years later (as of May, 1972) the *New York Times'* "giant step" has been reduced to a marching in place as DDT's use on many major crops, including cotton (which accounts for 70 percent of DDT's sales), remains unrestricted.

Efforts by outsiders to force the Government to place further restrictions on DDT have failed. On October 1, 1969, the Environmental Defense Fund petitioned the Secretary of Agriculture to ban immediately all uses of DDT. When the Secretary refused, EDF challenged the refusal in court. On January 7, 1971, the U.S. District Court for the District of Columbia ordered the Environmental Protection Agency (responsibility for pesticide regulation had shifted from USDA to EPA the previous December) to cancel all remaining uses of DDT and to reconsider its failure to "suspend" these uses. On March 18, 1971, EPA announced it would not suspend further uses of DDT but instead would convene a public hearing to weigh the evidence for and against DDT.

EPA's decision to cancel the uses of DDT, not suspend them, is very significant. While the term cancellation sounds very final, in effect it achieves no ban at all if a pesticide maker objects and takes advantages of appeal procedures under the law. Cancellation allows the accused product to continue to be sold while administrative and legal proceedings take place. Suspension, while it sounds more tentative, in fact removes the product from the marketplace while its case is being heard.

The cancellation proceedings are now well into their second year with no immediate end in sight. In the meantime it is business as usual for the makers of DDT.

EPA's insistence on further hearings and reviews of DDT seems unnecessary. DDT is the most thoroughly studied chemical ever released in the environment. Four governmental committees have studied DDT in depth between 1963 and 1969 and all have recommended that its use be phased out. In 1963, the President's Science Advisory Committee declared that "elimination of persistent toxic pesticides should be the goal." In 1969, the federal Commission on Pesticides and their Relationship to Environmental Health (the Mrak Commission) recommended that all uses of DDT not essential to public health be eliminated by December, 1971. EPA has allowed this deadline to pass, not because the scientific pros and cons of DDT require more study, but because the DDT case has a symbolic and political force which makes it very difficult for the agency to handle.

At first glance, there is an apparent paradox in the often emotional defense of DDT by the pesticide industry. DDT has been slowly dying from "natural" causes for several years, and is no longer a mainstay of profits for the pesticide industry. The amount of DDT used in this country has declined from 79 million pounds in 1959 to approximately 25 million pounds in 1970, largely because of a reduction in cotton acreage, the growing resistance of many insects to DDT, and public pressure in such states as Florida, Arizona, Michigan, and Wisconsin.

The fact is that DDT is more important as a symbol than a product. The preface to a 400-page defense of DDT prepared by its producers states that they are resisting the attack on DDT because the attacks are the "opening guns against all pesticides and against science and technology." DDT, which won a Nobel Prize for its role as a malaria fighter, enjoys a special reverence as the father of modern insecticides. In defending it, the industry sees itself as defending the concept of progress against a plague of Luddites who would dismantle the scaffolding of organic chemicals which, in their view, supports the technology of agribusiness. Dr. Charles Wurster, who had led the attack on

DDT for the Environmental Defense Fund, also acknowledges DDT's symbolic power: "If the environmentalists win on DDT, they will achieve and probably retain in other environmental issues, a level of authority they have never had before. In a sense, then, much more is at stake than DDT."

DDT is also very important to the farm politicians who control EPA's budget. Ruckelshaus, in justifying his refusal to suspend further uses of DDT, notes that cancellation has been successfully completed against nonessential uses of DDT. The problem is that EPA, following the lead of USDA, exempts from this category the use of DDT on cotton, which accounts for over 70 percent of all current domestic use.

By calling for more studies and hearings, Ruckelshaus has managed to postpone the day when he must choose between the environmentalists and the Southern congressmen. Despite all the scientific data amassed in the DDT proceedings, the decision will ultimately be made *de novo*, probably after political negotiations between Ruckelshaus and the White House. The deadline for decision is June 15, 1972.

## 2,4,5-T

In contrast to its failure to ban further uses of DDT, the Nixon Administration has been willing to pay the political costs necessary to maintain restrictions on the controversial herbicide, 2,4,5-T. This weedkiller causes birth defects in test animals and has devastated the ecology of parts of South Vietnam where it has been used as a defoliant. Under pressure from environmentalists and scientists associated with the American Association for the Advancement of Science, the Administration in 1970 restricted use of 2,4,5-T in Vietnam and banned some uses in this country. In May, 1971, however, an EPA science advisory committee secretly recommended that 2,4,5-T be cleared of all restrictions. The committee's report was leaked to a group of environmentalists and independent scientists, who held a press conference severely criticizing the recommendations. Both groups agreed that many key questions about 2,4,5-T (its contamination by highly toxic chemicals called dioxins, their presence and possible build-up in the food chain, and the weighing of risks against benefits) remained unanswered. Senator Philip Hart (D-Mich.), in opening his hearings on the herbicide in April, 1970, stated: "The questions . . . concerning the hazards of 2,4,5-T and related chemicals may in the end appear to be much ado about very little indeed. On the other hand, they may ultimately be regarded as portending the most horrible tragedy ever known to mankind." As Senator Hart's statement suggests, there is a lack of conclusive data that 2,4,5-T either can or cannot cause birth defects in man. The opinion of the independent scientists was that in view of the possibility that 2,4,5-T could cause birth defects, it was wise not to use the substance until it is either exonerated or finally condemned by further research. On the other hand, it was the opinion of the EPA advisory committee that since there is no conclusive evidence that 2,4,5-T is harmful, it should be used while the studies are being performed.

The significance of the 2,4,5-T decision transcended questions about its economic and potential health effects. 2,4,5-T had become a battleground of opposing philosophies about the relationship between technological risk and human safety. At stake was the question of the procedures and standards by which the safety of pesticides and other environmental pollutants are to be judged.

Taking advantage of the intervention by outside scientists, Ruckelshaus took the unprecedented step of repudiating the official advisory committee's recommendations and maintained the cancellation of 2,4,5-T uses on food and the suspension of its use around the home. His rejection of the committee's advice was also a rejection of the system that produced the advice. Ruckelshaus subsequently instituted an important change in the system by ordering that reports of science advisory committees on pesticides shall be made public as soon as they are completed. The old policy, which prevailed when pesticide policy was in the hands of the Department of Agriculture was to suppress the reports even after an official decision on their recommendations had been taken.

Ruckelshaus also moved decisively to open for the first time EPA's files of safety data on individual pesticides. He has also taken pains to invite the opinion of outside scientists on pending pesticide decisions. Defending his decision to bring pesticide policy into the "full glare of the public limelight," Ruckelshaus told the American Chemical Society: "Decisions such as the fate of DDT [and 2,4,5-T] are not decisions solely within the purview of the scientist to make in his laboratory. Rather they are basic societal decisions about what kind of life people want and what kind of risks they are willing to accept to achieve it."

The 2,4,5-T issue remains in limbo until a public hearing decides its fate. But Ruckelshaus, in rejecting the advisory committee's recommendation and removing some of the secrecy which discouraged public participation in pesticide policy, has made courageous and responsible decisions.

### Mirex and the Fire Ant

Every three or four years since 1957, the Department of Agriculture has launched a final campaign to wipe out the fire ant, and every year the fire ant responds by either holding its own or extending its range. This tiny red insect with a painful sting entered this country from South America about 1918. Originally confined to Mobile, Alabama, it is now spread over part of nine Southern states, building high, hard mounds which sometimes interfere with hay and mowing operations. Occasionally the ants, if disturbed, sting laborers, picnickers and school children. Despite its fearful name, the ant is not a major public health or economic problem. Yet this minor pest has been the target of this nation's longest and most expensive federal pesticide campaign.

The fire-ant issue dramatically illustrates the principle that with federal pest control the politics of ecology is far more important than the science of ecology. It is a fascinating case of how local politics, the power of appropriation subcommittees, and organizational rigidity in the federal bureaucracy interact to shape national priorities on pesticides.

In 1962, Rachel Carson described the fire ant campaign as "an outstanding example of an ill-conceived, badly executed, and thoroughly detrimental experiment in the mass control of insects, an experiment so expensive in dollars, in destruction of animal life, and in loss of public confidence in the Agriculture Department, that it is incomprehensible that any funds should still be devoted to it." At that time the program cost $2 million a year. In 1969, USDA and the Southern Plant Board jointly approved a twelve-year program to treat 126 million fire-ant-infested acres with Mirex, the only pesticide effective against the fire ant, this time at the cost of $238 million, almost $20 million annually. (By contrast, the annual amount spent on rat control is approximately $15 million.) In 1971, USDA backed away at least temporarily from this grandiose plan but intends to spray 16 million acres in 1972.

In 1971, the National Wildlife Federation, and the Environmental Defense Fund, were denied their request for an injunction against the spraying of Mirex in the 1971 season. The only chance to stop the program now is in the White House, which could freeze its funds. Seven million dollars for fire ant control in 1971 makes for an embarrassing item in President Nixon's austerity budget, but he will probably continue to support the program. The fire-ant campaign has become a hostage of the Southern strategy. In 1968, in a speech in Atlanta, Nixon promised to continue the ant war if elected.

Ruckelshaus acknowledged in September, 1971, that the fire-ant issue is a severe challenge for his young agency. His proposal to cancel the registration of Mirex earned him a rebuke from the floor on the House by Congressman Whitten, who described Ruckelshaus as having "more power than a bad man ought to have and more power than a good man would want." In April, 1972, EPA silenced its critics on Capitol Hill by approving, over objections from environmentalists, the continued use of Mirex for aerial bombardment of the fire ant.

## Predator Control Chemicals and the Bald Eagle

On May 27, 1971, Assistant Secretary of Interior Nathaniel P. Reed held a press conference to announce that at least twenty-five bald and golden eagles had been poisoned by Wyoming ranchers since May 1, 1971. He estimated that only 800 pairs of these majestic birds remain in the United States. The eagles were killed when they fed on carcasses which ranchers had baited with poison, ostensibly to kill coyotes. Their deaths are all the more tragic because they were needless: they were caused by a poison banned by the federal government for private use nearly six years ago.

Thallium, the poison used to bait the carcasses, was banned for all uses except by government and professional exterminators in 1965. These officials were permitted to use it for rat and mice control, but they were *not* authorized to use it for predator control. In this case, a manufacturer of thallium sent the pesticide in its technical form to Wyoming where it was to be prepared for use by these officials. It then got into the hands of the ranchers.

Although thallium's registration clearly states that it is not to be used by individual ranchers for predator control or any other purpose, the ranchers were subject to no legal sanctions under the Federal Insecticide, Fungicide and Rodenticide Act (FIFRA). It is, of course, against federal law to kill an eagle intentionally, but intent is very hard to prove when eagles die from feeding on carcasses ostensibly baited for coyotes. Remarkably, under FIFRA, there are no penalties for an individual who misuses a pesticide in defiance of its label. Federal law controls what goes on the label of a pesticide, but not what happens to the pesticide after it is sold.

EPA has taken two steps which should help curb the slaughter of predatory animals. First it has pressed for legal reforms to make it a federal crime to misuse a pesticide. These amendments to the Federal Insecticide, Fungicide and Rodenticide Act are likely to become law in 1972. Second, EPA braved the opposition of western ranchers and suspended interstate shipment of the toxic chemicals used in the predator control programs. This step won the praise of environmentalists.

## The Pesticide Reform Bill

The Nixon Administration's record on pesticide reforms has been on the whole positive. Legislative overhaul of the Federal Insecticide, Fungicide and Rodenticide Act is long overdue. FIFRA is basically a labelling act which provides no sanctions against misuse of a pesticide, no authority for stop-sale orders against dangerous pesticides, and only feeble penalties for pesticide companies who sell pesticides in violation of safety criteria.

In January, 1971, the Council on Environmental Quality prepared an excellent comprehensive pesticide reform package for the White House. As originally written, the bill would have come under the jurisdiction of environment subcommittees in both the House and Senate, and would have freed pesticide regulation from the dead hand of the agribusiness bloc on Capitol Hill. The farm committees balked, however, provoked no doubt by a CEQ staff member's indelicate admission in the press that the bill was designed to take pesticide control out of their hands. The White House refused to press a fight for jurisdiction in the House. Subsequently, the House Agriculture Committee completely rewrote and severely weakened the Administration bill.

The House bill, now before the Senate, has been branded by a wide coalition of environmentalists as "a disaster" and "backward step." Critical defects pointed out by environmentalists include:

- The definitions of key phrases vital to enforcement

appear to shift the burden of proof of safety away from the pesticide company, where it belongs, and introduce cost-benefit considerations at points where they are inappropriate. The effect will be to delay and restrict decisions to suspend dangerous pesticides.

- The authority of citizen groups to obtain judicial review and to participate in the hearing process, broadened by recent court and EPA decisions, has been clouded.
- The bill provides for an indemnity when a pesticide is suspended or canceled, thereby unfairly placing the burden of financial loss upon EPA and ultimately the taxpayer, rather than upon manufacturers and heavy users of those pesticides. This unique indemnity provision is inconsistent with the standard practice in comparable situations, such as with recall of products containing cyclamates, automobiles, soups and other products, in which manufacturers, retailers, or users have properly borne the risk. This indemnity provision also discourages self-policing of the pesticide industry by removing an otherwise important deterrent to promotion and sale of a pesticide whose safety and potential environment effects are known by its maker to be in question.
- The issue of work safety for farm laborers and chemical producer employees is completely ignored, even though it is not dealt with adequately in other laws.

While these defects are serious, the bill does have many useful provisions. For the first time, it gives EPA control over the uses of pesticides as well as their labelling, with new civil and criminal penalties against violators; it extends federal control over pesticides marketed within a state as well as those which move in interstate commerce; and it gives EPA authority to do expanded research and monitoring in order to find ways to reduce human exposure to pesticide residues.

Anxious to get a major pesticide reform bill passed in

an election year, Ruckelshaus has been reluctant to endorse efforts to strengthen the House bill in the Senate. This conflict was fueled by a controversial memo prepared by one of Ruckelshaus's aides (later disavowed by Ruckelshaus) which was leaked to the *New York Times*. The memo, written by Howard Cohen, who handled congressional affairs for EPA, stated that "the President is in an election year and needs some legislative victories." The Administration was therefore willing to accept weakening amendments to the pesticide bill to help speed its passage and mollify the farmers. The memo further urged that any further hearings on the pesticide bill in the Senate be avoided since "they would put EPA on the spot in trying to defend the House bill or attacking the House bill as being too weak." "Under no circumstances," the memo continued, "should EPA attack the pesticide bill as being too weak. This would cause serious problems for the President in farm states. The environmentalists will strongly object," but "they will not, for the most part, be voting for the President."

Cohen was subsequently fired for his indiscretions, but EPA has remained largely on the fence in the fight for strengthening amendments in the Senate.

But legal reforms will have little effect on the federal pest control programs themselves. The attack on the fire ant, the gypsy moth, and the other hardy perennials of federally subsidized pest control remains in the agribusiness network of USDA and the Congressional farm committees. The White House has done very little to force USDA to reduce the environmental damage from these chemical campaigns. Moreover the Nixon Administration's support for USDA research of biological controls and other alternatives to pesticides has been at best ambivalent. In 1971, for example, the White House refused to spend $1 million specifically allocated by Congress for nonchemical pest control research.

Legal reforms, if enacted, will have no effect on Jamie Whitten's influence over pesticide policy. When EPA was created, many observers expected that the appropriation committees would create new subcommittees to oversee environmental protection. This would have freed pesticide regulation from Whitten's control. Whitten, supported by Allen Ellender (D-La.), Chairman of the full Senate Appropriations Committee, counterattacked with a stunning move. His subcommittee on agricultural appropriations was given control not only over pesticides, but also over air and water pollution and the other regulatory programs of EPA, the Federal Trade Commission, the Food and Drug Administration, and the Council on Environmental Quality.

Nixon's pesticide policy has been cautious, reactive rather than innovative, and frequently frustrating to environmentalists and industry alike. But by any standard, it is a vast improvement over the apathy and nonfeasance which characterized pesticide regulation under the Johnson Administration. The political pragmatism of the Nixon White House has been its salvation. Despite the outrageous behavior in the Pesticide Regulation Division revealed by the General Accounting Office and the congressional committees, the White House showed little interest in pesticide reform until the ecology movement, and Senator Muskie, threatened President Nixon politically in 1970. This threat eventually outweighed his campaign debts to the pesticide patrons among Southern farm congressmen. Similarly, most of EPA's positive actions were forced by a succession of lawsuits, congressional investigations, and press exposées initiated by public interest groups not on the scene during the previous administration. But while Ruckelshaus has given pesticide reform its first articulate spokesman in the Executive Branch, his rhetoric is still to be tested by major pending decisions on DDT, 2,4,5-T, and the pesticide reform bill. By seeking the advice of environmentalists and permitting pesticide policy to be thrashed out in public forums, Ruckelshaus has been able to extend his initial honeymoon with pesticide reformers, but is working on borrowed time—time borrowed by postponing his major decisions. The real tests are still to come.

# POPULATION

## CARL POPE

Serious concern about the domestic population problem in the United States began to develop in the late 1960's. Although birth rates had declined from their post-World-War-II peak in 1958, the nation's population passed the 200 million mark in 1967. The harmful consequences of this rapid growth became clear in overcrowded schools, traffic congestion, increased pollution, and a general stress upon social services and the environment. Even though the birth rate (now roughly 2.3 children per family) is declining, the population increases, and the Census Bureau projects that the country will have between 220 and 285 million people by the year 2000, an increase of 40–60 percent over the 1967 population. Worse, no public policies have been developed to insure that population growth will be stabilized by the end of the century. Without such action, growth will continue into the 21st Century, and the nation may find itself with an eventual population of over 400 million.

Since these projections for population growth are

---

*Carl Pope has served as Zero Population Growth's representative in Washington, D.C. since March of 1970. He graduated from Harvard College in 1967 with a B.A. degree in the social sciences. He served as a Peace Corps Volunteer for two years in India, where he worked on family planning projects. Mr. Pope is also the author of* Sahib: An American Misadventure, *published by Liveright in 1972, based on his Peace Corps experience.*

coupled with the assumption that the American standard of living will continue to increase, students of resource depletion and environmental quality have become increasingly alarmed. In 1970, the United States, with 6 percent of the world's population, was using 40 percent of the world's natural resources. By the year 2000, if projected growth occurs, it will be using at least 60 percent. Writing in the *New Republic*, Wayne Davis suggested that an appropriate way to measure overpopulation is to calculate the degree to which a nation's population puts stresses on its environment. Citing American consumption patterns, he argues that the average American produces about 50 times the environmental stress of the average Indian, and that it is thus the United States, not India, which has the most serious population problem.

Increasing concern has also been voiced over the psychological effects of crowding and the increasing depersonalization of modern life, with the computer card and its "Do Not Fold, Spindle, or Mutilate" instruction as a prime target. People complain about lack of involvement with or responsibility for others in the large cities. (At the National Institute of Health, Dr. John Calhoun conducted experiments with rats which indicated that overcrowding, even in the presence of adequate food and water, produces severe social pathologies and eventual refusal of the overcrowded population to reproduce, leading to the extinction of the colony.)

In 1967 and 1968, a serious drought in north India brought home the fact that large sections of the world teeter at the narrow edge of famine and seem likely to be pushed over by continued population growth. Larger and larger numbers of Americans feel that the United States has to take the lead and set an example in achieving zero population growth.

President Nixon broke a precedent of silence on July 19, 1969, by delivering to Congress the first major Presidential Message on population. His central point was that rapid population growth is a major factor in many of

America's social and environmental problems. He said the government could no longer ignore the effects of future population growth, and that the nation should prepare itself to deal with them. The President proposed three major initiatives. First, he pledged a major expansion of federal support for family planning programs, declaring that no American family should be denied access to family planning services because of its economic situation. Second, he instructed his Committee on Environmental Quality (the forerunner to the Council on Environmental Quality) to examine the relationship between population growth and environmental quality. Third, he called for the formation of a Commission on Population Growth and the American Future.

The President's Message was revolutionary in the context of past governmental caution toward discussion of population problems. But it delicately skirted many key, and controversial, issues, and the rhetoric was much stronger than the program. These characteristics reflected the views of the Presidential advisor most responsible for the message, Daniel Patrick Moynihan.

Moynihan had long been concerned with family planning and population problems, and he believed that the failure to deal with population distribution is an essential element of the urban crisis. But Moynihan also believed that the government should avoid raising issues which might provoke a political and social furor among ethnic or religious groups.

So the Message was careful to duck the central issue in the debate over population policy: does the government have the right and responsibility to develop public policies designed to influence population size and growth? The stance taken by the Nixon Administration was for the most part accommodationist: the government would prepare for projected population growth, rather than try to reduce it. Leaving the question of numbers simply to chance or to fate was exactly what population activists most feared.

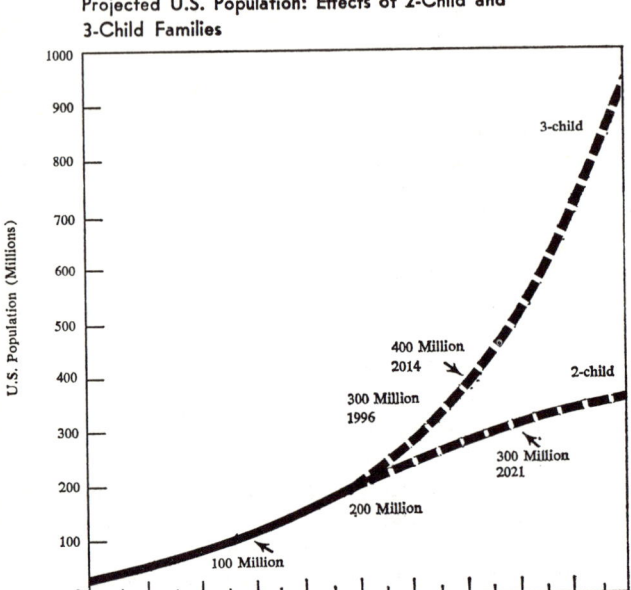

## Projected U.S. Population: Effects of 2-Child and 3-Child Families

[Graph showing U.S. Population (Millions) from 1870 to 2070, with curves for 3-child and 2-child family projections. Key points labeled: 100 Million, 200 Million, 300 Million 1996, 400 Million 2014, 300 Million 2021.]

SOURCE: Commission on Population Growth and the American Future.

In developing, or failing to develop, the themes outlined in the 1969 Message, the Nixon Administration was motivated by confused and sometimes contradictory impulses. First, Nixon and Moynihan had a genuine desire to grapple with underlying social factors which they believed had been ignored by the traditional Democratic approach of solving problems by spending money. Moynihan wanted to get at causes instead of symptoms, an approach which appealed to the President as being different from that of his predecessors. But this approach, if followed to its logical conclusion, would have revealed to the President that we needed a policy to avert, rather than accommodate, growth. And this conflicted with his personal moral vision. The rhetoric of the population movement, with its strong suggestion that the traditional ideas of the family and the importance of children were outmoded and irresponsible, was in strong conflict with the President's traditionalism. A major government role related to population would mean a confrontation on issues like abortion, contraception for minors, and sex education, issues with which the President was not comfortable, and which he felt were better left to private action or tradition. Moynihan took the same attitude from a more subtle line of reasoning: government intervention in this field was undesirable, in his view, because it violated the moral sensibilities of certain religious groups on highly emotional subjects and therefore might disrupt the fragile social fabric.

But the impetus for the Message, almost certainly, came in large part from political motives, from the new awareness of the U.S. population problem and its emergence as part of the environmental agenda of the ecology movement. In the environmental movement the traditional population groups found an ally with mass support and an appealing, and at the moment, "safe" cause. The environmentalists brought to the population movement an evangelism, a grass roots orientation and an aggressiveness it had lacked. As long as the political situation reflected this new constituency, the Administration was inclined to take a position on population which would satisfy it; thus the Message. But at the same time, as the population movement won its first major victories on the abortion issue at the state level in Hawaii and New York, the hierarchy of the Roman Catholic Church was preparing a major counterattack. Shortly after the Population Message was delivered, it became clear that abortion was a major political issue, one that was beginning to cut against the environmentalists.

The first clash between the Nixon Administration and

the environmental and population groups came in April, 1970. Phillip Berry of the Sierra Club questioned the Administration's population policies during a meeting between the President and environmentalists. The questioning led to an exchange of letters, with Moynihan arguing, "Who is to say with any confidence what would be the 'optimum size' of the American population? It is, in my view, largely a matter of judgment." Berry replied, "Frankly, your letter does not tell me that the President is willing to assume strong moral leadership on this question. Until he does that, the other *small* steps in the 'right direction' are not going to have any significant impact."

The Administration gave its full-fledged response to this challenge in the spring of 1970 with the publication of the report from the President's Commission on National Goals. Entitled *Toward Balanced Growth: Quantity with Quality,* it stated that the essential population problem in the United States was distribution, rather than growth itself. During the press conference announcing the report, Moynihan laid great stress on this finding, and staff members of the Commission indicated privately that he had strongly influenced, or even dictated, their report's section on population. The same thesis was repeated in the 1971 annual report of the Council of Economic Advisors, which stated that "many of the problems that are commonly attributed to excessive population in the United States are actually caused by uneven distribution."

The Administration's argument that the essential population problem was distribution was blasted by reports from the Commission on Population Growth and the American Future, which acidly pointed out that redistribution of population had no impact on resource consumption. Wherever a family lives it drives a car built in Detroit, of steel refined in Pittsburgh, from iron ore mined in Minnesota and by coal strip-mined in Appalachia. Further, the distribution argument is logically separate from the question, "Do we need or want more Americans?" For the accumulated economic and social forces making for population concentration simply cannot be reversed rapidly enough to prevent most of the population growth which will occur before the year 2000 from locating in the major metropolitan areas. While about 70 percent of the U.S. population is now concentrated in metropolitan areas, 85 percent is expected to reside there in the year 2000. Russell Train, the chairman of the President's Council on Environmental Quality, has said that, "The anticipated distribution of future population makes clear that under even the lower population growth projections we may have to make substantial sacrifices in the quality of our lives to accommodate large numbers of people in our urban regions."

## Commission on Population Growth and the American Future

The proposed Commission on Population Growth and the American Future posed a potential challenge to the Administration's position. Indeed, some of the bills introduced in Congress to create the Commission assumed that the goal of population stabilization was self-evident. One bill, introduced in 1970 by Rep. Morris K. Udall (D-Ariz.), explicitly declared the achievement of zero population growth a national policy. The bill supported by the Administration, however, would have limited the Commission to examining the specifics of accommodating growth.

The Senate passed the bill essentially as proposed by the White House. The House Government Operations Committee, however, was presented with two amendments drawn up by the Sierra Club. These would have expanded the Commission's duties to include consideration of the relationship between the environment and the population, and would have directed the Commission to consider means by which the nation could stabilize its population level. The Subcommittee at first rejected the Sierra Club amendments. But eventually, under pressure from some religious and conservation groups, and after a personal lobbying effort by Republican Rep. Pete McCloskey of California, the amendments were written into the law. When signing the bill on March 16, 1970, President Nixon said he "welcomed" the House amendments.

The President named John D. Rockefeller III, a veteran in the population field, and the chairman of President Johnson's Commission on Family Planning, to head the new commission. When Moynihan drew up his list of commission nominees, however, Rockefeller is reported to have insisted that the list was too heavily dominated by Republican campaign contributors, and demanded that Moynihan revise it. It was not until July, four months after the Commission was to have begun its work, that a final list of members was completed, comprising a good cross-section of experts and the general public.

With Moynihan's departure from the White House on January 1, 1971, the Administration's interest in the Commission dwindled. The Commission's interim report, issued in March, 1971, was met with a resounding silence from the White House. The Commission's final report, issued in March, 1972, called for "a deliberate population policy" employing voluntary means to achieve population stabilization. The highlights of its recommendations are as follows:

1. The federal government should enact a Population Education Act to assist school systems in establishing well-planned population education programs.

2. We should make sex education available through responsible community organizations, the media and especially the schools.

3. In order to neutralize the legal, social and institutional pressures that historically have encouraged childbearing, we should eliminate discrimination based on sex by adopting the proposed Equal Rights Amendment to the Constitution.

4. In order to avoid unwanted births we should increase investment in the search for improved means by which individuals may control their own fertility; establish subsidized family planning programs; liberalize access to abortion services; extend and improve the delivery of health services related to fertility; and provide contraceptives to minors.

5. In order to improve the federal government's population-related programs and its capacity to evaluate the interaction between public policies, programs and population, specific organizational changes should be made. These include the creation of a National Institute of Population Sciences within the National Institute of Health, and an Office of Population Growth and Distribution within the Executive Office of the President.

The report ended, "And finally, this nation should welcome and plan for a stabilized population."

Nixon rejected several of the Commission's key proposals in a statement issued on May 5, 1972, after his meeting with Rockefeller to receive officially the report. Liberalized abortion, and the supplying of contraceptive devices to minors without parental consent, "would do nothing," said the President, "to preserve and strengthen close family relationships."

The press release failed to mention the Commission's basic conclusion that the nation should work toward stabilization. But the President said, "I have a basic faith that the American people themselves will make sound judgments regarding family size and frequency of births."

## Family Planning Services and Population Research Act of 1970

Congress moved swiftly to act on the Administration's proposal to make family planning services available to an estimated five million low-income women. A comprehensive bill, S. 2108, the Family Planning Services and Population Research Act of 1970, had been introduced by Senator Joseph Tydings (D-Md.). The Administration vacillated on this bill until the eve of hearings before the Senate Labor and Public Welfare Committee, when, at the last moment, it rushed its own bill to Senator Jacob Javits of New York, the committee's ranking Republican. This Administration bill would have provided funds for family planning, but would have eliminated the proposed expansion of population research embodied in S. 2108. Javits was publicly apologetic for having presented the bill so late, a maneuver widely interpreted as a last-ditch Administration attempt to kill the Tydings bill. Senator Thomas Eagleton (D-Mo.), chairing the hearings, dubbed the Javits measure "the Midnight bill," while Javits himself called for stronger legislation.

The Tydings bill, with some modifications to meet Administration objections, was finally passed by the Senate on July 14, 1970. In testimony before the House committee, Secretary of Health, Education and Welfare Elliot Richardson declared Administration support for S. 2108 in general, if not for all its specific provisions. Later in the fall, the White House placed it on a list of "must pass" legislation. The House responded and cleared it for the President's signature. Indicative of the Administration's ambivalence, officials within the White House Office of Management and Budget considered a veto of the bill. But the President signed the legislation on December 24, 1970.

When HEW issued its guidelines for implementation of the Act, it included for the first time reference to a means test for all families with incomes over $4,000 a year. HEW had never had a means test before, and its own *Five Year Plan for Population Research and Family Planning* (required by the Tydings Act and released in November, 1971) indicated that such an approach would be demeaning and self-defeating and would reduce utilization of facilities. HEW now justified the test by arguing that the Tydings bill had required it to give "priority" to low-income families. Population groups argued that giving priority had never meant exclusion of others, that priority could better be given by establishing clinics in low-income neighborhoods, and that, in any case, all of HEW's own studies indicated that $4,000 a year was far too restrictive a definition of "low-income." Such a definition would exclude about 2 million of the 5 million women mentioned by the President himself in his Population Message. Under this pressure, the HEW Office of Population Affairs backed down, raised the income ceiling to $6,000 and made the means test optional for local clinics.

The Administration's funding for the law has been disappointing. The Tydings Act envisioned a budget for population research in fiscal 1972 of $78 million, but the Administration only asked for $39.3 million. For fiscal year 1973, the bill authorized $103 million for population research, but the Administration has asked for only $44 million. The Administration's *Five Year Plan* had called for a population research commitment in fiscal 1973 of $75 million.

Funding for family planning services has been somewhat better. Of the $79 million increase authorized by the Tydings Act for fiscal 1972, the Administration asked for $52.9 million, to make a total of $98.9 million for family planning services. In fiscal 1973, the Administration has requested $140 million, an increase of $40 million over the fiscal 1972 funds.

While the Commission on Population Growth and the Amercan Future has rightfully called for increased funding for family planning services, the low funding for population research disturbs population groups. If solutions are to be found to domestic and international population problems, population research must be greatly expanded. Family planning is seen by the Administration as a health issue, and considered politically safe, whereas population stabilization is regarded as a broader social and environmental problem of which the President is wary. To get around this problem the President's budget terminology calls all population programs "family planning," and his annual messages on the environment have failed even to mention population.

In addition, the Administration showed its unwillingness to endorse reduced family sizes by the total silence with which it greeted proposals in March, 1970, by Senator Robert Packwood (R-Ore.) and Rep. Pete McCloskey (R-Cal.) to eliminate income tax deductions for third and subsequent children born. Packwood, in introducing the measures, confessed that the dollar value of the deduction was probably insufficient to lead people to have more children than they otherwise would have. But he argued that the fact of the exemption, if not the amount, represented an implicit governmental endorsement of large families. Removing the exemption after two children, he suggested, would be a clear signal to Americans that the nation had an interest in smaller families.

Although the proposal was greeted with wide publicity, and was promptly followed up with similar bills in half-a-dozen state legislatures, the Nixon Administration never made any response to the idea. In the 1971 session of Congress, however, Packwood declined to reintroduce his tax proposal, with the explanation that its educational value had been exhausted and that it would possibly disdiscriminate against middle-income families. Population groups such as Zero Population Growth agreed.

From the beginning, however, the Administration has permitted highly-placed officials personally concerned about population to speak out even where their concerns clearly go against Administration policy. Thus Presidential advisor and former HEW Secretary Robert Finch told a group of students that those concerned about the environment could begin by limiting their families to two children. The President's former science advisor, Dr. Lee Dubridge, pleaded that every human institution make the achievement of zero population growth a major goal. In April, 1971, long after the official Administration position had shifted from concern to silence, Secretary of the Interior

Rogers C. B. Morton told the White House Conference on Youth that stabilization of population is essential for environmental preservation. EPA Administrator William Ruckelshaus also has warned repeatedly that control of environmental degradation will depend upon population stabilization. Such strong statements would have been unthinkable in any previous Administration, and are still unthinkable in official Nixon Administration statements.

## Abortion

White House silence has partly been the result of the President's personal conservatism, but politics has played a part too. Since the message of July, 1969, there have been two major changes in public attitudes on population. Most Americans, especially the young, have moved from relative indifference to a position of great concern. Public acceptance of means to stabilize population, such as contraception, sterilization, and abortion, has increased dramatically to the point where there is majority support for all significant policies called for by the population movement.

At the same time, however, strong opposition to the idea of liberalized abortion laws has continued. Organized largely by the Roman Catholic Church as the "Right to Life Movement," it has demonstrated spectacular political clout in several areas of the country.

During the early part of the Nixon Administration, Dr. Louis Rousellot, Assistant Secretary of Defense for Health and Environment, declared that military hospitals could perform abortions on "eligible beneficiaries in accordance with sound medical practice, subject to the availability of space . . . and the capabilities of the medical staff. Neither state laws nor local medical practices will be a factor in making these determinations." Angry Roman Catholic physicians in the armed services protested to the White House. With the help of their civilian counterparts in the Right to Life Movement, they mounted a quiet but powerful campaign against the ruling. On April 3, 1971, the President told the nation that he was reversing the policy because he was personally opposed to abortion. "From personal and religious beliefs," he said, "I consider abortion an unacceptable form of population control. Further, unrestricted abortion policies, or abortion on demand, I cannot square with my personal belief in the sanctity of human life—including the life of the yet unborn."

One year later, however, the final report of the Commission on Population Growth and the American Future assailed prohibitions on abortion "as obstacles to the exercise of individual freedom." The Commission said "women should be free to determine their own fertility" and "avoid unwanted births."

The President rejected this proposal on May 5, 1972, however, and simultaneously, in a letter released to the press, assured New York's Cardinal Cooke that he fully supported the efforts of the Roman Catholic Church to repeal New York's liberalized abortion law and restore the 19th Century statute. "The unrestricted abortion policies now recommended by some Americans," the President wrote, "seem to me impossible to reconcile with either our religious traditions or our Western heritage." The letter seemed to indicate an eager willingness to use issues related to sex and morality for political gain, and its release by the Archdiocese of New York greatly embarrassed Governor Rockefeller, who had repeatedly said he would veto the repeal measure. On May 10, John D. Ehrlichman, Assistant to the President for Domestic Affairs, attempted to ease the situation by saying that the letter was intended as private correspondence, and that granting permission to the archdiocese to publicize it was a result of "sloppy staff work." But under intense pressure, the State Senate by a vote of 30 to 27 that same day gave final legislative approval to the bill repealing the two-year old liberalized abortion law and reinstating the old statute. True to his word, Rockefeller vetoed the measure on May 13, saying, "I can see no justification now for repealing this reform and thus condemning hundreds of thousands of women to the dark age once again." Pointing out that the well-to-do could obtain abortions elsewhere if the law was repealed, and that the "poor would again be seeking abortions at grave risk to life in back-room abortion mills," Rockefeller concluded that, "I do not believe it right for one group to impose its vision of morality on an entire society."

## Population Education

The Environmental Education Act was passed by Congress in 1970 with language indicating that population issues were to be an integral part of the environmental education program. Commissioner of Education James Allen, who had called the 1970's the "Decade of Environmental Education," told the Senate that he expected population to be a major part of the majority of programs funded under the Act. Unfortunately, Allen left the Office of Education, and the Act's main impetus left with him. Of the fiscal 1972 authorization of $15 million, the Administration asked for only $2.5 million. A year after the Act was passed, the Office of Environmental Education had yet to be created, the Advisory Committee had not been constituted, and only 8 percent of the first year's grants had gone toward population education. In fiscal 1973, the Administration requested only $3.2 million of the $25 million authorized, an actual reduction from the $3.5 million appropriated by Congress for fiscal 1972.

## Women's Rights

The Nixon Administration has a distinctly mixed record with regard to women's rights. A large body of evidence indicates that a key element in any strategy to stabilize our population will be to encourage women to take jobs and careers instead of continuing in their traditional roles of wife and mother. The Nixon Administration has boasted of its record in appointing women to high places within the government, has established a

Talent Search to seek out women for more top federal positions, and has officially endorsed most of the major pieces of legislation dealing with women's rights. This record is better than that of the preceding Administration, but in light of the changing political climate, and the emergence of a strong feminist movement, it is less impressive. In an August, 1971, letter to the Republican National Finance Committee, Wilma Scott Heide, Chairwoman of the National Policy Council of the National Women's Political Caucus, wrote, "In his campaign, Mr. Nixon stated he supported the Equal Rights Amendment to the U.S. Constitution. So far, he has done nothing to manifest that support and much to deny that he even favors it. His own Task Force on Women's Rights and Responsibilities Report was not even released until six months after he received it and then without comment. Only on prodding and direct questioning has Mr. Nixon even spoken about women for the news media, and he generally relates to women as 'the wife of.' President Nixon allows the Secretary of Labor and every other Cabinet officer to daily violate Executive Orders and Civil Rights Laws forbidding sex discrimination in employment. These are only a few of the substantially more reasons why I could not support and would actively oppose Mr. Nixon's candidacy for re-election."

The Equal Rights Amendment cleared Congress on March 22, 1972. The President had quietly reaffirmed his support for the amendment in a letter to Senate Republican leader, Hugh Scott of Pennsylvania. But most women's groups still feel that the President's efforts on behalf of the amendment, which now must be ratified by the states, have been negligible.

In summary, the Nixon Administration has failed to deal with population problems in any meaningful way. During Senate hearings in 1971 on the National Population Stabilization Resolution, the Administration ducked the issue entirely. Although EPA snuck in Ruckelshaus's concern about the relationship between population and the environment, it joined other federal agencies in asking the Senate not to act on the Resolution until after the final report of the Population Commission—even though the Commission, as the Administration had feared it would, already had endorsed the Resolution. At the same hearings, the Administration's unenthusiastic record on implementation of the Tydings Act, preparation of the Five Year Plan for Population Research and Family Planning, and funding of the Environmental Education Act, was strongly attacked by a host of witnesses from population and environmental organizations. The Administration's resounding silence on the Resolution, and the evidence presented by witnesses at the Senate hearings, bore out the fears first expressed by Phillip Berry in his letter to Daniel Patrick Moynihan: that the President is unwilling "to assume strong moral leadership on this question."

# TRANSPORTATION

BOB WALDROP

A little more than sixteen years ago, the 85th Congress passed and President Eisenhower signed into law the Federal Aid Highway Act of 1956. Title II of the Act established the Highway Trust Fund (HTF) which, among other things, has made it possible for Americans to drive coast to coast with much greater ease than was thought possible only twenty-five years ago. The trust fund has also brought us streets so congested with cars that the average suburban commuter spends up to fifteen hours a week stalled in traffic. We have come a long way since 1956, but the going is getting more and more difficult—especially in urban areas.

By almost every measure, our cities are becoming less livable, less lived in, and looked upon as work islands to be visited only on work days. Air, noise, and water pollution are driving out those who can afford it, leaving the poor and the rats behind to fight over what's left. Air-

---

*Bob Waldrop has been Assistant to the Washington, D.C. Representative of the Sierra Club for the past six-and-a-half years, and is a founder and co-director of the Highway Action Coalition. He has been actively involved for several years in national legislative battles over transportation issues, such as the SST. Waldrop previously worked with the Conservation Foundation, and is also the Washington Correspondent of* Clear Creek, *a monthly environment magazine. Working with him on this chapter was research assistant Cliff Preminger.*

borne toxicants spewed from our tailpipes are readily detectable in our bodies. People of marginal health are commonly warned to stay indoors on bad smog days, or to relocate in safer areas if they can. City dirt, which accumulates on windowsills and shirt collars as well as in our lungs, contains a higher percentage of lead than the richest body of ore. And it comes entirely from vehicles which travel on federally subsidized highways.

In fiscal year 1973, as in the past several years, the Highway Trust Fund will pump more than $4 billion into highway programs—principally the Interstate System. Public transportation—buses, rapid rail, subways—will be lucky to get 20 percent as much, even though it is four to twenty times more efficient. The imbalance in funding brought about by the 1956 Act is clearly apparent. Over the last eighteen years, 268 public transit operations have been driven out of business. Meanwhile, highways continue to be built with as much as 90 percent federal money, an incentive which helped build 11,000 miles of new highways in 1969.

What was initiated while he was Vice President, Richard Nixon has perpetuated with a flourish as President. At a critical juncture in the 1956 Senate debate over the Highway Act, Vice President Nixon cast a tie-breaking vote and opened the way for passage of the legislation. In 1969, President Nixon cast aside recommendations to open the Highway Trust Fund for financing other modes of transportation, proposing instead a mediocre public transit program which left the trust fund untouched. Flashy transportation like the SST and Tracked Air Cushion Vehicle programs have also been a consistent gleam in the President's eye.

Shortly after taking office in January, 1969, President Nixon appointed a task force to bring him up to date on the nation's transportation difficulties. "Powerful new transportation systems," the report said, "have powerful consequences. Their impact on man's environment is rightly a source of deep concern throughout the nation. Dislocation of people and neighborhoods, air and water pollution, noise, and traffic fatalities are important side effects of our transportation investments which should now receive full attention."

## Nixon and Volpe

Nixon's selection of former Federal Highway Administrator John Volpe for the post of Secretary of the newly created Department of Transportation (DOT) seemed at first to be in keeping with Nixon's strong highway bias. From Nixon's point of view, Volpe's credentials were impeccable. He was the first Federal Highway Administrator, an untiring advocate of freeways while Governor of Massachusetts, and a former President of the Associated General Contractors of America. As Governor, Volpe had fought hard to ram a freeway through Boston, despite community protest that the public had been excluded from the planning process. "The point comes," he said, "when you consider and consider and consider and you never get a road built." During the 1968 election campaign, Volpe arranged a meeting between Nixon and the leadership of the American Association of State Highway Officials (AASHO), a major component of the highway lobby. At the meeting, they discussed recent DOT attempts to slow down the highway program, its designs for opening up the HTF, and its oversensitivity toward ghetto neighborhoods in the path of proposed highways. His subsequent appointment as Secretary of Transportation naturally set off rounds of applause from the highway lobby.

*The New York Times*, echoing widespread sentiment over Nixon's selection, editorialized that the appointment of Volpe "pays a political debt that would have been better left unpaid, particularly in the sensitive post to which he has been named." By all indications, Volpe would provide the American public with the additional 41,000 miles of Interstate freeways, which, in a 1968 statement, he said the nation needed.

One of the first actions of the new Secretary effectively

reinforced the grip of the highwaymen on the Nixon Administration. Frank Turner, a forty-year veteran of the now redesignated Bureau of Public Roads, and a close colleague of Volpe's, was named Administrator of the Federal Highway program. With a peculiar logic, Volpe justified his selection by saying, "Some people suggested that I appoint a city planner or a psychologist to the Highway Administration. But you don't go to a doctor with a legal problem, and I needed an experienced man to run our massive highway program." His logic seemed a little shaky to many at the time—it later crumbled when he appointed Carlos Villarreal, a sales executive with an aerospace corporation, to oversee the Urban Mass Transportation Administration. This time Secretary Volpe stated, "He's not a transit man and that was deliberate. I wanted someone who wasn't wedded to old concepts but someone who could think fresh. . . ."

But the view from the top floor of the new DOT building, which Volpe's construction company built, seemed to have an expansive effect on his transportation outlook. It did not come immediately, and by many standards he is still quite stodgy, but the longer he busied himself with transportation, the broader his conception of transportation became. Slightly more than a year after the Nixon/AASHO meeting, the Secretary granted $5 million for a study to find other transportation means which would make his once-cherished and now held-up Boston inner loop obsolete. He said later, "There is no government order decreeing that rapid transit must perish while highways become parking lots for miles of angry commuters." Although the Highway Trust Fund does not order the death of rapid transit or the overcrowding of highways, Volpe soon came to the realization that the fund had that effect and began searching for ways to loosen the highwaymen's grip on the fund.

Volpe's renaissance has come in stages. Over his three-and-a-half years in DOT, he has seen what is happening to the country as it becomes more and more dependent on the automobile, and has set out to remove the roadblocks to other modes of transportation. Several times he tried, unsuccessfully, to share his illumination with the President. But he found that if getting Nixon's attention was difficult, convincing him was nearly impossible. During the intra-administration debate over Amtrak, it took a burst of anger from Volpe even to get past Presidential aides and into Nixon's office. But getting the President's ear did little good; later Volpe threatened to resign if Nixon made good on his intention to veto the Amtrak legislation. Similar resistance from the White House awaited virtually every proposal Volpe sent up.

By early 1970, the Secretary had isolated the Highway Trust Fund as a critical element in the rapidly worsening transportation situation. Many of his speeches during that time were aimed at the trust fund and suggested that the fund should be made available for other forms of transit. Since the Administration had not yet sent its recommendations for the 1970 Federal Aid Highway Act to Capitol Hill, many hoped that the Secretary's suggestions might find their way into a legislative request. But all departmental requests going to Congress are routed through the White House, and after a great deal of non-public debate within the executive branch, Volpe's proposals were struck and a request for $14.6 billion for new highways was sent up instead.

## 1970 Highway Act

Highway legislation, for reasons having to do with construction commitments, is customarily considered by Congress every two years, and two years in advance of actually spending the money. When the Highway Trust Fund was created in 1956, its major project, the Interstate System, was scheduled to be completed in 1972. More importantly, the fund, on which a sizable portion of the American economy had become dependent, was also scheduled to expire in 1972, with completion of the Interstate.

## The Highway Trust Fund

The Highway Trust Fund was established by the Federal-Aid Highway Act of 1956. Its coffers are constantly replenished through federal excise taxes on gasoline, oil, tires, and other automobile related products. Currently, the flow of money into the trust fund is approximately $5 billion a year. The initial goal was the construction of 41,000 miles of interstate highways connecting all major cities with populations of over 50,000 by 1972. Since that time, these figures have been revised to 42,500 miles by 1977.

The trust fund makes interstate highway building a relatively inexpensive undertaking for the states—90 percent of the check is picked up by the federal government. Even though mass transit systems may be cheaper to construct, only one half to one third federal money is available, which obviously makes mass transit a more expensive alternative for the states. Consequently, the Highway Trust Fund has been a major factor in the deterioration of mass transit systems.

## HTF Expenditures, Revenues, and Balances: 1969-1971
(in millions)

| Fiscal Year | Revenues | Expenditures | Cumulative Balance at Close of Fiscal Year |
|---|---|---|---|
| 1969 | $4,690 | $4,151 | $1,521 |
| 1970 | 5,469 | 4,378 | 2,612 |
| 1971 | 5,725 | 4,685 | 3,652 |

In 1956, it was estimated that the program of interstate construction would cost approximately $41 billion, but recent calculations have shown that projected costs will be closer to $76.3 billion. In fiscal year 1971, $5,725 million in revenues flowed into the trust fund, as compared to only $1,482 million in 1957; $4,685 million was spent in fiscal 1971, leaving a yearly balance of $1,040 million, and a cumulative balance of $3,652 million.

If anything was going to be done about restructuring the trust fund, 1970 was the year.

Many people, including at least one Presidential advisor (John D. Ehrlichman, Assistant to the President for Domestic Affairs), saw 1970 as the logical year for a reexamination of the usefulness of the trust fund mechanism. Several of Secretary Volpe's speeches during the first half of 1970 reflected his conviction that the fund should be made available to other forms of transportation. Pressures were also building from outside the federal government for redirecting the billions in the Highway Trust Fund. The National Governor's Conference had only recently resolved in favor of giving the states limited authority to transfer federal transportation money from one mode of transportation to another, depending on the needs of the state.

On the other side, highway proponents had no trouble finding reasons for extension of the fund. The Interstate System was badly behind schedule and well ahead of earlier cost estimates of $41 billion. Only 70 percent of the project was ready for traffic and the predicted cost had skyrocketed to $70 billion (estimates now run to $76 billion). In addition to completion of the Interstate, the highway lobby sought to include in the 1970 act a couple of new highway programs as well, and to secure another long term federal commitment to highway construction similar to the 1956–1972 obligation.

Both House and Senate Public Works Committees held lengthy hearings at which numerous members of the pro-highway forces presented testimony in favor of enlarging the federal-aid highway program. Then, having concluded the public portion, the committees retired behind closed doors to get down to the real business of writing the legislation.

Ironically, as central as the Highway Trust Fund was to the debate, not a single day of hearings was held about its extension. Since the House Ways and Means Committee has primary authority over all revenue raising measures, responsibility for the future of the trust fund fell to Chairman Wilbur Mills and his powerful committee. The Chairman spent a few hours one afternoon with his committee colleagues and concluded that the fund should be extended for three years. After talking to the Public Works Committee, he stretched it to five.

By November, both houses had passed their versions of the highway bill and six Senators and seven Congressmen began the long complicated series of Conference Committee meetings to iron out their differences. The Administration had been in evidence throughout the hearing and mark-up process, but as the conferees met, the White House sent in a more specific memo stating what the President would and would not accept. Should a substantially different bill emerge, the implication of a veto was quite strong. The instructions pertained mostly to budget ceilings and altering the federal-state matching fund formula. Ruled out, therefore, was the possibility of any major modifications of the highway program structure.

The bill which Congress eventually passed and which Nixon signed into law contained two new highway programs of great potential—a Federal-Aid Urban System of highways for metropolitan regions, and an Economic Growth Center Development program to stimulate highway construction in underdeveloped regions of the nation. Both new programs start small but both have ominous potential.

The bill did, to a small extent, reflect some of the growing discontent with the present limited focus of the highway program. Although still strictly limited to highway projects, money from the trust fund could now be used, under certain narrow conditions, for the construction of preferential bus lanes and to finance highway safety projects. Another section of the act directed the Secretary of Transportation to submit guidelines to Congress which would help to minimize adverse social, economic and environmental impacts of highway construction.

In summary, the 1970 Federal-Aid Highway Act took several giant steps for highway programs and a few smaller ones for public transit and the environment. The Highway Trust Fund was revived for another five years, the Interstate will continue to plow ahead at least until 1977, and two new construction programs for urban and undeveloped areas were approved.

## SST

By 1970 the federal government had invested $708 million and eight years assisting the Boeing Corporation design and construct prototypes of a U.S. supersonic jet transport. The closer it came to getting off the ground, the more infatuated with the plane its supporters became and the noisier its opponents.

Attacked were the plane's cost, noise, effect on the environment, technical feasibility, and the diversion of money needed for other federal programs. So widespread was the criticism, that experts had almost to stand in line to make their public statements opposing the development of the SST.

Technical problems included dangers from intense sonic boom, airport noise, small and marginal payload, short range, and excessively high landing speed. Lesser sonic booms than those expected from the SST rocked Oklahoma City in 1964 during tests by the Federal Aviation Administration and caused damage running to more than $200,000. Wide body jets, like the 747, are able to carry a payload weighing 20 percent of their weight; the SST payload would be an only marginal 7 percent. Furthermore, the plane's landing speed would be 180 mph necessitating elongation of runways to a length of more than two miles. For these characteristics, there was no solution; if the plane was to go into service, these would be features with which Americans would have to live.

Environmental dangers, not so conclusively identified, would spread out to affect life on other parts of the planet. Russell Train, Chairman of the Council on Environmental Quality, warned that "a fleet of 500 SST's would soon increase the upper air's water content by 50 percent to 100 percent and could lead in a few years to a sun-shielding cloud cover with serious consequences on climate." Scientists argued another serious environmental threat: 500 SST's could cause one half of the ozone in the upper atmosphere to decompose, allowing damaging ultraviolet rays (which can penetrate cloud cover) to reach the earth's surface. A meteorological chemist, Dr. Harold Johnston, declared, "All animals in the world (except of course those that wore protective goggles) would be blinded if they lived out of doors during the daytime."

If the technical and environmental information seemed too confusing or unsubstantiated to members of Congress, the facts brought to their attention by a large group of economists made a definite impression. Until the economists began to speak up, the Nixon Administration had been asserting that construction of the SST would improve the nation's balance of payments since foreign nations would want to buy the American SST. John Kenneth Galbraith, Paul Samuelson, and other well-known economists did away with several such arguments. On the balance of payments question, Galbraith said, "The truth is that these calculations are strictly fraudulent and should detain no one." Walter Heller, former Chairman of the Council of Economic Advisors, addressed himself to the priorities issue and reminded Congress that they should also look toward "balancing the dubious potential gains from the SST against the desperate dangers of failing to fund our critical social programs."

Scientists, economists, and environmentalists of every political leaning joined in blasting the project. In 1969 the President appointed a special panel to review the plane's justifications. That group, the President's SST ad hoc Review Committee, released its report in October, 1969, finding that the plane was a threat to the country's balance of payments position and questioning the assumption that Americans would grow accustomed to the sonic blasts produced in the plane's wake. The full report was a strong indictment of the project, recommending that it be discontinued.

Ignoring his own panel's advice, President Nixon chose to push for further federal funds for the SST, and asked Congress to include $290 million in the fiscal year 1971 Budget to allow the Department of Transportation to construct two prototypes of the airplane. On this issue, Volpe stood side-by-side with the President.

As the controversy raged, word came of another highly critical Presidential study on the SST. But unlike the first panel, composed of high governmental officials, this committee consisted of well-known scientists and technicians, headed by Richard Garwin, who served on the President's Science Advisory Committee. The committee's report was not released to the public despite repeated requests by citizens and Congressmen alike.

Garwin, however, was quite open about saying that the report was highly critical of the SST project, and he testified to the plane's environmental, technical and economic problems. (Long after Congress had decided the fate of the SST, the courts overruled the President's use of "executive privilege" in refusing to release the "Garwin Report" and it was made public in August, 1971, some six months after the final vote.)

As House and Senate Conferees met to write the 1970 Federal-Aid Highway Act, Senator Proxmire and a handful of colleagues were long-windedly holding forth on the Senate floor (as they had been for several days) on the foolishness of the SST project. The filibuster was a last ditch attempt by Senators, angered that the recent Senate vote on December 3, 1970, deleting all funds for the SST from the DOT budget, had not been reflected in the conference committee meetings. Although heavy public pressure had successfully persuaded the Senate to strike the whole program, the House of Representatives, responding to Administration lobbying, had approved the appropriation measure containing the SST money. Conferees on the issue were stacked in favor of the project and reported back only a slight reduction, from $290 million to $210 million.

As the 1970 session of Congress drew to a close, the Senate accepted temporary funding for the SST in exchange for a decisive vote on the SST project, isolated from the other programs in the Department of Transportation budget. When that vote came, in March, 1971, both houses of Congress voted to cancel all federal funding for the controversial plane. The House voted 217-203 against the SST on March 18, the Senate 51-46 on March 24. President Nixon said the vote "could be taken as a reversal of America's tradition of staying in the vanguard of scientific and technological advance." Earlier he had predicted an "ideological majority" would uphold his support for the project. He found the defeat "distressing and disappointing," and a "severe blow" to the aerospace industry. He was "determined" not to let it halt American technological leadership.

Hailed at the time as a victory for the environment, the defeat of the SST seems about to be outflanked by an Administration intent upon committing the country to its gadgetry-loaded concept of good transportation. In March, 1972, a short innocent-looking press release from DOT announced a contract had recently been let to determine "the effect high-flying aircraft might have on climate." Secretary Volpe, announcing the study contract, said, "This study, vigorously endorsed by President Nixon and this Department, is a major effort to separate fact from fiction." "Led by President Nixon himself," *Newsweek Feature Service* reported in January, 1972, "a quiet campaign has begun to put the U.S. back into the international supersonic transport competition. . . . 1973 looks like the year of the big push."

## Mass Transit Tokenism

If the Highway Trust Fund could not be used to assist public transit, which it had already nearly put out of business, something else had to be done. Fully aware of this situation, Volpe went to the White House with several proposals, all to no avail. He first proposed a Transportation Trust Fund, to unify funding for all modes of transportation and insure an equitable share of the money for each. When this plan was rejected, Volpe asked for a Mass Transportation Trust Fund to finance mass transit much as the highway fund does for highways and roads. But President Nixon's White House advisors opposed any additional funding mechanisms, such as the highway fund, which operate outside the standard budgetary process.

President Nixon, however, was beginning to realize that urban congestion was threatening to become coagulation. Six months after his Inauguration, he took a 45-minute helicopter ride with Secretary Volpe and City Councilman Gilbert Hahn, observing Washington, D.C.'s workday snarl which Volpe described as "the longest parking lot in the world." "I sure am glad," responded Nixon, "I don't have to drive to work."

Clearly something had to be done. The question was how much, when, and how.

Nixon's answer came on August 7, 1969, when he proposed to Congress that we spend $10 billion out of the general fund for developing and improving public transport over a twelve-year period. The President proposed authorizing $3.1 billion during the first five years, but supported only single-year authorizations.

Compared to Volpe's suggestions, the Nixon approach was a sharp disappointment. "Volpe gave it everything he had, no question about it," said James Braman, then Assistant Secretary of Transportation for Environment and Urban Systems, "but he just couldn't shake the President's key economic advisors." But months after proudly presenting his trust fund proposals to the White House, the Secretary reversed himself and was out drumming up support for the President's tepid compromise.

"If Nixon would listen to Volpe," said one DOT official, "he'd be ten times better off." Why? The legislation drawn up by the White House and sent to Congress

## Federal Transportation Outlays

Since 1956, when the Federal-Aid Highway Act was passed, federal outlays for highway construction have far outstripped outlays for other transportation modes. The following table shows the trend since 1955 of budget outlays for transportation. (Dollar amounts are rounded to nearest million.)

### Budget Outlays for Transportation

|  | 1955 | 1960 | 1965 | 1970 | 1971 |
|---|---|---|---|---|---|
| Department of Transportation | | | | | |
| Highway | $636 | $2,978 | $4,069 | $4,642 | $4,588 |
| Aviation | 122 | 508 | 756 | 1,252 | 1,636 |
| Railroad | 2 | 3 | 3 | 21 | 23 |
| Coast Guard | 190 | 238 | 367 | 593 | 597 |
| Urban mass transit | 0 | 0 | 11 | 158 | 280 |
| Proprietary receipts (–) | 0 | 0 | –20 | –26 | –121 |
| Subtotal | 950 | 3,727 | 5,209 | 6,673 | 7,049 |
| Other agencies: | | | | | |
| Army Corps of Engineers (navigation projects) | 118 | 202 | 396 | 385 | 400 |
| Civil Aeronautics Board | 61 | 67 | 92 | 48 | 42 |
| Maritime Administration | 163 | 270 | 330 | 318 | 333 |
| Subtotal | 343 | 539 | 818 | 751 | 775 |
| **TOTAL** | 1,292 | 4,266 | 6,027 | 7,424 | 7,824 |

SOURCE: Reprinted from "Setting National Priorities: The 1971 Budget," by Charles L. Schultze, with Edward K. Hamilton and Allen Schick, © 1970, the Brookings Institute, Washington, D.C. (Figures for 1955, 1960 and 1965 were taken from an unpublished paper, "Future Federal Transportation Budgets: Basic Numbers and Anticipated Budget Issues," by James R. Nelson.)

---

promised implicitly much more than it could possibly deliver. And although Volpe did what he could for the President's proposal, others in DOT had a more difficult time explaining away the bill's serious shortcomings. Assistant Secretary Braman realized it would be a waste of time trying to convince the cities to support the bill because it gave DOT almost no ability to make long-term obligations. Without the support of the cities, the bill would go nowhere.

Multi-year contract authority was essential to the cities because they would have to raise up to half the project costs in order to receive federal money. The President, however, only proposed single year authorizations. How much would actually be appropriated, obligated, and then spent remained an open question. Without long-range assurances that the federal money would be available when needed, the cities would have exceptional difficulty raising their share of the funds. Just the year before, public transit bond issues had been rejected in Los Angeles, Seattle, and Atlanta. The absence of meaningful contract authority prompted the powerful National League of Cities—U.S. Conference of Mayors to reject the Nixon program soon after it surfaced.

Perhaps not very much surprised, Volpe and Braman worked to convince the White House that long-term financing was crucial. On November 19, 1969, Volpe was able to announce that the Administration had agreed to a five-year contract authority making the full $3.1 billion ready for immediate obligation. This went a good part of the way toward meeting the cities' objections, and the legislation, known as the Urban Mass Transit Act of 1970, was passed by Congress on October 5 and signed by the President on October 15 of that year.

Still, the program fell some $23 billion short of what the cities estimated was needed to bring their systems up to even moderate standards. In fact, within two years the backlog of applications for Urban Mass Transit Administration capital assistance grants totaled more than $4.5 billion. Unlike the highway program, having its own trust fund, public transit would have to fend for itself among other programs needing money from the Federal Treasury.

## Amtrak

Rail is the only form of popular transportation in the U.S. which has experienced a decline in ridership since 1956. Buses have managed to hold their own, while air and auto use have increased dramatically. Car ridership, for example, is approaching one trillion passenger miles annually, up 30 percent since the Highway Trust Fund was initiated in 1956.

Railroads haven't had smooth going since the peak demand during World War II fell off. In an effort to assist nearly extinct and definitely bankrupt inter-city rail transportation, Congress enacted on October 14, 1970, the National Railroad Passenger Corporation, now known as Amtrak. The railroads were to sell their passenger service to the public corporation, and Amtrak would then consolidate routes and manage their operation on behalf of the public. Once established by Amtrak, service may not be discontinued until July, 1973, the end of the trial run period.

Secretary Volpe, verbally a vigorous supporter of Amtrak, was directed by the act to designate terminals to be served by a system designed in detail by a board of directors. Under pressure from the White House and the rail industry to limit Amtrak's scope, however, Volpe announced route assignments including only nineteen lines. The number of inter-city passenger trains in service was cut from 364 to about 180.

The rail industry, which seems to be in good standing with the White House, has endorsed Amtrak publicly but quietly and effectively encumbered its operation. Passenger trains, which are supposed to have priority over freight, are frequently shunted on to side rails to make way for freight trains. Reimburseable costs for operating passenger service are inflated by railroads before being submitted to Amtrak, aggravating an already painful debt.

The rail industry's subcutaneous dislike of Amtrak stems from their fear of nationalization of all rail service, combined with the fact that they don't really want people getting in the way of better-paying freight operations.

President Nixon had never listed Amtrak as priority legislation. The Administration had promised Congress a rail-passenger bill by January, 1970, but the Department of Transportation's proposal was rejected by the White House for budgetary reasons. Faced with a popular Senate bill, however, the Administration accepted a compromise measure. A number of Presidential advisors who had fought the concept were not pleased with its enactment. They have subsequently worked in the executive branch against effective implementation of the act, trying, as one rail advocate puts it, "to choke the baby in its crib." Lead voice in the Amtrak opposition belongs to George Shultz, director of the White House Office of Management and Budget, and nominated by the President for Secretary of the Treasury. He didn't want Nixon to sign the bill in 1970, and he opposes badly needed increased federal assistance today.

## The 1972 Federal-Aid Highway Act

Secretary Volpe had failed to sell his unified transportation trust fund in 1970. Instead, the President pushed through two separate programs—one for highways and another for mass transit. An Airport and Airways Trust Fund and Amtrak were also created in the interim. Although Volpe officially endorsed the White House plans, he did so with little gusto and continued to apply steady pressure for a single source of funding for all modes of transportation.

In March, 1972, the Secretary received White House clearance to send his latest reform program to Congress. The 1972 National Highway Needs Report proposed that all surface transportation be consolidated into five categories, each with its own separate account. The divisions were: the Interstate Highway Program, a Single Urban Fund, a Rural Federal-Aid highway system, a Rural General Transportation System, and a fund for Safety and

Miscellaneous programs. The Single Urban Fund and the Rural General Transportation accounts would be open to finance any form of surface transportation, with certain restrictions.

Essentially the concept establishes the Highway Trust Fund as the sole source of money for all five categories of surface transportation construction. Considerable autonomy is given to local government, especially in the case of the Single Urban Fund, to decide on the transit mode to be funded. This partial diversion of Highway Trust Fund money would slow down construction of the Interstate Highway System, which is now scheduled for completion in 1977, but which could be delayed at least until 1979.

The proposal was greeted with mixed feelings. Highway people, as expected, blasted the plan to divert money from the Highway Trust Fund. Public transit organizations, such as American Transit Association and the Institute for Rapid Transit, expressed suspicion over the

## Volpe's 1972 Proposal For Transportation Funding

### AUTHORIZATIONS

($ in millions)

| Fiscal Year | 1974 | 1975 | 1976–1979 |
|---|---|---|---|
| Interstate | 3,250 | 3,250 | 3,000 |
| Single Urban Fund | 1,000* | 1,850 | 2,250 |
| Rural Federal-aid System | 800 | 800 | 800 |
| Rural General Transportation | 200 | 200 | 400 |
| Safety and Other | 400 | 400 | 400 |
| TOTAL | 5,650 | 6,500 | 6,850 |

* In FY 1974, UMTA Capital Grant authority of $850 million in existing program will be available in addition to the amount shown.

Administration's motivation, and politicians wondered about its workability. The surprisingly strong criticism from public transportation groups focused on the amputation which the plan would perform on the Urban Mass Transportation Administration. As Volpe presented it, the plan would eliminate UMTA's mass transit assistance program by using the Highway Trust Fund as the source for all surface transportation. With the disappearance of UMTA, mass transit proponents foresee its assimilation by the highway administration, which would probably not be very generous toward mass transit.

The city-transit coalition also sees co-option behind the timing of the report. Momentum had been building in Congress for a larger boost than would come from the Single Urban Fund. They see a situation similar to that in 1970, when Nixon substituted his moderate transit assistance program for the far reaching program proposed by Volpe. Even if not 100 percent accurate, that viewpoint has factual and historical foundation. Although the White House has tried to appear publicly as an ally of transit, it has often worked quietly to block city requests for financial assistance with endless red-tape hassles. Senator Gordon Allott (R-Colo.), customary supporter of Nixon, is openly critical of the White House for "moves by the Office of Management and Budget to develop criteria so strict that it would preclude federal funding of any non-bus system."

Up to the time of the Nixon proposal, badly needed transit legislation seemed a near certainty. Now, the Administration plan and the proposals backed by the city-transit lobby appear to be mutually exclusive—it's one or the other. Perhaps not, but the chances for rapid passage of the transit legislation is surely jeopardized. Why did the Administration make such a move? A one-time DOT administrator who often stood between the White House and urban interests makes one point clearly: "There has been an underground war going on between the Nixon Administration and the city and transit lobbies."

The Administration's transportation balance sheet isn't entirely a list of debits. On the plus side are several items—$3.1 billion for public transit and authorization for the use of the Highway Trust Fund for bus lanes. The Single Urban Fund, if passed by Congress, might work out to be an improvement over present funding methods.

But time and time again promising opportunities like Amtrak, and Volpe's Transportation Trust Fund, have been bypassed in favor of more politically expedient courses of action. Occasionally the public catches a glimpse of the inner workings of the Administration. More often, however, the evisceration is conducted cautiously, out of public view. The Nixon machine seems to work like a vast political Rube Goldberg contraption, into which flows a steady stream of reports, opinions, recommendations, and influential people. Too often its output consists not of new programs to meet today's needs, but of mediocrity and political expediency.

# THE INNER-CITY ENVIRONMENT

## JAMES RATHLESBERGER

Thirty thousand urban poor marched past the White House on March 25, 1972, and rallied at the Washington Monument. Their message was "Nixon Doesn't Care," and while the President's proposal for family welfare assistance was the immediate target of their discontent, their anger sprang from the overall low quality of their lives.

While degradation in the cities is borne by all, it falls most crushingly on the poor. When the environmental stresses are added to the already straining tensions of poverty, the poor cannot escape without physical and mental damage. As a hushed-up task force report for the Environmental Protection Agency says, the urban poor are "our most endangered people."

The deteriorating environment of crowded urban slums aggravates their problems. Overflowing garbage accumulates on their streets and alleys, lead paint on the

---

*James Rathlesberger is the Research Director for the League of Conservation Voters. He is also a columnist for* Not Man Apart, *and the Washington Correspondent for* Environmental Quality Magazine. *He has written articles for other environmental journals, including* National Parks *and* Conservation Magazine. *Rathlesberger graduated from the University of California at Berkeley in 1971, and previously served as a Vista Volunteer for one year in West Virginia. During the 1970 congressional campaigns, he was research director for the Bipartisan Congressional Clearinghouse.*

walls is eaten by their children, air pollution frequently exceeds federal standards for health, highways displace them from their homes, rivers in the city are usually too polluted for swimming, and parks are rare and decreasing in number.

Of the 130 million urban Americans, about 8 million fall below the official poverty line (an annual income less than $3,968 for a non-farm family of four). Of these, 3.1 million are black and 4.5 million are white. Another 8 million are "near poor," having incomes slightly above the official poverty line but essentially sharing the same living conditions as those below it. Not only are they confronted by a seemingly non-caring Administration, but their life situation is actually growing worse. The 1971 State of the Cities report from the National Urban Coalition found that slum conditions have actually deteriorated since the riots of the 1960's.

There are, however, people in the Nixon Administration who do care. George Romney, Secretary of Housing and Urban Development, has spent three unsuccessful years beseeching the White House to take a major initiative on urban problems. His last proposal, Total American Community Living Environment (TACKLE), has been rejected several times and is now apparently dead. Lonely and rebuffed within the President's Cabinet, Romney has toured the country urging local political, civic and business leaders to try on their own what the President has rejected: metropolitan area planning to help people out of the ghetto. With inspiration and persuasion, Romney calls for "one city" which can serve as a model for the rest of the nation. Accepting the White House policy that city problems are city, not federal, concerns ("Detroit cannot be saved by Washington"), he has only government reorganization, revenue sharing, and welfare reform to offer as the Federal contribution. William Ruckelshaus, Administrator of the Environmental Protection Agency (EPA), has shown some concern, but has failed to overcome his agency's bureaucratic resistance to focusing on the inner-city environment. After receiving an EPA task force report listing forty recommended actions, Ruckelshaus disclaimed the report and argued that his agency could do nothing without more research.

The President himself is aware of inner-city squalor. "The violent and decayed central cities of our metropolitan complexes," he said in January, 1970, "are the most conspicuous area of failure in American life." But this rhetoric has helped the urban poor no more than the unfulfilled promises of a "Great Society" which President Johnson offered to the nation in the 1960's.

To some extent, the government's inaction is a result of disillusionment brought on by the Great Society itself. When Presidents Kennedy and Johnson were formulating proposals for the early poverty programs, it was believed that poverty could be eradicated in a number of years without radically reorganizing the social and economic system. Now we have come to believe that poverty will always be with us, at least until the social and economic systems are changed, not a policy evident in the Nixon Administration. President Nixon believes in making the system work through such reforms as his family assistance plan, government reorganization and revenue sharing. Furthermore, the 16 million endangered urban slum dwellers have never cast their votes in great numbers for Nixon and, being a very political president, it is not surprising that he will do little for them.

The President's proposal for family welfare "reform," for example, would set a "national minimum income standard" of only $2,400 for a family of four. His proposal for a new Department of Community Development would simply create a super agency out of already existing programs. It would offer a neater organizational chart, but it offers inner-city residents nothing new. Nixon's proposals for revenue sharing, especially Urban Community Development Revenue Sharing, have been praised by city officials, and are truly needed, but the White House Office of Management and Budget (OMB) has cut the funds for already existing inner-city programs.

## Lead Poisoning

It is estimated that 2.5 million children living in metropolitan areas are in danger of lead poisoning. Up to 600,000 are estimated to have excessive lead levels in their blood, and lead poisoning kills at least 200 children every year. Six thousand children are left with neurological handicaps each year, 800 are blinded, and at least 150 more suffer severe mental retardation. High lead levels in children also cause convulsions, delirium, coma and paralysis. Lead ingestion may also drastically reduce a child's ability to throw off bacterial infection, and at least one expert believes this may in part be a cause of "sudden infant mortality," or death with no apparent cause, which kills an additional 10,000 to 15,000 infants each year. Those fortunate enough to recover from lead poisoning may experience delayed effects in later life, such as kidney disease, gout, and abnormalities in fertility and pregnancy. There is no question that the danger is widespread. One report from the EPA says a mass screening of inner-city children found 25 percent with blood levels of lead exceeding what is considered a safe amount.

One source of lead poisoning in ghetto children is old paint chipping off residential walls. House paint contains little lead today, but before World War II it often contained as much as 50 percent lead. Young children will put most anything in their mouths, but lead poisoning is most prevalent among children ages one to three who exhibit pica, a compulsive tendency to eat non-food substances. Such children can get very sick by nibbling just a few small chips a week over a period of three to six months.

To combat this, in 1970, Congress passed the Lead-Based Paint Poisoning Prevention Act. Sponsored by Rep. William F. Ryan (D-N.Y.) and Senator Edward Kennedy (D-Mass.), the law authorized $30 million over fiscal years 1971 and 1972. The Department of Health, Education and

Welfare was given $25 million to detect and treat poisoned children, and the Department of Housing and Urban Development was given $5 million to determine the extent of lead paint in housing and to determine the best methods for removing it. But by mid-1972 nothing has been done. The President requested no funds for appropriation in fiscal 1971, nor did he spend any. In fiscal 1972, the President's budget requested $2 million, Congress appropriated $7.5 million, and, the Nixon Administration waited until the very end of the fiscal year to begin spending the funds.

President Nixon has promised to get these programs started during fiscal 1973. The budget requests $9.5 million for the HEW program, and these funds will be available along with those carried over from the previous year. HUD, for its part, still has not requested any funds, but does promise to use $2.2 million of its basic research money to begin its part of the program.

Even if the Administration does spend this money, however, it will be far from enough. In fiscal year 1971, for example, the government received program requests totaling up to $45 million. Rep. Ryan and Senator Kennedy, pushing Congress to authorize and appropriate the money, believe a fiscal 1973 budget of $50 million would be "a bare minimum."

Recently, there has been accumulating evidence that lead from the air also contributes to the problem. The National Institute of Mental Health issued a report in February, 1972, stating that airborne lead rather than lead in paint may in fact be the major source of lead poisoning among inner-city children. Dr. Ronald E. Engel, a scientist with the EPA, has concluded that lead levels in the air might cause lead poisoning in children who otherwise would have recovered from eating lead paint. Dr. Paul Craig, a physicist with the Atomic Energy Commission and the chairman of the Environmental Defense Fund's Committee on the Environmental Impact of the Automobile, estimates that "at least one-third of the total lead absorbed by average American urban dwellers arises directly from atmospheric lead." These findings are not surprising in view of a conclusion from a 1971 report from the National Academy of Sciences. "Due largely to the combustion and dispersal of lead additives in gasoline," said the report, "the air in the largest American cities has a concentration of lead 20 times greater than air over rural areas and as much as 2,000 times greater than air over the middle of the Pacific Ocean."

So for those children who might escape lead paint, the danger is still present. Dr. Engel calculated that a one-year-old child, living within 100 feet of a roadway, could accumulate a toxic level of lead by ingesting "less than one-sixth of a gram of atmospheric particulate fallout daily, an amount equivalent to one-twenty-fourth of a teaspoon." Almost everything in the inner city is within 100 feet of a roadway with heavy traffic, and any child can breathe the lead-filled dust (the most potent way to take lead) before it settles.

Unfortunately, the Administration's response to lead in the air has not been much greater than its effort to implement the Lead-Based Paint Poisoning Prevention Act. President Nixon's first initiative was the 1970 proposal to put a tax on leaded gasoline, thereby gradually reducing the use of such gas by making it more expensive than unleaded gas. The House Ways and Means Committee, however, which held hearings on the measure in 1970, gave the proposal little consideration. In 1971, President Nixon promised that "I shall again propose" the lead tax, but he never did. And it was not even mentioned in his Environmental Message to the Congress in 1972. To be sure, one doesn't take lightly opposition from the House Ways and Means Committee and its Chairman Wilbur Mills, but the White House has chosen not to mount even the most minimal campaign for its own proposal.

William Ruckelshaus and the Enviremental Protection Agency have been equally sheepish. On May 12, 1971, for example, it acknowledged that it had, for more than a year, withheld from the public a study indicating that excessive amounts of lead had accumulated in the air over

Los Angeles. The study, made available only after harassment from Clear Creek, a California-based environmental group, showed that lead in L.A.'s air had risen from an average of 2.29 micrograms per cubic meter in 1961–1962 to 3.58 micrograms in 1968–1969. The latter figure is more than double the California State Health Department safety standard of 1.5 micrograms.

Fortunately, lead in gasoline can be banned. It would be much easier to eliminate this generalized source of lead than to remove the lead paint from hundreds of thousands of ghetto homes. All that is required is an Administration —unlike Nixon's—with enough courage to deal firmly with the petroleum industry, which added about 300,000 tons of lead to its gasoline in 1970.

As long ago as 1967, the Technical Advisory Board to the Department of Commerce recommended that the "Federal Government should establish standards immediately for lead content of gasoline which will prevent any further increase in the total quantity of lead emitted to the atmosphere." On May 5, 1970, after three years of governmental inaction, the Environmental Defense Fund filed a petition with HEW asking that such standards be issued. However, except for the President's order requiring all Federal vehicles (less than two-tenths of one percent of all the cars on the road) to use unleaded or low-lead gasoline, there was no action through 1971. In November, 1971, the Environmental Defense Fund and the Center for Science in the Public Interest again petitioned the government (the Federal air pollution control program had now been transferred from HEW to the EPA) to move against lead. They requested a deliberate national phase-out program beginning in 1972, to eliminate completely lead emissions from automobiles by 1976.

The EPA Task Force Report on the Environmental Problems of the Inner City, given to Ruckelshaus in September, 1971, argued that the "Bonner & Moore report just completed for EPA shows that adoption of the most rapid lead removal schedule would result in all gasoline being lead free by 1977. The report further reveals that total lead removal is both technically feasible and economically reasonable. The task force concludes that the lead burdens of the urban poor dictate adoption of this most rapid lead removal schedule. The task force, therefore, recommends that the Administrator promulgate by January 1, 1972, a regulation requiring all gasoline to be lead-free by 1977."

Under increasing pressure, EPA finally acted on February 23, 1972. Ruckelshaus announced that EPA was proposing regulations to require large volume (why not all?) gasoline stations to carry one grade (why only one?) of near lead-free gasoline by mid-1974 (not the mid-1972 date considered necessary to achieve total lead elimination by 1977). EPA's proposed regulation also requires a gradual reduction of lead in all regular and premium high-octane gasolines.

This is not a plan for a total elimination of lead. First, the proposed regulations define "lead-free" as a maximum of .05 grams of lead per gallon of gas. Secondly, the lead content of regular and premium gasolines would only have to be reduced to 2 grams per gallon by January 1, 1974, and eventually down to 1.25 grams by January 1, 1977. (Regular gasoline now contains 2.2 grams and premium contains 2.7 grams.) These gradually reduced ceilings are expected to achieve only a 60 percent to 65 percent reduction in vehicle lead emissions by mid-1977. While lead levels in the air over some major urban areas now range over 5 micrograms, EPA's proposed regulation is expected to bring them down to 2 micrograms or less on a nationwide basis. The level of 2 micrograms, says EPA, is "a level, based on present scientific evidence, which is fully protective of public health." This level is generally considered safe, but it does not provide as much a margin of safety as would a limit of 1.5 micrograms.

EPA will issue its final regulations for "lead-free" gasoline (perhaps weaker, perhaps stronger) sometime during or after June, 1972. Hopefully, the agency will move more in the direction of total lead elimination—but it is not expected to do so.

## A Legacy of Parks

As the construction of urban highways and urban renewal increases, parks and recreation areas within the inner city are becoming scarcer and scarcer. Studies from the Departments of Interior and HUD show a loss of more than 22,000 acres of urban parkland in the last six years alone. Of the 491 million acres of public recreation area in the U.S., less than 3 percent is within forty miles, or one hour's driving time, from the center of metropolitan areas with more than 500,000 population. Because only 30 percent of the poor own automobiles, they are in effect being deprived of recreation. The National Advisory Commission on Civil Disorders found that out of twenty cities where the most serious disorders occurred in the summer of 1967, there were grievances about recreation in fifteen, and that these grievances were the major cause of the problem in three cities. A 1970 study on recreation problems of urban impact areas in California showed an inverse relationship between family income and desire for recreation. In families with an annual income under $2,000, the desire to participate in outdoor activities was almost double that of families with an income above $9,000. In response to these needs, President Nixon has initiated a "Legacy of Parks" program which he says will bring "parks to the people." Essentially, the program has meant increased budgets for the Land and Water Conservation Fund and the Open Space Lands program, and has succeeded to some extent in channeling greater portions of these funds into urban parkland.

During President Nixon's Administration, the authorization for the Land and Water Conservation Fund has been increased from $200 million to $300 million annually, and since fiscal year 1971 the President has seen that it is fully funded. Unfortunately, the fund's potential for acquisition of urban park land has not been fully realized.

Both the Land and Water Conservation Fund Act, and the administrative formula for distribution of the money, weigh heavily against areas of population density. In fiscal 1972, for example, the per capita allocations for such open space states as Wyoming and Idaho were $6.44 and $3.28 respectively, while states with denser populations had to be content with far less—$1.26 for Maryland, $1 for New Jersey, and 87 cents for New York.

In his Environmental Message of 1971, President Nixon talked about this problem very directly, explaining that a "relatively small percentage" of the funds have been used in and near urban areas, and he proposed that the allocation formula be changed in several ways to give the urban areas a better shake. Unfortunately, the House and Senate Interior Committees, dominated by representatives from the lesser-populated Western states, have not given the proposal serious consideration.

Funding for HUD's Open Space Lands program has steadily increased during the past several years. For fiscal year 1972, for example, the President's Budget requested $200 million, compared to a budget of only $75 million in fiscal 1971. $100 million was already authorized for fiscal 1972, and the Administration was successful in having Congress pass an additional authorization for the $200 million total. But the additional authorization of $100 million was passed after the year's appropriation legislation, so the program level in fiscal 1972 was kept at half the level requested by the President. The additional authorization of $100 million, therefore, carries over into fiscal 1973, and it was hoped that the Administration would request another $100 million to fulfill its promise of a total program of $200 million. Unfortunately, the Administration requested no new funds for fiscal 1973, and the program will remain at the $100 million level. Secretary Romney pushed for the full $200 million, but was unable to influence the President's Office of Management and Budget. The White House has also initiated a policy of limiting the Federal grants to only 50 percent of the project costs, even though the Housing and Urban Development Act authorizes grants at the 75 percent level.

There is no lack of demand for the program—in fact, there is a backlog of project requests now totaling over $500 million. But the program seems to have been cut back for budgetary reasons. According to HUD Assistant Secretary Floyd H. Hyde, the additional program money is not being requested "in the interest of the national economy and as a part of the fight to control inflation." Inflation is certainly a serious national problem, but the needs of inner-city residents, and the President's policy to bring parks back to the people who need them most, suggest that there are other programs which would perhaps be better cut.

The suppression of the Interior Department's "Nationwide Outdoor Recreation Plan" is another disappointment. Congress ordered the Department's Bureau of Outdoor Recreation to produce the plan by 1968, but it still was not completed when the Nixon Administration took office. Then, on September 17, 1969, Nixon's Secretary of Interior Walter Hickel previewed the plan and said that it called for a major, innovative urban orientation—to the tune of $6.3 billion over a five-year period. The plan was about to be released when the White House Office of Management and Budget balked at the price tag. Then, according to one observer, a "sanitized version" was drafted "without the dollar signs and with some of the gutsier recommendations taken out. Then it was set in page proofs. But they never even got that one out." When Rogers Morton took over at Interior, he said he doubted that such a plan was necessary. But subsequently he told the Bureau of Outdoor Recreation to work up a second, altogether new plan. This plan is not scheduled to be finished until sometime in 1973.

## Rats

About 60,000 Americans are bitten each year by rats, according to HEW's Bureau of Community Environmental

Management. Sixty to ninety percent of these bites occur in the inner city. Most victims are helpless infants and young children. Many of the bitten children are permanently disfigured by bites on their ears, nose, or mouth. Rats also spread disease by biting, contaminating food and water with urine and feces, and by carrying disease vectors such as fleas, lice and mites. The more common diseases for which rats are responsible include rat bite fever, leptospirosis (a mild to severe infection), salmonellosis (food poisoning), trichinosis (infection of intestines and muscles), and murine typhus fever. Rats also eat or destroy an estimated $1 billion worth of food per year, and destroy hundreds of millions of dollars worth of buildings, clothing, and other valuables. Having teeth that grow some five inches a year, rats keep them ground down by gnawing through almost anything, including lead pipes, planks, and poorly mixed concrete. Rats are extremely difficult to exterminate, especially because of the overflowing garbage found in inner-city alleys and yards. The Council on Environmental Quality's 1971 annual report pointed out that the presence of rats in a building "often has nothing to do with the particular building's cleanliness. Substandard housing often is replete with holes in basement walls or around windows and pipes, giving rats entry points from which they fan out through a building." To the urban poor, the rat is a gruesome and repulsive symbol of environmental degradation. Said one slum dweller, with understandable bitterness, "I live with the rats."

Since fiscal year 1969, HEW's Bureau of Community Environmental Management (BCEM) has funded a limited number of community rat control projects with a budget of approximately $15 million each year. Thirty-three cities have so far taken part in the program, and HEW plans six new projects during fiscal year 1973. In those communities where the rat control program has gone on for at least one year, HEW has good evidence to believe that the rat population has been cut by 50 percent. During fiscal 1973, it believes the rat populations in some of the communities can be cut by 61 percent.

By any criterion, this is an outstanding success, and one would expect and hope that the Administration, having found a successful program, would broaden and enlarge the scope of the project. But the Nixon Administration's basic conservatism has constrained it from such an undertaking. The Administration's philosophy says that rat control is a local problem to be solved by the municipalities, even though the Federal effort, as limited as it has been, has been remarkably effective. "The Urban Rat Control Program," says BCEM's director Robert Novick, "demonstrates the feasibility of comprehensive community programs for rat control. As such demonstrations are successfully completed, projects will be phased out of the Federal program and, hopefully, carried on entirely by state and local governments."

Thus the Administration has no plans to increase the rat control budget, and, in fact, plans to terminate Federal assistance during fiscal 1973 in five projects "having achieved a satisfactory reduction of rat populations and correction of causative conditions."

The problem with this approach is that 1) a 50 percent reduction in a city's rat population should not be considered "satisfactory," 2) many cities will not be able to continue a successful program without Federal assistance, 3) the rats will come back if the programs are discontinued or lose effectiveness, 4) there are many more than forty cities in the U.S. which have significant rat problems, and 5) many of HEW's projects have not covered the total city area but only very limited neighborhoods.

As Novick says, "You just can't kill rats and be rid of them." Rats multiply and migrate. There are approximately 100 million rats in the United States, and the female Norway rat (the one which gives us most of the problem) can produce five or six litters a year, of up to twelve rats each. So far, the Urban Rat Control Program has had no national impact whatsoever, and Novick's assertion that cities will "hopefully" pick up the slack in the Federal effort won't help those living with the rats.

## Noise

Noise in the inner city is increasing at the alarming rate of nearly one decibel each year. In another fifteen years, the level is expected to double. Motor vehicles are the chief source of this noise, and poor city planning practices and opportunism route it often through the ghetto neighborhoods. In some ghetto communities, over 60 percent of the traffic noise is generated by people who live elsewhere.

The poor are exposed to more noise than other income groups because they are less able to shut it out of their homes. While middle-income groups escape outside noise by turning on the air conditioner, the poor have to keep their windows open on hot summer days. This makes a significant difference. One study by the Department of Housing and Urban Development found that people keeping their windows open are exposed to ten times more the noise intensity than the air-conditioned affluent. A 1967 study by the Public Health Service indicated that the prevalence of binaural (both ears) hearing impairment decreased as the amount of family income increased. Fifty-five percent of the persons with binaural hearing loss were found to have family incomes of less than $4,000.

In addition to disturbing abilities to sleep, hear and concentrate, noise is linked with cardiovascular diseases, nervous disorders and gastrointestinal problems. The EPA inner-city report, April, 1972, warned that: "Unnecessary noise seems to be particularly provoking and has been blamed for triggering murder, suicide, and insanity. Less dramatic and probably too common to document are the cases of sudden loss of temper, child abuse, headaches, depression and irritability caused by the intrusion of noise into our private lives."

Federal involvement to control and limit excessive

noise was initiated by Senator Edmund Muskie, who authored the Noise Pollution and Abatement Act as Title IV of the Clean Air Act Amendments of 1970. The act required the establishment within EPA of an Office of Noise Abatement and Control (NOAC). NOAC was required to monitor the activities of other Federal agencies and to report back to Congress concerning the national problem of noise and recommend what the Federal government should do.

In response, President Nixon proposed in his 1971 Environmental Message noise legislation which would set Federal noise emission standards for the principal sources of noise, such as transportation and construction equipment. Unfortunately, confronted with tougher proposals from Congress, the Nixon Administration is unenthusiastic about pushing legislation for which Muskie would undoubtedly receive much of the credit. Senator Muskie's legislation, considered infinitely stronger than the Administration's bill, would require quicker action from EPA in setting the standards, and would authorize criminal penalties and imprisonment for violation. It also authorizes citizen suits to make certain that EPA enforces the standards, and provides grants to state and local noise control programs to insure their effectiveness. The Administration's bill has no such provisions for criminal penalties, imprisonment, citizen suits, and state and local grants. Indeed, the Administration's proposal would even amend the Clean Air Act to dissolve the Office of Noise Abatement and Control as a major division within the EPA.

Meanwhile, NOAC reported back to Congress on December 31, 1971, with its *Report to the President and Congress on Noise*. While insiders who worked on the report complain that the White House Office of Management and Budget deleted or watered down key sections, the report still speaks strongly: "The projections of noise impact conducted for this report indicate the need for aggressive efforts at all levels of government." On the positive side, it finds that "current technology and that which is expected to be available in the next five to ten years indicate that a substantial reduction in the noise from various sources is feasible."

But the "aggressive efforts at all levels of government" has not been forthcoming. NOAC staffers say off-the-record that "the noise legislation is bottom priority for EPA's office of congressional affairs." Having passed the House, the legislation languishes in the Senate with little pressure for passage coming from the White House.

The day-to-day activities of NOAC have been almost pathetic. With its report now submitted, NOAC's prime responsibility is to monitor the noise activities of other Federal agencies and to encourage a lessening of the noise which Federal projects might create. But with a staff of only twenty-five persons, of whom only twelve are full-time, it has simply not been able to do an effective job.

The EPA task force report on the inner city charged that, "on the Federal level, practically nothing is being done to alleviate the noise problems of the inner city." The task force also found that NOAC "is inadequately staffed" and that EPA has done little to pass the pending legislation giving it more authority. The report recommended "as a first and primary action that the Administrator [William Ruckelshaus] adopt as a personal challenge the passage of the pending noise legislation."

## Transportation

Transportation systems in the inner city have generally been developed not for the needs of the inner-city residents themselves but for commuters coming into the city to work. Highways are a major burden. Because only 30 percent of the poor own automobiles, compared to 90 percent of the non-poor, highways don't increase their mobility. Public transit, upon which the poor must rely, is dying in many cities. Meanwhile, highways add to the noise and air pollution of inner-city neighborhoods and tend to displace the poor from their homes. Not surprisingly, the Los Angeles Riot Study by Nathan Cohen found that transportation-related problems were one of the major grievances of ghetto residents.

The air pollution hazard is the greatest threat. The EPA task force report says that "city residents must breathe the emissions of suburban automobiles which travel in to work every morning and out to escape the noise and dirt of the city in the evening. City children play in the streets over which the automobiles travel, inhaling the gases and dirt left behind." Based on the incidence rate of diseases related to air pollution, the problem is growing worse. In New York City, for example, deaths from emphysema alone have risen 500 percent in the last ten years. Twenty-five percent of the persons in Harlem Hospital are now suffering from asthma, compared with only 5 percent in 1952. And one study by experts from the Albert Einstein College of Medicine found that one out of eight deaths occurring from 1963–1968 in New York City were brought on by air pollution. Their report said that "about 10,000 deaths a year would not have occurred at the time they did if there had been no pollution on the day of the death or on immediately preceding days." These afflictions attack all economic groups, not just the poor.

The Administration's response to these problems has been mixed. While the White House gave priority to development of the SST, which would have committed the federal government to a subsidy of at least $1.3 billion for international travel, it has consistently opposed efforts in Congress to grant operating subsidies to the beleaguered public transit systems in our nation's cities. During debate on both the Urban Mass Transit and Housing and Urban Development Acts of 1970, efforts were made in Congress to establish such assistance. The Senate housing bill even set an authorization of $750 million, but the provision was deleted after the Administration promised to issue a study on the feasibility of operating subsidies.

Submitted to Congress in November of 1971, the Department of Transportation's (DOT) report on the *Feasibility of Federal Assistance for Urban Mass Transporta-*

*tion Operating Costs* admits that subsidies would lower transit fares, but argues that "low fares, per se, will be no help to the poor if the transit service is inaccessible or unresponsive." Francis Turner, the Federal Highway Administrator, has added insult to injury by deriding the "argument often heard that we must provide mass transit facilities in our cities in order to move the aged, the young, the handicapped, and the poor. This conclusion seems to be a pretty flimsy justification for such a system if this is the only reason for it.... For the poor, it would be cheaper to just issue them a car, or give them taxi coupons, like food stamps, than to provide an expensive system for them alone." DOT's *Feasibility* report makes the same basic points, suggesting "transportation stamps" for the poor, and argues that revenue sharing will solve the operation problems of urban transit systems. Fortunately, Congress is moving again in 1972 to grant the needed operating assistance.

On the other hand, the Nixon Administration has proposed a diversion of money from the Highway Trust Fund, partly for the purpose of assisting the construction of mass transit systems. Putting money into a Single Urban Fund, the money could be used for whatever purposes state and local governments desire. This proposal, along with the Urban Mass Transit Assistance Act of 1970, which the Administration proposed, has substantially increased federal assistance to mass transit construction.

But even as the Interstate Highway System is completed, highway interests and the Federal Highway Administration are pushing for a new Urban Highway System, which they argue is needed to link further the cities with the interstate system. Initiated with a budget of $254 million in fiscal year 1971, $380 million is proposed for fiscal year 1973. Beginning in 1974, the Administration proposes that the system be funded through the Single Urban Fund, which will also be the budget source for mass transit construction. It is possible that this Urban Highway System could choke mass transit funds and develop into a hazard for the urban poor equal to the Interstate.

## Our Most Endangered People

There has been much talk of a renewed "war on poverty" under the banner of ecology. A government and people who forgot the poor after the passing of the "Great Society" might well remember the commitment under the new concerns of pollution and environmental degradation. This may yet occur, but the Nixon Administration's opportunity has come and been discarded.

The logical government agency to take up such a challenge is the Environmental Protection Agency. A relatively new agency, still carving out its domain, and led by an energetic young administrator, EPA could begin a new crusade against rats, lead poisoning, noise, air pollution, water pollution, displacement of housing, and elimination of parkland rampant in the inner city. And a "total mobilization" of the kind which President Nixon called for in his 1970 Environmental Message could easily transform this into the kind of effort attacking the causes of poverty —lack of education and job training, unemployment and discrimination—as well as the symptoms.

The possible stage for such action came on July 9, 1971, when President Nixon and his key officials met with black community leaders at the White House. It was a very political meeting, an attempt by the President to convince blacks that there were indeed reasons why he should receive their votes. A key member of the President's party was William Ruckelshaus, Administrator of EPA. Ruckelshaus told his audience that he was setting up that very day a Task Force on Environmental Problems of the Inner City to report back to him on September 1, 1971, on actions that he could take to achieve improvements in the inner-city environment "by June, 1972."

"By June, 1972" placed an obvious limitation on the recommendations the task force could make: Ruckelshaus emphasized the need for immediate results rather than a commitment of long-term effort. The task force was given very little time to work, indeed—only two months. Still, it was the first time the Environmental Protection Agency placed an emphasis on inner-city environmental problems. One could not expect much at first, but a little action now could mean an expanding role in the future.

The task force report, entitled *Our Urban Environment and Our Most Endangered People,* was delivered to Ruckelshaus early in September. Among the more than forty recommendations, the task force suggested that EPA:

- Conduct a "National Operation Clean Sweep" in twenty major cities to clear away the backlog of trash and keep the cities clean. The task force recommended a special budget request of $50 million, with the explanation that "inner-city residents consider solid waste and the associated rat problem their Number One environmental problem."

- Initiate city clean-up programs to prevent litter from entering sewers and clogging drainage.

- Concentrate and coordinate EPA resources in a "Demonstration City Project" to show, in a way reminiscent of Romney's plan, the possibility of achieving environmental improvements within nine months.

- Take action to encourage clean air pockets within inner-city areas by reducing traffic and planting trees and shrubs.

- Recommend and support legislation in Congress giving EPA increased authority to deal with the problems of noise, solid waste and toxic substances.

- Accelerate agency efforts to require lead-free gasoline and move toward a total elimination of lead.

- Initiate agreements with HUD, FHA, VA, OEO, and other Federal Agencies to correct the deteriorating plumbing and inadequate installation of sanitation facilities.

- Establish an EPA Urban Affairs Office and an Administrator's Urban Advisory Council to coordinate and plan inner-city programs and recommend future budget proposals.

As it turned out, the task force recommendations were stillborn. The report was not officially released to the public until April 7, 1972, when the Senate Commerce Committee's Subcommittee on the Environment was finally able to get a response to the report from Ruckelshaus himself. Before this, the report had been hushed up within the agency until columnist Jack Anderson wrote a series of articles revealing that the EPA had no plans to implement the recommendations.

When Ruckelshaus finally appeared before the Environment subcommittee, he announced that the "report does not represent EPA's official position on this critical issue." He also announced with pride that "we established an Office of Civil Rights and Urban Affairs, consistent with one of the major recommendations of our Task Force." Otherwise, he said, "EPA plans to expand research."

The testimony was a major disappointment to environmentalists who hoped that the agency would begin placing more emphasis on inner-city problems. It was well known that other EPA officials were shocked, even frightened, by the report's orientation towards action rather than study and delay. Thomas Carroll, Assistant Administrator for Planning and Management, and David Dominick, Assistant Administrator for Categorical Programs, had been especially uncooperative and antagonistic to the Task Force. Dominick was shocked by the National Operation Clean Sweep proposal requiring $50 million, feeling that this would set a precedent for federal involvement in local solid waste efforts and raid the federal treasury. But Ruckelshaus himself had responded well to the task force, and it was hoped that he would find enough merit in the recommendations to guide them through his agency's bureaucracy.

From the beginning, it should have been obvious that EPA was not about to put itself out on a limb of commitment. Of the eighteen people assigned to the study, eleven were student interns working with the agency for the summer. No one in the agency's upper echelon was really serious about the task force, and nearly all the task force members report little cooperation from their superiors.

The White House meeting of July 9, 1971, was held to convince blacks that the Nixon Administration deserved some black votes, and the promise of the task force report was part of the evidence it gave of its concern. The report was designed to outline the minimum that a conservative Administration could do in return for a small, but perhaps significant, portion of the black vote in 1972. As the *Washington Post* remarked in a February 21, 1972, editorial, "The government is about to issue a 'task force' report on inner-city ecology. It will repeat the tired old facts, offer recommendations, and the administration will have proof, in a campaign year, of its concern." Not only has the Administration lost a chance to regenerate the war on poverty, it has lost a prime opportunity to show 16 million urban poor that the government does indeed care.

# THE WORKPLACE ENVIRONMENT

## FRANKLIN WALLICK

President Nixon, when signing the Occupational Safety and Health Act of 1970 on December 29 of that year, called it "perhaps the most important piece of legislation ever passed by Congress from the viewpoint of the workers," and, potentially, it may be. Of the total national workforce of 80 million, the law covers 57 million workers and contains sweeping authority for the federal government to make their workplaces clean and safe. Unfortunately, most workers have never felt any impact of the law's mandate for workplace inspection, abatement of workplace hazards, and research into workplace environmental quality. The law has been swallowed up by a hostile bureaucracy, with only a tiny band of union officials and environmentalists pressing the Nixon Administration to initiate effective enforcement.

The dimensions of workplace hazards are virtually unknown. Business and industrial interests, so successful in tying the hands of state programs for occupational safety and health, have always maintained, with the active collaboration of the National Safety Council, that work-

---

*Franklin Wallick began working for the United Auto Workers in 1951, and in 1963 became the editor of the weekly United Auto Workers Washington Report. He was active in the campaign for the Occupational Safety and Health Act, and is the author of a book on this subject published by Ballantine, 1972.*

ers are safer on the job than at home or on the highways.

The National Safety Council reports about 14,000 deaths, and 2.2 million injuries, from industrial accidents each year. Dr. Sidney Wolfe, head of Ralph Nader's Health Research Group, estimates the actual number of occupational deaths is more on the order of 50,000, if deaths stemming from workplace health hazards are counted.

For years, the National Safety Council has also undercounted injuries. Only "lost time" accidents were counted (workers had to lose a day's work before their injuries would show up in the statistics), and workers scoff at the Council's awards for "no lost time accidents" which hang on company walls. One 1970 Labor Department study estimated that there are actually 25 million serious injuries each year.

The U.S. Public Health Service has cited the figure of 336,000 recognized job illnesses annually, but this is only from a projection based on data collected in California in 1965. The Public Health Service further estimates that as many as 50 million employees work in an environment with potentially dangerous health hazards.

A study conducted by the University of Michigan's Survey Research Center found 71 percent of a national sampling of workers rating work injury or illness as a "very important problem"—the highest percentage registered on a list of problem areas which included salary, fringe benefits, and unsteady employment.

Prior to the passage of the 1970 law, the federal government had accepted industry's notion that occupational health and safety is the responsibility of the states. Outside of limited authority in some selected industries, and over certain types of employment under federal contract, the federal role was limited to research and technical assistance to the states.

President Johnson, noting in 1968 that this resulted in "a patchwork of obsolete and ineffective laws," proposed a fairly tough and broad reform. But meeting massive resistance from business interests, such as the U.S.

### Estimated Number of Workplaces and Workers Subject to Provisions of the Occupational Safety & Health Act of 1970
(in thousands)

| Industry | Total Workplaces | Total Employees |
|---|---|---|
| Total United States | 4,152.4 | 57,011 |
| Agriculture, forestry, and fisheries (excluding farms) | 31.5 | 228 |
| Farms | 417.0 | 1,315 |
| Contract construction | 308.0 | 3,500 |
| Manufacturing | 299.2 | 19,512 |
| Transportation | 44.9 | 2,166 |
| Wholesale-trade | 298.4 | 3,869 |
| Retail trade | 1,197.5 | 11,067 |
| Finance, insurance, and real estate | 395.1 | 3,695 |
| Services | 1,073.0 | 11,659 |
| Unclassified | 87.8 | |

SOURCE: Department of Labor.

Chamber of Commerce, Johnson's bill died a swift and silent death before the House Rules Committee. President Nixon, already having begun a campaign to woo workers into the Republican party, made his own proposal on August 6, 1969. In a special message to Congress, Nixon said that government protection of the workplace had been "haphazard and spotty." He then outlined a measure which Ralph Nader's task force report *Occupational Epidemic* called "worse than no bill at all."

Republican Senator Jacob Javits of New York, when introducing the Nixon bill in the Senate, simultaneously issued a statement of his own reservations about the weaknesses of the bill. Business and industrial interests, on the other hand, found the Nixon proposal so "responsible" that some even supported it.

Organized labor and the White House were at log-

## The Occupational Health & Safety Act of 1970

• The Secretary of Labor must "promulgate the standard which assures the greatest protection of the safety and health of the affected employees."

• The Labor Department has authority for safety and health inspections. Its inspectors may issue citations listing violations of standards and giving timetables for corrections. Inspectors may also assess penalties.

• Either employers or workers may appeal citations before the Occupational Safety and Health Review Commission.

• In cases of "imminent danger," the Secretary must ask the federal district court for a temporary restraining order to shut down the unsafe operation.

• To keep workers informed of alleged violations in the workplace, the employer is required to post citations at or near each place of violation.

## State Programs

• State health and safety codes remain in effect wherever untouched by federal standards.

• Secretary of Labor may allow states to continue enforcement of their own health and safety standards for up to two years (until 1973).

• States may then continue to retain authority by submitting program plans to the Labor Department. A plan will be approved if the Secretary determines it "is or will be at least as effective" as the federal Act.

• After plans are approved, the Labor Department can no longer enforce federal standards in areas governed by state plan. If a state fails to comply substantially with its plan, however, the Secretary must withdraw his approval after a hearing, and the federal standards and enforcement powers go back into effect.

## Worker Rights

- Workers may initiate a standard setting procedure by writing a petition to the Secretary.

- Any workers (more than one is required) who believe a violation of a standard exists which threatens physical harm or imminent danger may request an inspection. An inspection must then be made "as soon as practicable" or the Secretary must explain in writing why one hasn't been made.

- Workers may accompany inspectors during inspection.

- If inspectors do not issue citations on the basis of a written request, the worker or his representative may ask the Department of Labor for an informal review.

- Workers may participate in any proceedings of the Occupational Safety and Health Review Commission, and may appeal to the courts to modify or set aside any Commission order.

- Employers must record exposures to substances included in the annual list of toxic substances issued by the Secretary of Health, Education and Welfare (HEW), and give workers the opportunity to observe the monitoring process.

- If the Secretary of Labor refuses to petition the courts for a temporary restraining order, after receiving the results of an inspection revealing an imminent danger, workers may bring court action against the Secretary to force him to act.

- Employers are forbidden from discharging or discriminating against workers who exercise any employee rights.

---

gerheads from the start. Labor wanted all the law's authority put under the Secretary of Labor to assure maximum effectiveness and minimum delay. The President was proposing that an independent board set standards for health and safety. The Secretary of Labor would then have to ask employers to comply with these standards voluntarily. If employers didn't volunteer to comply, the Secretary could take a complaint back to the standard-setting board. After holding a hearing, and after determining that a violation existed, the board would issue compliance orders. If the employer still did not comply, the Secretary would have to seek a court order. The unions saw such procedures as crippling the proposed federal authority.

Labor also sought the right of federal inspectors to "red tag" or close any operation which posed an "imminent danger" to the lives of workers. This authority was especially needed because as many as twenty-one states don't have it. The Nixon Administration was, however, against it.

As finally passed, the law is a compromise more to the liking of the unions than to the White House. The Secretary of Labor has authority to set the standards. Federal inspectors have authority to issue citations ordering corrections and to assess penalties. An Occupational Safety and Health Review Commission is established to consider appeals from either employers or employees, and workers are guaranteed numerous essential rights.

But the Administration won many of its points. Federal inspectors are not authorized to red tag a workplace no matter how dangerous it is to the workers. Instead, the Secretary is forced to go to the courts for a temporary restraining order. A weakened law passed because Republican members of the House-Senate conference committee, which thrashed out the final version of the law, threatened a Presidential veto if the bill came out too tough. Men like Rep. William Steiger (R-Wis.), who later claimed credit for the legislation, did what they could to gut it behind closed doors. "The legislative history of the Occupational Safety and Health Act," says the Nader report, "removes the gloss from the Nixon Administration's blue-collar strategy, and unmasks a cynical attempt to deceive the American worker. For while the President and Vice President were making rhetorical pronouncements that purported to support working class goals, the Nixon Administration was struggling to perpetrate a bill that would furnish no more than cosmetic protection for employees in an area which concerned them in the most vital ways imaginable."

## The Occupational Safety & Health Administration

The Occupational Safety and Health Administration (OSHA), which the Act established within the Labor Department, has been permeated from the day of its birth by an administrative sabotage of the law's activist intent.

George C. Guenther, formerly the director of the Bureau of Labor Standards, was appointed by President Nixon in March, 1971, as Assistant Secretary for Occupational Safety and Health. During his Senate confirmation hearings, Guenther emphasized fairness to business, mentioned unions once and workers not at all. Subsequently, Guenther has filled OSHA with corporate yes-men. The only exception is Maywood Boggs from the AFL-CIO, who was hired after severe criticism of OSHA from the unions. Underescretary of Labor Laurance Silberman has also played a key role in forming OSHA policy. Above Guenther in the department's hierarchy, Silberman was one of the Administration's key lobbyists trying to gut the law before it was even passed.

For the first full year of operation, fiscal 1972, the Labor Department requested a total of $31 million, an increase of $24 million over past programs, but still only 42 cents per worker. For fiscal year 1973, the President's budget requested $67 million, more than double that for fiscal 1972. Almost half ($29 million), however, is earmarked for assistance to state programs. The Labor Department's own enforcement program is allotted $23 million, which will allow it to have only 500 safety inspectors on duty by mid-1972. The government has no plans to increase this force even though it would take 500 inspectors fifty-eight years to inspect all of the 4.1 million workplaces covered under the law. The number of industrial hygienists, to perform more sophisticated health inspections, is even more inadequate. The Labor Department planned to have only fifty, meaning a ratio of one hygienist for every 1 million workers, by mid-1972. During hearings before the Senate Labor Committee in 1969, government witnesses said there ought to be one hygienist for every 35,000. Based on this estimate, there ought to be a crash training program to put 8,000 hygienists into the field, but the Nixon Administration has no plans to expand the present force.

The Act itself specifically prohibits advance notice of inspections, and provides a fine and possible imprisonment for anyone giving such notice without authorization from the Secretary of Labor. Secretary James D. Hodgson, however, found a loophole. He issued regulations allowing advance notice in cases of imminent danger, where special preparations might be necessary, and in order to make sure the employer and employee representatives are present. These regulations will allow companies to continue their practice of mounting temporary clean-ups before the inspector arrives.

The first 5,000 inspections have brought an average penalty of $18 for over 19,000 cited violations. One employer, Kawecki-Berlyco, a beryllium company, was fined $6.00 because workers had to eat their lunch near dangerous toxic substances. OSHA is finding violations in only 78 percent of the workplaces, compared to 95 percent under the Walsh-Healy Act of 1936 (which gave the federal government authority over job safety on certain federal contract employment). Obviously, it is turning its back on a significant number of violations, and Assistant Secretary Guenther admits this by explaining that the Nixon Administration doesn't want to "nitpick." Guenther generally downplays the importance of enforcement. "The Training and Education Office," he says, "is looked upon as the key to the ultimate success of the program. It will reach more people in a more effective way than the heavy club handed us by the Act."

The "public service spots" sent out by OSHA might

serve to illustrate what Guenther means by "education." The radio and television announcements are condescending to workers, with an assumption that catchy warnings will prevent clumsy clods from catching their hands in a machine:

Department of Labor
Radio PSA: 30 seconds

| | |
|---|---|
| Music: | *Up full and fade to bg for singer* |
| Singer: | Grab a sack of safety, let it fill your bag, workin' where you're careless is a hurtin' drag, yeah, take a sec and check around your own two feet, then sing a song of safety—it's a hap, happy beat, yeah! |
| Announcer: | (with music under) Think about job safety while you work—it can save your life! |
| Singer: | So sing a song of safety, it's a hap, happy beat. |
| Music: | *Out to time* |

Department of Labor
Radio PSA: 10 seconds

| | |
|---|---|
| Celeb: | Hi. This is Joanne Worley. Don't get hurt on the job! Stay alert and practice job safety full time! For more information, contact the nearest office of the U.S. Department of Labor . . . Um Humm. |

There is no attempt to tell workers their rights, to warn them that the air they breathe on the job may be dangerous, or that their hearing may be damaged by intense noise levels. There are worker rights in the law, such as the right to ask for an inspection, the right to have harmful substances properly labelled, the right to accompany inspectors, and the right to have citations posted at the workplace, but these are not spelled out in the "public service" spots. A worker trapped in a hot, dusty and noisy job is told to be careful and "work safely."

The "target industries" program initiated by the Nixon Administration was heralded with fanfare as an example of government sincerity, but this has also been a cruel joke. These industries, including longshoring, roofing and sheet metal, meat packaging, mobile home manufacturing, and lumber and wood products, employ only 1 million of the 57 million workers covered under the law. While they have high accident rates, the more insidious health hazards found in the chemical, textile, rubber, plastic, and steel industries are largely overlooked. Chemical workers, for example, are exposed to chemicals and fumes which can be debilitating and fatal. Workers like Harold Smith, of the Oil, Chemical, and Atomic Workers, Local 8-447, complain that, "When I go home at night, I have roast beef and the fumes. I can taste it, still taste it when I get home. If I have dessert, I can still taste some of these chemicals." Agriculture workers are totally overlooked, even though they have the third highest injury rate and the highest death rate.

Another example cited by the Nixon Administration, as evidence of its commitment, is the emergency asbestos standard of 5 fibers per milliliter of air which OSHA issued in late 1971. The existing standard had been 12 fibers, but the unions wanted this brought down to one, and ultimately zero fibers. OSHA issued its emergency standard only after Dr. Irving J. Selikoff, of Mount Sinai School of Medicine, wrote a stern warning to Secretary of Labor Hodgson. Selikoff had done years of research and showed that asbestos workers die of lung cancer at five times the rate of the general population. Asbestos can also cause asbestosis, a disease which is irreversible, and mesothelioma, a cancer for which a cure still hasn't been found. There are an estimated 200,000 asbestos manufacturing and construction workers in the United States, and as many as 5 million workers are exposed to some degree of asbestos dust. Selikoff tested 1,117 asbestos workers in 1962 and found radiological evidence of asbestosis in half of them. Selikoff has also done research on 632 asbestos workers who had been members of two local New York unions in 1942. As of June 30, 1971, 425 had died, whereas only 285 would be expected to be dead according to mortality tables for the general population. Selikoff found that 11 percent of these workers died of asbestosis, and that nearly 38 percent died of cancer. Asbestosis and lung cancer take twenty to thirty years to develop, so the death of these workers is probably the result of asbestos exposures dating thirty years ago. During the last thirty years, the amount of asbestos in use has greatly increased.

## The National Institute for Occupational Health & Safety

The kind of scientific evidence which Dr. Selikoff has prepared on asbestos is extremely rare. There is very little of such tough, irrefutable evidence for noise, chemicals, dusts, and other workplace hazards. Much of the existing data has been gathered by people who have mortgaged their scientific souls to business and industry. The long fight to get legal and scientific recognition for black lung, or coal miner's pneumoconiosis, which kills 1,000 miners each year in Pennsylvania alone, is symptomatic of the grand-scale failure to pinpoint the cause of worker illness and disease as it relates to the workplace. In Europe, black lung was officially recognized as an occupational hazard of coal miners as early as the 19th Century, but only since 1969 have American coal miners with this disease been compensated by federal law. Almost to the day that the Coal Mine Health and Safety Act of 1969 was passed, a determined group of doctors with corporate ties were claiming that black lung was really asthma with no job-related cause. Dr. Lorin Kerr of the United Mine Workers Retirement Fund estimates that at least 125,000 coal miners suffer from black lung today.

Company doctors have inherent conflicts of interest. Litigation may arise on the basis of what they diagnose, and they might even be summoned to testify against their employers. Dr. Hawey A. Wells explained this problem to the House Labor Committee in 1968:

> Dr. John L. Zalinsky came up to us in Detroit and told of thirty cases of chronic beryllium disease caused by exposure to . . . beryllium dust. He was told by the company that if he published this material in the medical literature he would have to look for another job. He was torn between professional honesty and personal security and before he resolved this dilemma he died of his second heart attack. His material has never been published.

The problem has been further discussed by Dr. Sidney Wolfe of Ralph Nader's Health Research Group:

> A worker hospitalized with mercury poisoning was asked if the company doctor had stopped to see him in the hospital. He grimly replied, yes, and added that the company doctor had angrily said, "What are you trying to do, shut the plant down?" Another company doctor in a second plant was asked why all workers in the mercury cell area had elevated urine mercury levels. He replied that they might be stealing mercury and taking it home.

To fill the gap in our knowledge of workplace health hazards, the 1970 Act established the National Institute for Occupational Safety and Health (NIOSH) within the Department of Health, Education and Welfare (HEW). The law requires NIOSH to research all workplace hazards and to suggest safe limits, which are to be embodied in standards set by the Secretary of Labor. There is an urgent need for more relentless research into the harmful effects of such potentially dangerous substances as enzymes, lead, silica, beryllium, metal fumes, cadmium, cotton dust, mercury, and many many more. Cadmium, for example, a metal used as a coating on iron, steel and copper, is released in fumes during firing or welding. Cadmium fumes are so toxic that they were once considered for use in chemical warfare. Inhalation of these can cause a severe form of emphysema as well as damage to the kidneys and bone marrow. The $4 million in the Nixon budget for research grants in fiscal 1973, will hardly begin the investigation which must be done on such dangers. It would take more than $4 million just to research properly the health effects of workplace exposures to noise, the standard for which (90 decibels for eight hours) actually condemns 15 percent of the working population to occupational deafness and a host of other afflictions ranging from heart trouble, sleeplessness, loss of appetite, increased susceptibility to infection, and lowered sex drives.

The Act required the Secretary of HEW to publish a list of toxic substances and their known exposure levels by June 29, 1971, and at least annually thereafter. But on July 23, 1971, Secretary Elliot Richardson's list included only 8,000 of the estimated 12,000 toxic substances in current industrial use. NIOSH is developing criteria packages (on which Department of Labor standards will be based) for each substance, and each will cost $40,000 to $80,000. NIOSH officials estimate that within two years they might be able to produce twenty to thirty criteria packages, a rate which will take them about 1,000 years to cover the basic list of toxic substances. NIOSH claims it takes nine months to produce a criteria document, a procedure which really should take no more than a few weeks if the data collection is done efficiently.

NIOSH was a bitter disappointment from the beginning. Congress established the Institute (replacing the old Bureau of Occupational Safety and Health, BOSH), hoping to raise within the HEW establishment the importance of workplace health and safety. NIOSH is staffed with competent and dedicated people, but it languishes several layers of bureaucracy below the Secretary (Secretary, U.S. Public Health Service, Health Services and Mental Health Administration, and finally NIOSH), and has not received the attention it deserves.

Even though the low position probably came more from bureaucratic jealousy than political malice, the decision to place NIOSH so low in the HEW chain of command rankles every friend of occupational health who expected more out of the new law.

## OSHA and the National Safety Council

To the American worker, the Nixon Administration's appointment of Howard Pyle (president of the National Safety Council) to serve as the chairman of the twelve member National Advisory Committee on Occupational Safety and Health, was a major letdown. Pyle is a conservative Republican, whose Safety Council is the complete creature of corporate America. Almost all of the Council's funds come from corporations, as do 95 percent of its board members.

The National Safety Council did not work for passage of the Occupational Safety and Health Act, and it provided no constructive input during the law's gestation. Yet Pyle presides over a citizen advisory committee which has the duty to see that the law is properly administered. Only two members of this committee are from labor, compared to six from industry, although the purpose of the law is to protect workers from injury, illness, and death.

One legacy of the close tie between OSHA and the National Safety Council has been the emphasis of safety at the expense of workplace health hazards, which is evidenced in OSHA's public service announcements, its target industries program, and its inspection program (with 500 safety inspections, but only fifty industrial health hygienists). Assistant Secretary Guenther himself has admitted that 60 percent of the first 868 complaints received by OSHA were for health hazards, such as dust, noise, fumes, chemicals, heat and cold stress. But OSHA continues to reflect the ideology that safety is 90 percent of the problem and that carelessness by the workers is responsible for 90 percent of the accidents: even if a machine is only marginally safe, it is the machinist who is responsible for any accident.

## Back to the States

Particularly grating to the unions has been the Nixon Administration's almost panicky campaign to throw the law back to the states, which have demonstrated a chronic inability to gear up effective safety and health programs for working people. Federal authority was sought just because the states had failed to protect workers. But the 1970 Act also provides Secretary of Labor Hodgson wide loopholes through which he can approve the continuation of ineffective state programs.

States are allowed by the Act to continue their own programs until 1973; but, to avoid a federal take-over from that time on, the states must prepare plans to make their own programs as tough as the requirements of the federal Occupational Safety and Health Act. The Secretary of Labor may approve a state plan only if it "is or will be at least as effective" as the federal law. This is fine on paper, but in the past, the states' record of implementing their own requirements was very poor.

Hearings before the House and Senate Labor Committees in 1968, 1969, and 1970, for example, documented endless accounts of how states would not spend enough money, would not hire trained and vigilant personnel, would rarely inspect the workplace, would not let workers know what hazards they found, and would not shut down unsafe or unhealthy operations.

A Bureau of Labor Standards survey found that the average budget for occupational safety in thirty-eight states was only 48 cents per worker in 1968. Inspectors lack authorization in twenty-one states to shut down operations where there are imminent hazards, and 75 percent of the states that have such authority have never used it. Sixteen states provide no criminal sanctions against employers who deliberately violate safety laws. In five states, inspectors do not even have the right to enter the workplace.

Out of 24,845 violations of Massachusetts' standards in 1968, only twenty-eight prosecutions and twelve fines resulted. New York reported only six fines in 1968. Carl A. Merritt, the director of occupational safety in Kentucky, can't recall any penalties ever being assessed for violations of the law.

And lastly, over the past ten years, the number of physicians employed by state occupational health units has actually dropped, primarily because of budget cuts, from fifty to thirty-five. The number of nursing consultants has dropped from thirty-six to twenty-two, five of whom are part time. Only twelve states and six local units employ these twenty-two nurses.

Secretary Hodgson announced on February 26, 1971, that the Nixon Administration is "giving highest priority to the development of procedures which will enable the States to continue their current programs . . . as quickly as possible." To do this "as quickly as possible," OSHA is making a mockery of the law's strong language that the state programs must be "as effective as" the federal law in order to be approved. In September, 1971, for example, Undersecretary Silberman said that it would exceed the "legal and policy guidelines of the Department to require specific Federal rights in the States plans," unless these rights were specified in Section 18, the state plan section of the Act. As an example of a right which wouldn't have to be specifically required, Silberman mentioned one of the most important rights guaranteed to the worker by the federal law: the right to accompany inspectors during inspections. This right is specified in Section 8 of the law, but not in Section 18, which Silberman mentioned. Section 18 only says the state plan must be "at least as effective as that provided in Section 8."

If allowed to go unchallenged, this "back to the states" policy will gut the federal law. The plan submitted by Massachusetts, for example, does not give workers the right to accompany inspectors. But the plan claims to be as effective as the 1970 federal Act by asserting that Massachusetts inspectors "welcome employer and employee representatives on tours of the plants." As the Nader report,

*Occupational Epidemic*, puts it, "a welcome is not the same as a right, for a welcome can always wear out."

Fortunately, although forty-nine states have filed notices of intent to submit plans, many of them may not do so. To even approach the effectiveness of the Safety and Health Act of 1970, many states would have to pass new state legislation. And since the law provides federal grants for only 50 percent of costs for administration of state programs, many states may find it much cheaper simply to let the federal government assume jurisdiction. But the Nixon Administration has committed itself to see that as many state plans as possible are approved. Legislation providing more federal financial assistance for state programs may be introduced, clearing away the main obstacle to the states.

The first two years of the Nixon Administration's implementation of the Occupational Safety and Health Act of 1970 have revealed a strong bias towards industry, a contempt for workers, a lack of candor and imagination, and a maze of legalisms which can only confuse and delay. So far as the workplace environment is concerned, the Administration has fallen short on many counts: it has failed to tell the working population of the nation what is in the law or how it can be used, it has failed to mobilize the nation's talent and resources to combat workplace pollution, and it has not even attempted to train workers in the rudiments of workplace pollution detection, measurement, and prevention. It adds up to a sorry record of timidity and neglect.

# SOLID WASTES

## JANET SCHAEFFER

"Last year New York City at the height of its garbage strike was only days, if that, removed from a major disaster. Flash fires from the mounting garbage and refuse increased more than sevenfold. It illuminated the vulnerability of our entire archaic waste control system. The paralysis of that city serves as a dramatic illustration that large-scale environmental disasters in densely populated areas are always possible."

Secretary Robert H. Finch, September 30, 1969. Testimony before the Senate Subcommittee on Air & Water Pollution.

The United States is producing 4.3 billion tons of municipal, industrial, mineral, and agricultural solid wastes each year. While the population increases only 1 percent annually, the wastes are increasing at a rate of 5 percent. Very little of these 4.3 billion tons is recycled, and, as a result, our natural resources are shrinking as the volume of trash increases.

Though municipal wastes (residential, commercial, and institutional refuse) constitute but 250 million tons

---

*Janet Schaeffer is the Assistant Editor of* National Parks & Conservation Magazine. *She was previously the co-editor of* Environmental Action, *and was a contributor to the* Earth Tool Kit *(Pocket Books, 1971). Diane Krasner, a student at Johns Hopkins University, served as a consultant for the writing of this chapter.*

of the total waste burden, they present the most immediate problem and have received the most attention from government. About 190 million tons of this municipal waste is collected by municipal collection agencies each year, at an annual cost of $4.5 billion, a municipal expense surpassed only by schools and roads.

Each American now discards about 5.3 pounds of "trash" every day, but this amount is expected to increase to eight pounds by 1980 and to ten pounds by the year 2000. To put these numbers into perspective, the municipal waste generated in 1970 was enough to cover an area of 17,000 square miles, about half the size of Connecticut, with a layer of garbage one foot deep. Increased use of packaging, disposable containers, and other materials which do not readily burn or decay, in contrast to traditional organic garbage, aggravates the disposal of these wastes. In 1970, for example, we threw away, along with other trash, 28 billion bottles, 48 billion cans, and 4 million tons of plastic containers. The technology for collection and disposal has not kept pace with this trend.

Nearly all municipal waste ends up in city dumps (84 percent), in "sanitary" landfill (6 percent), or in municipal incinerators (8 percent). The remaining 2 percent is flushed down the drain, converted into compost, or salvaged for reuse. The government reports that nearly all land disposal (dumps and landfills), and 75 percent of municipal incinerators, are unsatisfactory from the standpoint of human health.

Many cities, overstrained by rising municipal costs in general, have had to cut back on garbage collection, aside from being able to keep up with the increasing volume of trash. Finch told the Senate Subcommittee on Air and Water Pollution in 1969 that, "Rats, flies and fleas are common in neighborhoods that do not have adequate waste disposal services; these pests serve as disease vectors, spreading illnesses such as diarrhea and dysentery and many others. The results of one of our recent studies indicate a relationship between solid waste and no less than twenty-two human diseases prevalent in this country, including such diseases as encephalitis and hepatitis."

## Dumps, Landfills and Incinerators

The open dump, where some 14,000 cities and towns allow their trash to lay inadequately buried, is the oldest method of waste disposal. These disease-breeding and rat-infested eyesores are the most unsatisfactory disposal method. Three-fourths of them (those in which trash is burned) also create air pollution problems, and half of them contribute to water pollution.

Sanitary landfills, properly located and managed, can be clean and attractive. Each day's refuse is deposited in a depression, spread and compacted, and covered with a layer of dirt that is finally sealed over. But the Public Health Service reports that only 6 percent of our sanitary landfills are actually very sanitary. The other 94 percent don't meet "even the most modest criteria" defining sanitary landfills. Even proper landfill, however, will not be a long-term solution to solid wastes. Cities are running out of space and money for any kind of land disposal. New York City, for example, having nearly exhausted other landfill areas, is exerting pressure to utilize park areas.

The 300 large municipal incinerators still in operation are clearly obsolete in terms of today's needs. The Environmental Protection Agency estimates that 75 percent of them are burning refuse without even the most rudimentary air pollution control equipment.

## The Resource Recovery Act of 1970

The Solid Waste Disposal Act of 1965 left the states and local governments with primary responsibility for collection and disposal, but established the Bureau of Solid Waste Management in the Department of Health, Education and Welfare. The Bureau began a modest federal program of research, training, demonstration of new technology, technical assistance, and grants for state and interstate solid waste planning. The Act financed a number of research and development projects, as well as several projects demonstrating new collection and disposal techniques.

Once these R & D and demonstration projects were under way, it would have been quite natural for the federal government to help municipalities with financing construction of improved solid waste facilities. Senator Edmund Muskie (D-Me.), Chairman of the Senate Subcommittee on Air and Water Pollution, introduced legislation in 1969 to do just that. His Resource Recovery Act of 1969 also would have put an increased emphasis on recovery and recycling.

But the Nixon Administration opposed federal aid for constructing new facilities, as the government had done in the field of water pollution. Finch appeared before Muskie's Subcommittee on September 30, 1969, to oppose the major provisions of Muskie's bill: "I do not believe," he said, "that the solution lies in passing more federal legislation. Specifically, I oppose the new program of federal construction grants."

President Nixon himself explained his position in his first Environmental Message, delivered to the Congress on February 10, 1970. "One way to meet the problem of solid wastes," he said, "is simply to surrender to it: to continue pouring more and more public money into collection and disposal of whatever happens to be privately produced and discarded. This is the old way; it amounts to a public subsidy of waste pollution. If we are ever truly to gain control of the problem, our goal must be broader: to reduce the volume of wastes and the difficulty of their disposal, and to encourage their constructive reuse instead."

The President was correct that increased emphasis had to be put on recycling and reuse, but his arguments against the Resource Recovery Act seemed inappropriate because the legislation was designed to increase this very emphasis. The construction grants authorized by the legislation were geared to encourage recycling and recovery of resources, and, while they certainly would have created a new area of government spending, they hardly would have meant the "surrender" which President Nixon had warned about in his Environmental Message. The $4.5 billion a year paid out by municipalities is 85 percent for collection and transportation, expenses which neither Muskie nor anyone else had suggested the federal government assume.

But any increased expenditure was apparently too much for Nixon, especially as his economic advisors reviewed their difficulties in managing the economy. As Secretary Finch explained in his Senate testimony, the Administration's "effort to cool off the economy in view of the inflationary spiral we find ourselves in" meant that the White House wanted to cut back on government spending whereever it thought it could.

But Secretary Finch's alarm over solid wastes reflected the mood of Congress, and the Resource Recovery Act was enacted on October 13, 1970. The Act switched the emphasis from disposal to recycling and resource recovery, and it authorized $409 million for the Environmental Protection Agency's (EPA) solid waste programs. This amount included $80 million in fiscal 1972 and $140 million in fiscal 1973 "for the demonstration of resource recovery systems or for the construction of new or improved solid waste disposal facilities." This was precisely what President Nixon had opposed, and though the word went out that a Presidential veto was in the works, Nixon did sign the measure on October 26th. In announcing the signature, White House Press Secretary Ronald L. Ziegler said the President had indeed considered vetoing the bill because he had "some concern about the ability of the Federal government to effectively spend" the money authorized. But Ziegler said the President's "concern for dealing with problems of the environment was the overriding factor in his signing the bill."

Subsequently, the President has thwarted the intent of Congress through his control over the budget almost as

## EPA's Funding of Solid Waste Programs
(in millions)

| Fiscal Year | 1971 | 1972 | 1973 |
|---|---|---|---|
| Authorized by Congress | $41.5 | $152 | $216 |
| Requested by President Nixon | 15.3 | 28.4 | 23.3 |
| Appropriated by Congress | 19.7 | 35.9 | * |
| Obligated by Administration | 18.0 | 26.8 (e) | 36.4 (e) |
| Spent by Administration | 9.6 | 23.9 (e) | 26.3 (e) |

(e) Budget estimate.

\* Appropriation for 1973 pending before Congress.
SOURCE: The Budget, Fiscal Year 1973 & EPA.

well as he could have by vetoing the bill. Of the $409 million authorized under the law for the EPA over the three-year period, the Nixon Administration has requested only $67 million. Of the $220 million authorized for the demonstration of resource recovery systems and the construction of improved disposal facilities, the President's budgets have requested only $15 million. The $15 million was requested for fiscal 1972, but the Administration still has not spent a penny of it. No new funds were requested for recycling or construction in the fiscal 1973 budget. EPA's Office of Solid Waste Management Programs (OSWMP) plans to begin four resource recovery demonstration projects with the $15 million during fiscal 1973, but there are no plans to use the authorized millions for construction grants. When asked about this, some officials within EPA are completely ignorant of the fact that construction grants have been authorized.

## The U.S. Bureau of Mines

The Interior Department's Bureau of Mines has been conducting research on the recycling of mineral-based waste material since 1910, and the Solid Waste Disposal Act and the Resources Recovery Act both reaffirmed this authority. Ironically, the greatest successes which EPA is

## How Much Is Recycled?

There are 4.3 billion tons of solid waste produced in the United States each year:

|  | *Million tons* |
|---|---:|
| Residential, Commercial and Institutional wastes | 250 |
| Collected | (190) |
| Uncollected | (60) |
| Industrial wastes | 110 |
| Mineral wastes | 1,700 |
| Agricultural wastes | 2,280 |
| Total | 4,340 |

SOURCES: Bureau of Solid Waste Management, Department of Health, Education, and Welfare; Division of Solid Wastes, Bureau of Mines, Department of the Interior.

Virtually none of this waste is recycled. The 4.3 billion tons is the amount discarded, and once we throw something away we almost never recover it. In 1970, we threw away 28 billion bottles, 48 billion cans, 4 million tons of plastic containers, 30 million tons of paper, and 100 million tires.

Recycling is nothing new to many industries, but the industrial materials "recycled" are primarily "secondary materials," scraps which for the most part were never thrown away. Even this recycling, however, has been decreasing in recent years. The use of scrap in the making of aluminum, copper, zinc, and lead, for example, increased between 1963 and 1965, to reach a peak of 40.9 percent of materials used, but then declined to 38.6 percent in 1967, the latest year analyzed. And even in the major industries which do recycle, scrap materials account for only about 25 percent of the total material used for production purposes. The American Iron and Steel Institute pointed out, "We spend $4.5 billion annually to collect refuse, and we throw away metals alone that are worth more than $5 billion."

Much more must be recycled and reused, while at the same time we must cut down on consumption. High grade reserves of most metals, for example, have long since been exhausted in the United States; and the National Academy of Sciences report, *Resources and Man*, states "it is clear that exhaustion of deposits of currently commercial grade is inevitable."

A major problem is that economic disincentives exist for industrial recycling. Freight rates set by the independent regulatory Interstate Commerce Commission, for instance, discriminate against scrap in favor of virgin materials (e.g., it costs two-and-one-half times as much to transport a ton of scrap as a ton of virgin iron ore).

---

ever likely to achieve in the recycling field have already probably been surpassed by the Bureau of Mines, yet EPA, in a classical battle of agency jurisdiction, has prevented the Bureau from using any of the funds to which the Bureau is entitled under the Resource Recovery Act.

The Bureau has developed a number of remarkable resource recovery methods, and one of them, developed by its Energy Research Center in Pittsburgh, is nothing less than a miraculous short cut of nature's million-year process of converting animal and vegetable matter into petroleum.

Since mid-1971 the Bureau's scientists in Pittsburgh have been stuffing everything they can get their hands on, animal manure, wood chips, paper towels, dead mice, garbage, and what else, into an experimental "pressure cooker." The wastes, along with water and carbon monoxide, are heated to a temperature of 380 degrees centigrade under a pressure of two to four thousand pounds. After twenty minutes, the pressure vessel is cooled and opened. Incredibly, what is left is a small amount of clean, powdery solid waste, and oil—oil with an extremely low sulfur content.

Potentially, this process is not only a partial solution to solid wastes, but it could also help close the growing energy gap. The potential from the 3 billion tons of organic and animal wastes produced in the U.S. each year is some 2.45 billion barrels of oil—about half the nation's present annual consumption.

During hearings on February 24, 1972, before the House Appropriations Committee, Rep. David Obey (D-Wis.) asked Dr. Elburt F. Osborn, Director of the Bureau of Mines, "How many years away do you think you are from really being able to apply that practically?" Osborn answered, "I think the main factor is how much money we can put into it. . . . If this could be stepped up to something like a $2 million program, then, say, in two years."

But as Rep. Obey and other members of the committee learned, the likelihood of increasing the project's funding to $2 million a year is remote. The Resource Recovery Act authorized $50 million for the Bureau's solid waste research ($8.75 million in fiscal 1971, $20 million in fiscal 1972, and $22.5 million in fiscal 1973), but the President has requested none of this money.

The House Appropriations Committee asked Osborn why none of the funds were being requested, and to its amazement Osborn explained that the Environmental Protection Agency had been supported by the White House Office of Management and Budget in its view that "the funds available under the Resource Recovery Act are only for them to use." Rep. Joseph McDade (R-Pa.) responded that this "is just outrageous," but Osborn explained that that, simply, was the case.

Meanwhile, the Bureau's waste-to-oil project continues as a five-man operation with a budget of around $255,000 a year. Not spending much of its own money authorized by the law, the Environmental Protection Agency apparently wants to make certain that it isn't outdone by the

Bureau of Mines. That this inter-agency jealousy is supported by the White House is one of the most disappointing aspects of the Nixon Administration's solid waste program.

## Nixon's Initiatives

Solid waste and recycling have received steadily declining attention in President Nixon's Environmental Messages. In 1970, he gave the subject two pages, in 1971 he gave it half a page, and in 1972 he gave it two small paragraphs, using this space to discuss his alternatives to the construction program authorized by the Resource Recovery Act of 1970. Rather than have the government "surrender" by subsidizing municipal construction of improved solid waste disposal and recycling facilities, Nixon has called for incentives "directed especially at two major goals: a) making products more easily disposable; and b) re-using and recycling a far greater proportion of waste materials."

His first goal, making products more easily disposable, recognizes that many of the modern products are not as easily disposed of as traditional garbage, but does not deal with the fact that we are already throwing away too much. The President's second goal, recycling waste materials, is admirable, but it is difficult to understand why he considers recycling as something in opposition to helping municipalities construct resource recovery and recycling systems, which could be done under the Resource Recovery Act. One certain difference is that the Nixon alternatives have meant far less federal expenditure.

The President's first initiative, mentioned in his February, 1970, message, directed itself at the problem of junk automobiles. "I have asked the Council on Environmental Quality," the President said, "to take the lead in producing a recommendation for a bounty payment or other system to promote the prompt scrapping of all junk automobiles." This was a sound proposal. The number of abandoned cars littering the nation is estimated to be between 2.5 and 4.5 million. In New York City, 2,500 were abandoned in 1960, 25,000 were abandoned in 1964, and more than 50,000 were abandoned in 1969. The figure for 1971 is put at 82,000. Nationwide, an estimated 800,000 are abandoned each year. And as the President remarked, "Few of America's eyesores are so unsightly as its millions of junk automobiles."

Six months later, in August, 1970, the White House Council on Environmental Quality reported in its first annual report that it had "reviewed the range of alternatives leading to a Federal or State bounty system and concluded that under present conditions it is not practicable." Administration and enforcement of the system, it said, "would require excessive increases in government personnel and expenditures."

The President's other 1970 initiative was to ask the Council to work "with appropriate industry and consumer representatives" to develop similar incentives in other areas. As a result, the President was able to announce one year later, in his 1971 message, that the General Services Administration (GSA), the government's chief purchasing agency, had changed its specifications for buying paper. Though paper constitutes about half of all municipal waste, roughly 60 percent of previous GSA specifications had prohibited the purchase of paper products with recycled fibers (GSA purchases $100 million worth of paper products annually). Many common paper products now purchased by the GSA are required to contain percentages, varying from 3 percent to 100 percent, of recycled paper.

The President devoted one of his two solid waste paragraphs in the 1972 message to praise of this program. "Last year, at my direction," he said, "the General Services Administration began reorienting government procurement policies to set a strong Federal example in the use of recycled products." This it has done, to a limited extent. The second paragraph announced that the Treasury Department was "clarifying" the availability of tax exempt revenue bonds for financing construction of recycling facilities built by private industry to recycle wastes they otherwise would discard.

These, then, have been the President's "incentive" proposals: the proposed bounty on abandoned automobiles was scrapped, the GSA has begun a praiseworthy program of purchasing some recycled paper, and the Treasury Department is "clarifying" the availability of bonds which were already available.

## EPA Initiative

The initiatives emanating from the EPA's Office of Solid Waste Management Programs (OSWMP) are even more limited than those coming from the White House. Most of what OSWMP is already doing was required of it by the Resource Recovery Act. The Act, for example, requires OSWMP to undertake a study for a national network of disposal sites for radioactive and other hazardous materials. This study will be released sometime in late 1972. The Act also directs OSWMP to undertake other research, demonstration projects, training of public solid waste personnel, and to make grants for state, interstate, and municipal master plans for solid waste disposal (with emphasis on recycling). OSWMP's most important role under the Act, the disbursement of construction grants, has not been included as part of the Nixon Administration's program.

While the numerous studies, demonstrations, and plans being worked on by the EPA will have some long-term significance, the agency's only do-it-now initiative has been "Mission 5000." William Ruckelshaus of EPA told the National Solid Waste Management Association on June 17, 1971, that "the public quite naturally wants to see proof that you and I mean business in the here and now. That's why we in EPA have begun a campaign to improve environmental health by closing 5,000 of some 14,000 open dumps across the country by June 30, 1972. Traditionally, each little town has thought it had to have its own dump. Now Mission 5000 will encourage the consolidation of many such open dumps into sanitary landfill operations."

Mission 5000 participants can get technical and planning advice from EPA, but in keeping with the Nixon policy, no financial assistance. Since the program began, in the summer of 1970, about 1,600 dumps have been closed, but the original deadline has been extended fifteen months to September, 1973. Meanwhile, the Citizen's Advisory Committee on Environmental Quality, chaired by Laurance Rockefeller, has proposed in its 1971 report to the President that all open dumps be converted to sanitary landfill.

## Non-Returnable Beverage Containers

The battle over non-returnable bottles has been one of the symbolic struggles of the ecology movement, with environmentalists seeing the throw-away bottle as the epitome of the wasteful society. Compared to the overall waste growth of 5 percent each year, non-returnable, throw-away, or "convenience" bottles and cans are increasing at the rate of 7.5 percent. Of the 46.8 billion beverage containers (both cans and bottles) produced in 1969, 44.7 billion were non-returnable (28.5 billion cans and 16.2 billion glass bottles). There were only 2.1 billion returnable bottles.

It is estimated that twenty to thirty non-returnable containers must be produced for every returnable taken off the market. The 44.7 billion non-returnables in 1969, for example, were used for no more than 44.7 billion fillings, whereas the 2 billion returnable bottles carried a total of 41 billion fillings. If the non-returnable continues to decline, it is estimated that 100 billion beverage containers will have to be produced annually by 1980. Already beverage containers make up over 20 percent of the litter problem, and cost the public about $176 million each year for collection and disposal. Crusade for a Cleaner Environment estimates that abolishing the one-way syn-

## Soft Drink Containers By Type, 1957-76

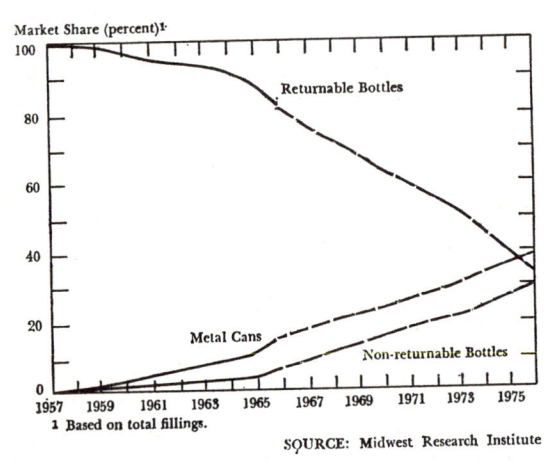

Market Share (percent)[1]

*(Chart showing Returnable Bottles declining from ~100% in 1957 to ~35% in 1975; Metal Cans rising to ~40%; Non-returnable Bottles rising to ~30%)*

[1] Based on total fillings.

SOURCE: Midwest Research Institute

drome could save consumers a total of $1.5 billion each year.

President Nixon, however, seems to have a poor grasp of the issue. While realizing that non-returnables are a problem, he told the Congress in his first Environmental Message that "we need incentives, regulations, and research directed especially at . . . making products more easily disposable—especially containers, which are designed for disposal."

This is precisely what the container industry likes to hear, because disposable bottles and cans have the certain virtue of increased profit. The manufacturers, of course, produce the twenty to thirty non-returnables for every returnable removed from the market. In short, they make each container twenty to thirty times. But while doing this, the industry uses more energy, and creates more pollution and solid waste. In a study of energy requirements of the soft drink industry, for example, Dr. Bruce Hannon of the Center for Advanced Computation at the University of Illinois showed that it requires 3.06 times as much energy to deliver a gallon of soft drink in eight non-returnable bottles than in one returnable bottle filled eight times.

To divert attention from this waste-producing trend, the container industry formed as early as 1953 an organization known as Keep America Beautiful (KAB). With an annual advertising budget of $100,000, Keep America Beautiful tells Americans that "People start pollution. People can stop it," "Please don't litter," and "Dispose of litter properly." The industry has also re-defined recycling. To the ecologist, it means re-use. To the container people it means remelt. This approach to recycling, apparently endorsed by President Nixon, has been criticized even by David Dominick, EPA's Assistant Administrator for Categorical Programs, which houses the Office of Solid Waste Management Programs. At a September, 1971, meeting sponsored by Keep America Beautiful, Dominick stated that making containers more disposable and remelting them will not significantly ease the nation's solid waste problem. In fact, he predicted that public opinion and scientific studies would force Congress to pass a law within two years either taxing or prohibiting non-returnables.

It was perhaps significant that Dominick said public opinion and scientific studies, and not pressure from the Nixon Administration, would force Congress to pass the restrictive legislation. EPA's official position has been "we do not believe enough information has yet been accumulated or that all pertinent factors have yet been adequately considered to warrant action at this time." The Administration has, in fact, opposed restrictive legislation several times in the past several years.

Ruckelshaus, for his part, has scored proposed throw-away restrictions. Speaking at a news conference before his dinner speech for the Aluminum Association on October 27, 1971, Ruckelshaus cited a study which he claimed backed up his position that returnables are more of a solid waste problem than non-returnables. No transcript of his remarks is available, but the *New York Times* (February 5, 1972) later reported his statements as follows:

Mr. Ruckelshaus said that people were not returning returnable bottles because it was too much trouble. Thus, he said, the returnable bottle, because it was much more durable and heavier, was adding more of a solid waste burden if it was thrown away after one use.

To back up his contention that returnable bottles may pose even more of a solid waste problem, Mr. Ruckelshaus cited what he termed a federally aided experiment that had shown that if the deposit on a bottle was raised high enough to encourage people to return it, counterfeiters would make the bottles just to collect the deposit.

The test was in California, he said, and the deposit price was put at 11 cents. At that point, Mr. Ruckelshaus reported, counterfeiters found they could make the bottles cheaper than that, so they simply made the bottles to collect the deposit.

The result, Mr. Ruckelshaus said, was even more bottles added to the solid waste glut.

These remarks greatly disturbed environmentalists, and the EPA was immediately asked for more information about the study. After much delay and prodding, EPA's Samuel Hale finally admitted, in a letter to *New York Times* reporter David Bird, dated January 26, 1972, that no such study had ever been conducted. "We have not been able to determine," wrote Hale, "that there has been any federally-aided test and we do not know of any other such test involving a high bottle deposit and subsequent bottle counterfeiting for profit. From all indications, therefore, it appears that erroneous information was received on this matter from somewhere within the Agency." Another spokesman for Ruckelshaus said, "Bill thought he had been told that such a study existed. He had apparently seized on some information and taken it way further than was true."

When arguing against restrictions on throw-aways,

EPA invariably calls for more research ("we do not believe enough information has yet been accumulated..."), but in attacking the returnable it seems to need very little study and research whatsoever. It is interesting that, when asked for information about beverage containers, EPA hands out along with its own information a packet of twelve industry-published brochures to explain the "industry point of view."

Reviewing the Nixon Administration's solid waste "initiatives," one can only hope that the situation is not nearly so grave as Secretary Finch believed it was in 1969. Having inherited a non-policy towards recycling, with the federal government emphasizing disposal almost exclusively, the Administration has failed to use the opportunities given it by the Resource Recovery Act to develop a re-direction in the nation's use and non-use of wastes.

Part of the problem is strictly political. Since Senator Muskie was the principal author of the Resource Recovery Act, the Nixon Administration seems to feel a need to prove the legislation cannot work. By refusing to fund recycling and resource recovery as the law envisioned, the White House has severely limited the impact of the Act.

The President is also motivated by his Republican conservatism, which leads him to believe that government should let private industry develop profitable recycling processes on its own. But private industry is watching for some direction from the government, and the result has been a mutual wait-and-see game, through which very little is being accomplished.

Afraid to offend big business, the Administration talks in broad, general terms about incentives towards recycling, but fights any movement towards specific proposals. Only lukewarm support is given to environmentalists pressuring the Interstate Commerce Commission to correct the freight-rate discrimination towards scrap materials; and proposals to restrict non-returnable bottles and to put a bounty on junked automobiles find little favor once they pass the discussion stage.

By the time this Administration decides its policy, and prepares to take substantive action (if indeed it ever does), the solid waste battle may grow to the proportion of Secretary Finch's "large-scale environmental disaster."

# DECISION-MAKING IN THE WHITE HOUSE

## JOE BROWDER

President Nixon is the first American chief executive to feel the pressure of a national political movement in behalf of a healthy environment. The President, and his Administration, have shown a curiously mixed reaction. Former Attorney General John Mitchell has been heard to question the sanity of those who would join the Sierra Club, but his wife Martha has waded through polluted streams to express her indignation against those who despoil the environment. Some members of the White House staff have an understanding and respect for the broad base of public support for pollution control and preservation of natural values, while others see the environment as a phony issue that died when the crowds walked away after the first Earth Day rally.

Just as the nature of environmental advocacy has changed rapidly during the past few years, White House

---

*Joe Browder is Executive Vice President of the Environmental Policy Center. For twelve years, from 1956 until he became Southeastern Representative of the National Audubon Society in 1968, he was a news reporter for radio and television stations in Texas and Florida. He moved to Washington, D.C. in 1970, and worked as Conservation Director of Friends of the Earth before joining other Washington environmental lobbyists in forming the Environmental Policy Center in March, 1972. He has written articles for* Audubon, Not Man Apart *and other environmental journals.*

response to the politics of conservation has also fluctuated. From the first days when Secretary of the Interior Walter Hickel (since dismissed) aggressively sought portrayal as the nation's chief environmental steward, to the more complex present scenario of multiple but low-profile environmental policy makers, the White House has seemed to contradict itself, as if the President were not really certain about how to deal with the problems. As illustrated by the conflicting memoirs of those close to President Kennedy, even the people who participate in White House decision making can't agree on what really happened, or how and why. Hickel's recollections of his time in the Nixon Cabinet don't coincide with those of others, in and out of government, who watched his performance.

Secretary Hickel, who played the tough-talking, nature-conquering pioneer when first responding to his nomination to the Cabinet, can take much of the credit for making the environment a national political issue. What should have been a routine appointment to one of the lesser Cabinet posts—the nomination of a western-state politician to become Secretary of the Interior—turned into the first political test Nixon faced as President. In defending Hickel's nomination, the White House acknowledged the legitimacy of public concern over conservation. After his confirmation, Secretary Hickel set out to show that he was a good guy after all, and involved the White House in major environmental conflicts.

Secretary Hickel's first effort to prove that he really cared about things natural took place in the Everglades on March 13, 1969. Accompanied by enough journalists and politicians to scare off any sensible alligators, or alligator poachers, the Secretary went on a demonstration night patrol to learn how Park Rangers try to protect the endangered reptiles. After spending a few hours with a very convivial Governor Claude Kirk, Hickel announced that, in addition to stepping up the poacher patrols, he was going to join the Governor in ending the 20-year-old feud about south Florida water rights, and see that Everglades National Park would not be deprived of water from its northern watershed, controlled by the State of Florida and the Corps of Engineers. The Secretary was also briefed on the threat to the Everglades from a new jetport, slated to handle 50 million passengers a year, under construction in the privately owned Big Cypress Swamp, an Everglades' watershed.

President Nixon's subsequent decision to withdraw federal support for the airport project, his use of the carrot-stick of federal funds to force Dade County (Miami) authorities to relocate the airport, and his proposal for federal purchase of the Big Cypress are well known. The President gave strong personal support to Hickel's view that the airport be moved, in spite of vigorous protests from another Cabinet officer, John Volpe of Transportation. The White House has continued to insist on relocation of the airport, in the face of persistent efforts by other federal officials to delay the move or sanction use of the Everglades site. The Administration, understanding that south Florida's economy and Everglades National Park's survival depend on reformed land use and water management, is working hard to try to convince Congress to protect the Big Cypress watershed.

While the White House paid special attention to the Everglades problems, the Administration resisted Congressional efforts to make general concern for the environment a truly high-priority issue. The White House Council on Environmental Quality was established by Congress near the end of 1969 over the objections of the White House itself. But the President adopted the CEQ as if it were his own creation, and pointedly nominated three indisputably qualified persons to fill the Council seats: Russell Train (the widely respected President of the Conservation Foundation), Gordon MacDonald (a distinguished academic), and Pulitzer prize winner Robert Cahn.

The newly-formed Council immediately played a major role in a key White House environmental decision:

President Nixon's order halting construction of the Cross-Florida Barge Canal. The Council, with the support of Secretary Hickel, confirmed the evidence Florida scientists and conservation leaders had amassed against the canal. Economically and environmentally, the canal would have been an obvious failure. At a cost of $180 million, it would have provided a completely unnecessary short route from the Gulf of Mexico to the Atlantic Ocean, and would have destroyed the beautiful Oklawaha River. When the Florida Defenders of the Environment and the Environmental Defense Fund won a court order temporarily stopping construction, the Corps of Engineers and canal proponents ran out of time in their efforts to work out a compromise. President Nixon, a few days after the court decision, directed the Corps to abandon its work on the project. Once again, accurate information had been given to the White House, and the President had acted to protect the environment.

Hickel's style seemed to attract plaudits for his good deeds while leaving the White House to explain away the problems—certainly a characteristic not many Presidents like to see in their Cabinet officers. Considering the impact of Congressional pressures that are difficult to assess, it would be hard to say how responsible Hickel's political problems were for early White House moves to diminish the importance and stature of the Department of the Interior. President Nixon's selection of Russell Train to head the Council on Environmental Quality had already established an alternative spokesman for the Administration's conservation policy. The President's decision to remove water pollution enforcement from Interior jurisdiction and place it under the newly-created Environmental Protection Agency further diminished Hickel's role. But as Hickel's alienation from the President became more apparent, so did the effectiveness of the Earth-children to whom Hickel was urging the President to listen. The young leaders of Earth Day helped give us the Clean Air Act of 1970, and gave the heavy-handed White

House lobbyists who fought the bill a thorough and embarrassing defeat.

President Nixon's 1971 flight to Mobile, Alabama, to take part in the dedication of the Tennessee-Tombigbee waterway looked little different from the 1960 Florida campaign tour of John F. Kennedy, who listened to local political leaders and promised to resurrect the long discredited Cross-Florida Barge Canal. President Nixon's handshake with Governor Wallace seemed the kind of standard cornerstone sacrament that strengthens the political foundations of most public works projects. But in light of events of the preceding months, President Nixon's homage to the waterways lobby was more than a routine political commitment. The politics of the environment had been considered, found less significant than the politics of the pork barrel, and rejected. The Council's advice, which weighed heavily inside the White House in 1970, was ignored in 1971, and by 1972 a bitter political rupture had left the Council on Environmental Quality—supposedly the chief instrument for guiding the President in setting policy to save the degraded American environment—isolated from President Nixon and his staff.

Even before the break between the White House and the Council on Environmental Quality, it was apparent that President Nixon had never set a clear environmental policy for his Administration. In contrast to Vietnam and other foreign policy issues, where differences among Administration leaders rarely surfaced, the Nixon environmental policy depended on who was doing the talking. The Council on Environmental Quality, the Department of the Interior, and Environmental Protection Agency spokesmen would generally speak of environmental problems as deserving priority. But even within those agencies, lower-level bureaucrats continued to deny that pollution, overpopulation, and resource consumption were serious. So while the Environmental Protection Agency talked of launching a campaign to save the Great Lakes, the chief of the U.S. Geological Survey made speeches denying that

Lake Erie was dead and minimizing the problems of industrial pollution. Dr. William Pecora, the Geological Survey chief, was made number-two man in the Department of the Interior when top administrators in the agency were purged by the White House after President Nixon fired Hickel. And the Great Lakes water purification program, like many other EPA proposals that might have forced industry to stop polluting, was changed to place the cleanup burden on underfinanced public facilities.

Such policy differences within the agencies nominally responsible for environmental affairs were minor compared to conflicting policies and values advocated by other departments. Secretary of Commerce Maurice Stans, who has returned to private life to raise money for President Nixon's re-election campaign, was the Administration's most outspoken foe of conservation. Stans, whose principal environmental credentials were trophies he bagged while hunting big game, convinced the White House to give his department jurisdiction over the National Oceanic and Atmospheric Administration, the agency created by a White House reorganization plan to oversee federal ocean resource activity. The Commerce Department had no previous experience in resource management, but since the Commerce Department's Weather Bureau had more employees than the Interior Department's marine fisheries and science programs, the White House decided that the new agency resulting from merger of the programs belonged in the Commerce Department. Conservationists, worried that the development-minded Commerce Department would be more interested in exploiting the oceans than cleaning them up, unsuccessfully opposed the move.

After Congress approved the President's reorganization, Stans met with national environmental leaders to give them assurance of his personal commitment to conservation. As evidence of his interest in the environment, Stans pointed to the National Industrial Pollution Control Council (NIPCC), created by President Nixon's executive order on April 9, 1970. Staffed through the Commerce

Department, and given an annual budget of $300,000, the Council is composed of the chief executives of the nation's leading industrial firms—all the principal polluters of America. According to Stans, the activities of NIPCC would demonstrate that the industrialists and the Commerce Department were working to protect the environment.

On October 14, 1970, shortly after Stans met with conservationists, the NIPCC held a closed meeting. Representatives of several environmental organizations, alerted by Ralph Nader's Public Interest Research Group, went to the Commerce Department to observe the NIPCC session. Commerce Department officials refused to let the conservationists into the meeting room, on the grounds that the industry leaders and Commerce Department officials could not talk freely about environmental problems if conservationists were present. The NIPCC staff refused to make public a record of the discussions between the polluting corporations and government officials. Conservationists were told the public would learn about NIPCC's activities when the Council published its formal report.

At the next meeting of NIPCC, conservationists were given another sample of the Commerce Department's environmental concern. Commerce officials, angered and embarrassed by the conservationists waiting outside the conference room during the previous NIPCC session, arranged for the meeting to be held at the State Department, where security guards were stationed in the lobby to stop conservationists who tried to attend. Three conservation workers were threatened with arrest because they gave copies of written statements to a Washington *Evening Star* reporter. A few hours later, President Nixon addressed the business executives and praised them for their concern for the environment.

Facts about White House decision-making are obscured and distorted by the same problems that complicate assigning real responsibility at any political level. Those who have much power often hide it, those who have less often exaggerate it. There is intense competition, among individuals and agencies, to appear to be involved in important decisions, and to seem to have been on the winning side of deliberations that led to decisions. Individuals and agencies assume one posture for their direct constituency, another for the opposition, another for the public, and another for their hierarchical superiors. Any or all of these positions may be changed, after the fact, to suit what the participants believe the record should show. This preoccupation with the form of policy making, as opposed to the substance of the issues at hand, is so intense within the federal bureaucracy that those who must actually make decisions, including the President, cannot rely on information coming from the bureaucracy, even at the highest levels.

Contradictory and unreliable advice from official channels makes decision makers give even more weight to their own instincts and to suggestions from personal associates, in and out of government. Given a bureaucracy ill-equipped and not particularly willing to meet the new environmental responsibilities demanded by the public, an industrial leadership profoundly suspicious of the wisdom and the motives of those who want reform of wasteful and polluting business practices, and an official family dominated by personalities with little personal or professional understanding of the importance of environmental integrity, it is surprising that the White House has responded as well as it has to the environmental crisis facing America.

Other White House actions in 1971 showed that Administration policy makers were having second thoughts about the environmental issue. The Council on Environmental Quality, and the prestige of Council Chairman Train, were used to lend credence to Administration attempts to convince conservationists of the merits of new EPA regulations for enforcement of the 1899 Refuse Act. Chairman Train and EPA Administrator William Ruckelshaus asked conservation leaders to give the new permit program a chance to work before rejecting it, and brushed aside warnings that the program would render the Refuse Act unworkable. In fact, top EPA officials had argued vigorously against the program and had been overruled by the White House. What was then thought of as one of the most potentially effective weapons against industrial water pollution has since been all but abandoned by the Administration. From the beginning of his job as the nation's top anti-pollution officer, it was clear that Ruckelshaus had no real control over his own agency's policies.

Another 1971 incident served as a warning of what could happen to agencies that ran afoul, even inadvertently, of White House staff members. Peter Flanigan (the Presidential assistant who has since become better known for bigger things) defied the law and the obvious intent of other executive orders and put federal Wildlife Refuges under the threat of a White House order that could lead to the sale of valuable Refuge lands. The Fish and Wildlife Service was forced to prepare a list of Refuge and Game Range lands it considered "surplus." Protests to the White House stopped the surplus classification of the Refuge lands, but in the process, the chief of the Service, John Gottschalk, wrongly accused of letting environmentalists know about the White House order, was transferred to an obscure post in a Department of Commerce fisheries office.

The same conflicts that brought disillusionment to citizens concerned about the environment produced similar feelings in the White House, but for different reasons. Nader's reports on failure and conflict of interest in federal programs exposed the Nixon Administration's weakness in pollution control, pesticides, and other regulatory responsibilities. Saving endangered species is one thing, curbing industrial abuse quite another. Any lingering doubts about White House policy were resolved, to the satisfaction of most people on both sides, by the battles over two Administration bonuses to industry—the Alaska pipeline and the SST. Both issues were so clearly drawn that the White House could not avoid open and sustained conflict with conservationists. The future of wild Alaska is still to be decided, and the Nixon Administration suffered a humiliating Congressional defeat over the SST. But the outcome of both questions had repercussions going far beyond the immediate issues. Whenever and however Alaska is developed, and whether or not our government ever subsidizes the SST, the determination and competence shown by environmentalists in those campaigns exposed, at last, Nixon's true policy on the environment. The White House began a firm and conscious campaign to defend itself against further embarrassment.

The changed mood of Administration officials could be felt in late 1971. Between Thanksgiving and Christmas, the Council on Environmental Quality, EPA's Ruckelshaus, Interior Secretary Rogers Morton, and lesser figures began talking, among themselves and to anyone else who would listen, of an impending environmental backlash. Presidential aides not officially responsible for environmental affairs were, as Flanigan did in behalf of Armco and Anaconda, letting agency chiefs know about White House displeasure over rulings which forced industries to obey pollution laws.

The firing of Hickel had already eliminated one potential contrast between the White House and apparent defenders of the environment within the Administration. Morton, Hickel's successor, worked quietly, keeping himself and his Department's cooperation with oil, mining, and development interests out of the public eye. EPA Administrator William Ruckelshaus, who began his job with a flair that brought considerable attention to the new agency, had become almost politically invisible.

Train, Chairman of the President's Council on Environmental Quality, was neutralized in a more ingenious manner. Widely respected as President of the Conservation Foundation, his appointment as Undersecretary of Interior was a move by the White House to reassure conservation-minded Nixon supporters who were, like many other Americans, dismayed by the nomination of Hickel as Interior Secretary. Train's subsequent appointment as Chairman of the Council on Environmental Quality reinforced the prestige of the Council and the Administration's apparent commitment to the importance of sound environmental policy. A Council Chairman enjoying Train's stature could have become a source of considerable discomfort to the White House as Administration decisions became more blatantly anti-environment. The problem was solved by making Train the chief apologist for Administration policy. The Council on Environmental Quality, and Chairman Train, were turned into salesmen for White House programs to erode water pollution legislation, delay regulation of strip mining, speed up construction of environmentally unsound power plants, whitewash destructive Agriculture Department stream channelization policies, and even weaken the National Environmental Policy Act. Train's painful acquiescence on so many issues greatly reduced his credibility with conservation leaders.

With Train's reputation diminished, even among his own following, there were no more environmental heroes within the Nixon Administration to serve as embarrassing contrasts to the President. Even the Chairman's efforts to keep the Administration on the conservation side of less controversial programs failed. In the late summer of 1971, the White House attached a message from President Nixon ("It is simplistic to seek ecological perfection at the cost of bankrupting the very tax-paying enterprises which must pay for the social advances the nation seeks") serving as a disclaimer to the Council's already watered-down Second Annual Report. When White House aides, spurred on by the President's Office of Management and Budget and by the Commerce Department, amputated much of both the substance and the style of the 1972 Environmental Message, prepared for the President by the Council, the repudiation was complete. By the spring of 1972, the Council no longer had a real working relationship with the President it was supposed to serve. Only a handful of Council staff members, like Program Director Al Alm, Secretary Boyd Gibbons and Counsel Timothy Atkeson, had anticipated and accepted White House change of policy well enough to stay on civil terms with Presidential advisors. The three Members of the Council had become figureheads. Chairman Train was rewarded for his loyalty to the President with undisguised personal scorn from senior White House officials. Gordon MacDonald was preparing to return to the academic community. Robert Cahn, the persistent reporter of the nation's environmental problems, was reduced to a wistful speechmaker.

Within the White House staff, the Council's fall from power brought other internal struggles into the open. John Whitaker, responsible for giving the President advice on matters of energy, agriculture, and the environment, is thought by some environmental leaders to be an exceptionally fair and honest man. Whitaker is credited by some conservationists with convincing President Nixon to go all out to save the Everglades and protect south Florida's water resources, in the face of strong criticism from the Office of Management and Budget and other White House aides. Though his steadfast support of the SST, the Alaska pipeline, offshore oil development, and White House efforts to weaken water pollution control should give him impeccable credentials within Administration circles, other White House advisors began hinting in 1971 that Whitaker was "soft on conservation." By the spring of 1972, Flanigan, the Wall Street fund raiser who has aggressively represented industrial interests inside the White House, had become directly involved in environmental affairs. Even other top Republican fund raisers, many of whom have deep roots in the conservation movement, were dismayed at the White House assignment of Flanigan to deal with environmental problems. But the move was consistent with the new White House policy of trying to contain the politically sensitive environmental issue by burying it within business as usual.

Taking their cues from President Nixon's statements ("We are not going to allow the environmental issue to be used sometimes falsely and sometimes in a demagogic way basically to destroy the system . . ."), Administration leaders stopped treating the nation's environmental crisis as a problem deserving priority consideration. The environment was redefined as a function of over-riding economic and national security decisions. While the Environmental Protection Agency was given increased funds for public relations projects, other agencies were warned that budget proposals dressed up in environmental language would be frowned on at the White House Office of Management and Budget. White House aides gave newsmen considered friendly to the Administration tips that the environment was a dead issue, not worthy of continued special attention.

In a world where the art of politics is the final arbiter over all the sciences, the White House has begun to treat concern for the environment as just another passing issue. The new policy is a triumph for those in the White House who don't believe there actually is an environmental crisis. Yet to end the illusion that protecting our environment would make political leaders rise above politics might, in the long run, be marked as the beginning of effective action on the part of millions of Americans. Politics is a synonym for power, and its concentration at the White House is great, but the desire to attain and keep that power makes all those who aspire to the Presidency vulnerable to well-directed citizen activity. If any President fails to respond to the need for environmental integrity, the politics of survival will hasten the breakdown of partisan loyalties and bring us closer to genuine participation by all Americans in decisions about what kind of community, country, and world we will live in.

# INDEX

Abortion, 171, 175-177
Adams, Sherman, 85
Air pollution, 9-29, 204-208, 216, 219
Alaskan Native claims, 122-125
Alaskan pipeline, 82, 87-89, 122, 123, 125-128, 265
Albert Einstein College of Medicine, 9, 216
Allott, Sen. Gordon, 198
Alm, Al, 267
Aluminum Association, 253
Alyeska Pipeline Service Company, 87
American Association for the Advancement of Science, 146, 154
American Association of State Highway Officials, 182
American Chemical Society, 156
American Iron and Steel Institute, 245
American Mining Congress, 95
American Motors, 24
American Petroleum Institute, 55
American Smelting and Refining Company, 21
American Transit Association, 197
Amtrak, 184, 195-196
Anaconda Copper Company, 21, 266

Anderson, Jack, 47, 48, 72, 77, 220
Armco Steel Company, 266
Asbestos, 13, 231-232
Aspin, Rep. Les, 88
Aspinall, Rep. Wayne, 113, 124
Associated General Contractors of America, 182
Atkeson, Timothy, 44, 48, 267
Atlantic Richfield Oil Company, 91, 127
Atomic Energy Commission, 99, 100, 101, 103

Bagge, Carl E., 94
Black lung, 232
Boeing Corporation, 188
Bolle, Arnold, 116
Breeder reactor, 102-103
Bureau of Community Environmental Health, 210-211
Bureau of Land Management, 111, 113, 114, 141
Bureau of Mines, 93, 244-248
Bureau of Outdoor Recreation, 210
Bureau of Reclamation, 62, 66, 68-70, 75, 77
Bureau of Sport Fisheries and Wildlife, 72, 73, 120
Bureau of Water Hygiene, 32
Butz, Earl L., 117
Byerly, Dr. Theodore C. 73

Cahn, Robert, 259, 268
**Calvert Cliffs Decision, 101**
Carroll, Thomas, 220
Carson, Rachel, 147, 148, 151, 157
Chamber of Commerce, 54, 224
Chrysler Corporation, 24, 25
Citizen suits, 13, 15
Citizen's Advisory Committee on Environmental Quality, 251
Clean Air Act of 1970, 11-26, 28, 29
Clearcutting, 111, 116-117, 144
Clement, Thomas, 77
Cliff, Edward P., 117
Clusen, Charles, 77
Coal, 64, 81, 83, 90-95
Coal gasification, 89, 90-91
Coffey, John J. Jr., 54
Cohen, Howard, 54, 161
Colgate-Palmolive, 47
Colson, Charles, 48
Commission on National Goals, 168
Commission on Pesticides and their Relationship to Environmental Health, 147-148, 153
Commission on Population Growth and the American Future, 165, 168, 169-171, 173, 176
Corps of Engineers, 37, 40, 42, 43, 56, 57, 61, 65, 66-68, 70, 75-78, 145, 260
Council of Economic Advisors, 168
Council on Environmental Quality, 9, 14, 31, 44, 48, 55, 59, 65, 73-75, 111, 117, 118, 159, 211, 248, 249, 259-261, 264, 266-68
Cross-Florida Barge Canal, 59-60, 63-65, 259-261

David, Dr. Edward, 108, 109
DDT, 65, 141, 145, 147, 151-154
Department of Agriculture, 61, 63, 72, 148, 150, 151, 156, 157, 161
Department of Commerce, 14, 21, 48, 51, 54, 55, 130, 133, 142, 144, 262, 263, 266
Department of Communty Development, 21
Department of Health, Education and Welfare, 32, 47, 49, 172, 173, 203, 204, 206, 210-212, 234
Department of Housing and Urban Development, 204, 209
Department of Interior, 62, 86, 88, 90, 91, 95, 106, 107, 121, 126, 130, 131, 133, 135, 143, 210
Department of Justice, 24, 39, 40, 41, 43
Department of Labor, 225, 226, 228-230, 237
Department of Natural Resources, 82
Department of State, 136, 137
Department of Transportation, 182, 190, 194, 216, 217
Department of the Treasury, 249
Dingell, Rep. John, 56, 57, 133, 140, 143
Division of Wildlife Services, 138, 140-142
Dominick, David, 220, 253
Dow Chemical Company, 53
Drinking water, 31-33, 53
Dubridge, Dr. Lee, 174
Dumps, 240, 241, 250-251

Eagleton, Sen. Thomas, 24, 172
Eckhardt, Rep. Bob, 97

# INDEX

Ehrlichman, John D., 19, 176, 186
Eisenhower, Dwight D., 84, 129
Electric utilities, 26, 80, 81, 97, 108-109
Ellender, Sen. Allen, 79, 162
Endangered Species Act of 1969, 131-133
Energy, 80-109, 244-248
Engel, Dr. Ronald E., 204, 205
Environmental Education Act of 1970, 177
Environmental Protection Agency, 12, 13, 17, 18, 21-26, 28, 29, 40-43, 46, 47, 54, 56, 64, 75-77, 90, 140, 150-154, 158-161, 205, 207, 218-221, 244, 246, 247, 250-251, 253-255, 264-266, 269
Equal Rights Amendment, 170, 177-178
Eutrophication, 31, 45-50, 60
Evans, Rep. Joe, 63
Everglades National Park, 112, 118-119, 128, 258-259

Fairbanks, Richard, 54
Family Planning Services and Population Research Act of 1970, 171-175
Federal Aid Highway Act, 180, 181, 184-188
Federal Aviation Administration, 188
Federal Highway Administration, 183
Federal Insecticide, Fungicide and Rodenticide Act of 1947, 148, 158, 159
Federal Power Commission, 89
Federal Water Pollution Control Act, 37, 38, 41, 42, 52
Finch, Robert H., 174, 239, 243, 255, 256

Fish and Wildlife Service, 265
Flanigan, Peter, 19, 48, 265, 266, 268
Food and Drug Administration, 49
Ford Motor Company, 24, 25
Forest Service, 115-118, 120
Freeman, Dr. S. David, 85, 96-97, 108
Fuel cells, 106

Galbraith, John Kenneth, 189
Gammelgard, P. Nick, 55
Garwin, Richard, 190
General Accounting Office, 149
General Motors, 24, 25
General Services Administration, 24, 249
Geological Survey, 93
Geothermal energy, 107
Gibbons, Boyd, 267
Glasser, Dr. Martin, 9
Gofman, Dr. John, 99, 102
Grant, Kenneth, 73
Great Lakes, 47, 49, 50, 58, 61
Greenberg, Dr. Leonard, 9
Guenther, George C., 228, 229, 235

Hale, Samuel, 254
Hamilton, Walter, 54
Hansen, Rep. Julia Butler, 132
Hardin, Clifford, 118
Harlow, Bryce, 47, 48, 116
Harris, Sen. Fred, 142
Hart, Sen. Philip, 155
Hartzog, George P. Jr., 121
Heller, Walter, 189
Hickel, Walter, 110, 118, 121, 122, 130, 131, 134, 135, 258-261, 266
Highway Trust Fund, 180-182, 184-188, 197-199, 217
Hodgson, James D., 229, 237
House Agriculture Committee, 159

House Appropriations Committee, 63, 112, 132, 151, 247
House Education and Labor Committee, 233, 236
House Government Operations Committee, 169
House Intergovernmental Relations Subcommittee, 149
House Interior and Insular Affairs Committee, 112, 113, 124, 209
House Merchant Marine and Fisheries Committee, 144
House Public Works Committee, 44, 55, 56, 186
House Rules Committee, 224
House Subcommittee on Conservation and Natural Resources, 49
House Subcommittee on Fisheries and Wildlife Conservation, 133, 140, 143
House Ways and Means Committee, 186, 205
Hubbert, M. King, 85, 91

Iacocca, Lee A., 25
Inner-city environment, 200-221
International Harvester, 25
Interstate Highway System, 181-182, 184-186, 197, 217
Institute for Rapid Transit, 197
Interstate Commerce Commission, 246

Jackson, Sen. Henry M., 113, 114
Javits, Sen. Jacob, 172, 224
Jensen, Malcolm, 49
Johnson, Lyndon Baines, 38, 115, 119, 151, 162, 170, 202, 223

Joint Committee on Atomic Energy, 96, 97
Jones, Rep. Bob, 79

Kennedy, Sen. Edward, 203-204
Kennedy, President John F., 202, 261
Kirk, Claude, 258
Kossack, Nathaniel, 72, 74

Lake Erie, 46, 50
Land and Water Conservation Fund, 119, 208-209
Land use planning, 19
Lead, 32, 181, 203-206
Lead gasoline, 205-208, 219
Legacy of Parks Program, 119, 208-210
Lever Brothers, 47, 50
Livestock grazing, 115
Lopez, Glenn, 77
Lynn, Jim, 48

MacDonald, Gordon, 259, 268
Megnetohydrodynamics (MHD), 106
Magnuson, Sen. Warren, 108
McCloskey, Rep. Pete, 170, 174
McDade, Rep. Joseph, 247
McKernan, Donald, 136, 137
Meidav, Dr. Tsvi, 107
Mercury, 13, 32, 33, 65, 145, 149, 233
Middleton, Dr. John T., 18
Mills, Rep. Wilbur, 187, 205
Mining Law of 1872, 112-114, 128
Mission 5000, 250-251
Mitchell, John, 257
Morton, Rogers, 47, 86, 105, 107, 114, 117-119, 125-128, 132, 133, 175, 266
Mountain, Pamela, 77
Moynihan, Daniel Patrick, 165-168, 170

# INDEX

Mullen, Joseph, 14
Muskie, Sen. Edmund, 11, 14, 15, 16, 18, 22, 25, 35, 50, 52, 55, 214, 242, 255

Nader, Ralph, 10, 25, 41, 57, 58, 62, 223, 233, 237, 265
Nassikas, John, 19, 89
National Academy of Engineering, 26
National Academy of Sciences, 24-25, 205
National Advisory Commission on Civil Disorders, 208
National Advisory Committee on Occupational Safety and Health, 235
National Agriculture Chemicals Association, 150
National Air Quality Standards, 10, 12-15, 28
National Association of Manufacturers, 54
National Cancer Institute, 147
National Coal Association, 14, 94
National Environmental Policy Act of 1969, 43, 65, 72-75, 86, 97, 101, 103, 125
National Forests, 113, 115-118, 128
National Industrial Pollution Control Council, 51, 54, 55, 262-263
National Institute of Health, 164, 171
National Institute of Mental Health, 204
National Institute for Occupational Safety and Health, 232-235
*National Journal*, 11, 53, 54, 123
National League of Cities, 35, 194

National Oceanic and Atmospheric Administration, 130, 133, 143, 144, 262
National Park Service, 110, 111, 118-121
National Research Council, 26
National Safety Council, 222, 223, 235
National Science Foundation, 24, 105
National Timber Supply Bill of 1970, 115-116
National Urban Coalition, 201
Natural gas, 81-83, 85, 86, 89-90
*New Republic*, 164
New York Medical College, 9
*New York Times*, 152, 161, 182, 253
Nixon, Richard M. vii-ix, 267, 268;
  Alaskan pipeline, 127;
  Abortion, 176;
  Addresses:
    Energy Message of 1971, 70, 81, 98, 102;
    Environmental Message of 1970, 10, 242, 248, 249, 252;
    Environmental Message of 1971, 26, 209, 248, 249;
    Environmental Message of 1972, 248, 249;
    Population Message of 1969, 164-167;
    State of the Union Address for 1970, 29;
  Clean Air Act:
    Legislative proposals, 10, 14;
    Signature of law, 16;
  Commission on Population Growth and the American Future, 171;
  Cross-Florida Barge Canal, 59-60, 260;

Executive reorganization:
　Department of Community Development, 202;
　Department of Natural Resources, 81;
Everglades National Park, 259;
Gateway National Recreation Area, 119;
Golden Gate National Recreation Area, 119;
Great Lakes, 47, 50;
Land and Water Conservation Fund, 209;
Meeting with environmentalists, 168;
Non-returnable containers, 252;
Nuclear power plants, 98, 102;
Occupational Safety and Health Act of 1970, 222, 224;
Oil and natural gas policies, 81;
Pesticides:
　Mirex, 157;
　Pending legislation, 161;
Recycling, 248-250;
Resource Recovery Act of 1970, 242;
Tennessee-Tombigbee Waterway, 64-65, 261;
Transportation:
　Federal Aid Highway Act of 1956, 181;
　Selection of Transportation Secretary, 182;
　Supersonic transport (SST), 191;
　Traffic congestion, 192;
Sulfur tax proposal, 26-29;
Water pollution:
　Legislative proposals, 50-52;
　Funding, 34-36;
　Water Resources Development Standards, 79;
Wildlife:
　Endangered species, 133;
　Establishment of National Oceanic and Atmospheric Administration, 130;
　Predator control, 138, 140;
　Whales, 136;
　Women's rights, 178
Noise, 188, 213-215
Nuclear energy, 81, 83, 98-104
Nuclear fusion, 103-104
Nuclear wastes, 101, 102

Oak Ridge National Laboratory, 99, 100
Obey, Rep. David, 247
*Occupational Epidemic*, 224, 238
Occupational Safety and Health, 95, 147, 151, 160, 222-238
Occupational Safety and Health Act of 1970, 222-238
Occupational Safety and Health Administration, 228-232, 235, 237
Occupational Safety and Health Review Commission, 225, 227
Office of Management and Budget, 14, 18, 19, 21, 22, 57, 65, 78, 79, 172, 196, 198, 202, 209, 210, 214, 247, 266, 268, 269
Office of Noise Abatement and Control, 214-215
Office of Science and Technology, 25, 96
Office of Solid Waste Management Programs, 244, 250-251

# INDEX

Off-shore drilling, 82, 85, 86-87
Oil, 27, 81, 82-89
Oil imports, 82-85, 88-89, 90
Oil shale, 70, 90-91
Oil spills, 88, 125
Okun, Dr. Daniel, 31
O'Leary, John, 84
Open Space Lands Programs, 209-210
Osborn, Dr. Elburt F., 247

Packwood, Sen. Robert, 174
Pecora, William, 126, 262
Pesticides, 60, 144, 146-162
Pesticides Regulation Division, 148-151
Peterson, Dr. Malcolm, 96
Phosphate detergents, 31, 45-50, 58
Population education, 170, 177
Population growth, 83, 145, 163-179, 239
Power plants, 13, 27, 96-98, 103, 107
Power plant siting, 97-98
Pratt & Whitney Company, 106
Predator control, 138-142, 158-159
Proctor and Gamble, 47, 48, 50
Proxmire, Sen. William, 190
Pryor, Rep. David, 142
Public domain lands, 114-115
Public Health Service, 32, 53, 213, 223, 241
Public Land Law Review Commission, 113-114
Public lands, 110-128
Pyle, Howard, 235

Quarles, John, 41

Radiation, 98, 99, 101, 102
Rats, 210-213, 240, 241

Recycling, 52, 53, 239, 245-246, 248-250
Reed, Nathaniel P., 72, 73, 74, 112, 158
Refuse Act of 1899, 36-45, 58, 264-65
Resource Recovery Act of 1970, 241-244, 250
Resources for the Future, 105
*Resources and Man*, 246
Reuss, Rep. Henry, 40, 49, 50, 56
Richardson, Elliot, 14-16, 172, 234
Rockefeller, John D., III, 170, 171
Rockefeller, Laurance, 251
Rockefeller, Nelson, 176
Roman Catholic Church, 167, 175, 176
Romney, George, 201, 209, 219
Ruckelshaus, William, 17-19, 23-26, 41, 48, 56, 57, 98, 151, 154-157, 161, 162, 175, 201, 202, 207, 215, 218-220, 250, 253, 254, 264-266
Ryan, Rep. William F., 203-204

Samuelson, Paul, 189
Sanitary landfill, 240, 241, 250-251
Sato, Prime Minister, 88
Saylor, Rep. John P., 56, 114, 124
Schlesinger, Dr. James, 98, 100, 102
Schultz, George P., 57, 84, 196
Science Advisory Committee, 153, 190
Selikoff, Dr. Irving J., 231-232
Senate Appropriations Committee, 68, 79, 112
Senate Commerce Committee, 108, 220

Senate Interior and Insular Affairs Committee, 94, 112, 113, 116, 209

Senate Labor and Public Welfare Committee, 229, 236

Senate Public Works Committee, 186

Senate Subcommittee on Air and Water Pollution, 11, 22, 24, 52, 240, 242

Senate Subcommittee on Environment, 220

Silberman, Laurance, 228, 237

*Silent Spring*, 147, 148

Sloan, Stephen, 74

Soil Conservation Service, 61-62, 70-75, 77

Solar energy, 104-106

Solid wastes, 10, 219, 239-256

Sonic booms, 188

Stans, Maurice, 54, 135, 262

Stansbury, Jeff, 74

Steiger, Rep. William, 227

Steinfeld, Jesse, 48

Stream channelization, 60-79, 145

Strip mining, 64, 70, 90, 91-95, 144

Sulfur pollution, 9, 10, 12, 26-29

SST, 188-191, 265-266

Tamplin, Dr. Arthur, 99

Task Force on the Environmental Problems of the Inner-City, 200, 202, 206, 215, 218-221

Task Force of Oil Import Quota Controls, 84

Tennessee-Tombigbee Waterway, 64-65, 261

Tennessee Valley Authority, 62-66, 70, 75, 76, 79

Toll, David R., 54

Toxic substances, 13, 32, 226, 234

Train, Russell, 44, 98, 136, 169, 188, 259, 260, 264, 266-268

Transportation, 10, 19, 21, 81, 180-199, 215-218

Trudeau, Prime Minister Pierre, 47, 50

Trussell, Douglas, 54

Turner, Francis, 183, 217

Tydings, Sen. Joseph, 172

Udall, Rep. Morris K., 114, 124, 169

Udall, Stewart, 74, 113, 122

Union Oil Company, 24

U.S. Conference of Mayors, 35, 194

*U.S. News & World Report*, 91

Urban Mass Transportation Act of 1970, 191-194, 217

Urban Mass Transportation Administration, 183, 198

*Vanishing Air*, 10

Veysey, Rep. Victor V., 24

Villarreal, Carlos, 183

Volpe, John, 182-184, 186, 190-198, 259

*Wall Street Journal*, 117, 127

Wallace, Gov. George, 64, 261

*Washington Post*, 24, 221

Waste water treatment, 32-36, 49, 52, 53, 56, 57

Water pollution, 30-58

Water quality standards, 38, 41, 42, 51, 53

Water Resources Council, 77-79

Water resources development, 59-79, 145

*Water Wasteland*, 41

Weinberg, Dr. Alvin, 100
Whitaker, John, 14, 48, 54, 57, 268
Whitten, Rep. Jamie, 151, 157, 161-162
Wilderness, 110, 112, 117, 120, 121
Wildlife, 14, 129-145

Wildlife habitat, 60, 69, 70, 88, 121, 144-145, 265
Wolfe, Dr. Sidney, 223, 233
Women's rights, 177-178
Workplace environment, 95, 147, 151, 160, 222-238

Ziegler, Ronald L., 243

The League of Conservation Voters is a national, nonpartisan campaign committee which works in close cooperation with the Environmental Policy Center and other major conservation organizations.